William Henry Egle

Centenary Memorial of the Erection of the County of Dauphin

And the Founding of the City of Harrisburg

William Henry Egle

Centenary Memorial of the Erection of the County of Dauphin
And the Founding of the City of Harrisburg

ISBN/EAN: 9783337118051

Printed in Europe, USA, Canada, Australia, Japan

Cover: Foto ©ninafisch / pixelio.de

More available books at **www.hansebooks.com**

DAUPHIN COUNTY CENTENNIAL MEDAL.

OBVERSE.

REVERSE.

OFFICERS OF COUNTY OF DAUPHIN---1885.

PRESIDENT JUDGE,
JOHN WIGGINS SIMONTON.

ADDITIONAL LAW JUDGE,
JOHN BAYARD McPHERSON.

SHERIFF,
ISAAC MUMMA.

PROTHONOTARY,
EHRMAN B. MITCHELL.

DISTRICT ATTORNY,
SAMUEL J. M. McCARRELL.

TREASURER,
ERASTUS JAY JONES

REGISTER,
WILLIAM B. MEETCH.

RECORDER,
PHILIP C. SWAB.

COUNTY SOLICITOR,
FREDERICK M. OTT,

CORONER,
GEORGE F. SHINDLER.

COUNTY COMMISSIONERS,
CORNELIUS BIXLER,
JOHN W. STOBER,
CHRISTIAN L. GINGRICH.

DIRECTORS OF THE POOR.
WILLIAM SWAN RUTHERFORD,
ISAIAH T. ENDERS,
ADAM H. SHOPE.

AUDITORS,
ISAAC M. BONAWITZ,
GEORGE F. GREENAWALT,
GEORGE W. FOX.

OFFICERS OF CITY OF HARRISBURG, 1885.

MAYOR,
SIMON CAMERON WILSON.

TREASURER,
ALFRED T. BLACK.

CONTROLLER,
WILLIAM K. VERBEKE.

SOLICITOR,
THOMAS S. HARGEST.

CITY ENGINEER.
MATTHEW BENJAMIN COWDEN.

MEMBERS OF THE SELECT COUNCIL,

First Ward—Charles P. Mason,   Fifth Ward—William L. Gorgas,
Second Ward—John A. Fritchey,   Sixth Ward—Israel L. Trostle,
Third Ward—Joseph B. Ewing,   Seventh Ward—James McCleaster,
Fourth Ward—S. Boyd Martin,   Eighth Ward—Henry H. Mueller,
                Ninth Ward—John C. Forney.

MEMBERS OF THE COMMON COUNCIL,

First Ward—Edward Drinkwater, James T. Walters, Michael H. Melvin and Harry L. Champlain.

Second Ward—John C. Lyme, Bartholomew B. DeVout, John W. Miller and Amos F. Fry.

Third Ward—J. Monroe Kreiter, Wilson Elder, Valentine Hummel, and Edmund Mather.

Fourth Ward—Samuel H. Ettla, Frederick K. Swartz, Samuel W. Fleming and John J. Hargest,

Fifth Ward—Charles Fisher, William E. Machlin, John R. Stoey, and George C. B. Swartz.

Sixth Ward—John D. Weeber, B. Riley Wilson, Alvin W. Weikert, and Henry Schuddemage.

Seventh Ward—William H. Sible, John J. Gehrett, David E. Leighton and Moses H. Brensinger.

Eighth Ward—James H. W. Howard, Augustus H. Frankem, John A. Krause and Patrick H. Ryan.

Ninth Ward—John C. Hutton, James G. M. Bay, Herman J. Wolz, and John M. Shearer.

PRELIMINARY.

As early as November, 1883, the Dauphin County Historical Society considered the propriety of a proper celebration of the One Hundredth Anniversary of the Formation of the County of Dauphin, as well as the Founding of the City of Harrisburg, which would occur in the year 1885. In February following, acting upon the suggestions made, a Committee from the Society was appointed to whom was entrusted this important duty. As the Founder of the town gave liberally of his land to the State, County, and City, it was deemed appropriate that all should be invited to join the people in giving eclat to the occasion.

On the 9th of March, 1884, His Honor, Mayor Wilson, sent the following communication to the City Councils of Harrisburg:

" In 1885, Harrisburg will have reached the Centennial year of its existence, having been founded by John Harris in 1785. Believing that this important event in our history should not be permitted to pass by the municipal authorities without proper recognition, I would respectfully suggest to your honorable bodies the appointment of a Joint Committee upon Centennial, for the purpose of arranging all necessary details for the proper celebration of the occasion, and that they be empowered to invite the co-operation of the Dauphin County Historical Society, an association to whom our citizens are greatly indebted for the valuable records relating to our history. I have addressed you thus early on the subject, for the reason that it will require a great deal of time and labor to secure such a celebration as will prove worthy of the Capital City of the Commonwealth."

Acting upon the suggestion just set forth, Charles A. Miller, of the Select Council, offered the following:

" Resolved, by the Select and Common Council of the City of Harrisburg, That a Joint Special Committee, to be composed of six members of the Common Council and three members of the Select Council be appointed by the respective chairs so that each ward of the city shall be represented on said committee, to take into consideration the celebration of the centenial anniversary of the foundation of Harrisburg: that the communication of the Mayor be referred to said committee, and said committee shall have power to devise the means and most expedient manner of appropriately celebrating said event, and report from time to time to councils."

After an amendment, increasing the number, the foregoing was promptly acted upon by those bodies and a committee appointed. Finding, however, that the original committees were too large, it was decided that sub-committees of three from those of the Historical Society and Councils be appointed, which should be designated the General Committee on the Centennial. The number promptly organized was subsequently increased to ten, and from that time onward have acted for the committees originally appointed.

As the date of the erection of the county was the 4th of March, 1785, and the Report of the Commissioners, which designated Harrisburg as the county seat, the 14th of April, 1785, at first it was deemed better to fix upon the latter date as the beginning of our century, and April 14, as the day of celebration. After due consideration, however, and at a conference of all the Centennial Committees, from the 13th to the 17th of September was fixed upon as the time for the Anniversary.

From that date onward the General Committee met at first weekly, then two, three, and four times a week, devoting themselves to the perfecting of all arrangements necessary for a successful celebration, which it proved to be in every particular.

Beside the appointment of special committees to superintend each day's commemorative exercises, there were other and just as important ones, which proved to be a far greater labor than generally supposed. The results of the work of the General Committee were fully shown in the magnificent celebration, which in every detail proved so satisfactory.

The Programme as originally adopted, herewith given, was carried out to the very letter :

1. That the celebration of the One Hundredth Anniversary of the erection of the county of Dauphin, and the founding of the city of Harrisburg be fixed for Monday, September 14th, 1885.

2. That the Clergy of all the congregations or churches in the county of Dauphin, be requested to deliver Commemorative Sermons or Discourses on Sunday, September 13th, 1885, and that a committee

of nine be appointed to confer with, and invite the co-operation of the Clergy in the performance of this request.

3. That Monday, September 14th, 1885, at the hour of 9 o'clock in the morning of said day, it is recommended that the Court House, Church, Public School, Fire Engine, Factory and all other bells througout the county be rung for the space of fifteen minutes; and that in all the Schools, public and private, of the county, or other assemblage at that hour gathered together, sing the National Hymm, commencing

"God Bless Our Native Land."

4. That the Inaugural Ceremonies be held at the Court House and in other parts of the county to be hereafter designated, at the hour of 11 o'clock in the forenoon. There shall be delivered an introductory address, with brief addresses by State, County and City officials. And that on the evening of the same day at the hour of 7.30 o'clock the concluding exercises shall consist of a Centenary Poem, an Historical Address, Singing, etc., and remarks by old citizens; and that a committee of nine be appointed to carry out this resolve.

5. That on Tuesday, September 15th, 1885, a parade of the Military, Grand Army, the civil and social societies or organizations in the county, shall take place in Harrisburg, at 10 o'clock in the forenoon of said day; and that a committee of nine be appointed to invite organizations of this character to participate.

6. That on Wednesday, September 16th, 1885, at 10 o'clock in the forenoon, there shall be an Industrial Display and Procession. That every department

of industry—the farmer, the artizan, the citizen from every portion of the county be requested to participate; and that a committee of nine be appointed to arrange the details of this display by the people of Dauphin county.

7. That on Thursday, September 17th, 1885, the Firemen of this and adjoining counties of the State, and others whom they may invite, will arrange and organize a display and procession commencing at the hour of 11 o'clock on said day, and that a committee of nine be appointed to confer with the committee from the Firemen's Union relative thereto.

8. That a Marshal be chosen for each day with power to designate special and other aids, to whom shall be committed and entrusted the order of parade or street displays on the days fixed therefor. Such Chief Marshal's designation to be a crimson sash, special aids blue and other aids white.

9. That an Antiquarian Display be held on the week of the Anniversary Celebration. That a room be provided for the collection and display of ancient farm implements, furniture, portraits, paintings, china, books, clothing, beds and bedding, and relics of all descriptions. That a moderate fee be charged for admission, to be applied to the purposes of the celebration. That all articles will be properly insured, and returned to their respective owners. That a committee of forty ladies and ten gentlemen be appointed to give effect to this resolve, conduct and have charge of said exhibition. The Antiquarian Display will be opened at Harrisburg on Wednesday, September 9th,

1885. To be closed at 10 P. M. of Thursday, September 17th, 1885.

10. That in the various Election Districts of the county, special committees of five shall be formed to attend to the furtherance of the celebration, and by their attendance during it, to add to the importance of it; and that a committee of nine be appointed who shall carry out the object of this resolve.

11. That the officers of all Boroughs in the county be invited and requested to attend the Centennial Anniversary, on the opening and succeeding days. And resolved that Mayor Wilson, ex-Mayors Verbeke, Boas, Patterson, and Herman, and the presiding officers of the Councils of the city of Harrisburg, be a committee to carry this resolve into effect.

12. That a cordial invitation to participate in this celebration is extended to the citizens of the county of Lebanon, which for twenty-eight years formed a part of the original county of Dauphin, and ever since has been closely united therewith politically.

13. That a Commemorative Medal with suitable device and inscription be prepared, to be of three values, gold, silver and bronze. That said medal be sold by the treasurer or under his direction at a reasonable advance on its cost, and that a committee of five be appointed to carry out this resolve.

14. That the General Secretary of the committee shall notify all persons appointed upon committees by circular inviting their consent to assume the duty, and upon an affirmative reply, announce the appointment.

15. That all committees appointed under the foregoing shall have power to appoint such sub-committees as they see proper to aid them in carrying out the objects of their appointment.

16. That Dr. William H. Egle is permanent secretary and is charged with the duty of conducting and supervising all correspondence and publications respecting the proposed celebration.

17. That a Treasurer be chosen, who shall have charge of all cash contributions, with power to appoint assistants in any part of the county. His payments shall be made by check upon orders approved by an auditor to be appointed by this committee. All disputed claims shall be laid before this sub-committee for adjudication.

18. That 321 Walnut street, Harrisburg, be rented for the use of this committee, other committees, and for all the general purposes of the Centennial.

19. That this committee hereby notify the citizens of the city and county that there will be a general finance committee hereafter appointed by this body to whom all citizens will be expected to contribute at the proper time.

20. As it may be found necessary hereafter to modify portions of this programme, any suggestions in that direction will be received in writing, addressed to the secretary, and proper action taken as soon as the propositions can be considered by the general committee.

In the pages which follow will be found, not only a brief resume of the duty each sub-committee performed, but a record of what the citizens of the county of Dauphin and the city of Harrisburg, may look to with great pride. Take it all in all, under Providence, it was a celebration unequaled in the annals of America.

THE FORMATION

OF THE

COUNTY OF DAUPHIN.

MARCH 4TH, 1785.

INAUGURAL CEREMONIES.

WEDNESDAY, MARCH 4TH. 1885.

At noon, on this day, the bells and whistles throughout the city announced the completion of the first century of Dauphin county. The event would have been more formally celebrated. had not the absence of so many citizens and officials at the inauguration of President Cleveland interfered. However, the bells rang out in joyous peals and the whistles of the various industrial establishments screamed as though in full sympathy with the important occasion. Here and there the flags were flying, but the important transactions at the city of Washington, at the very hour, seemed to absorb all other questions, and the local event neglected, save as here noted.

The following data is appropriate in this connection : The "act for erecting part of the county of Lancaster into a separate county," to be called Dauphin, was passed on the 4th of March, 1785. The first officer commissioned was Capt. Alex. Graydon, as prothonotary, March 9, 1785; the second, Rev. Joseph Montgomery, as register and recorder, March 11, 1785. Thus it will be seen that very little time was lost in the organization. The first will was proved on the 27th of April, 1785, while the first deed was recorded on the 26th of April, 1785.

THE
FOUNDING OF HARRISBURG,

April 14th, 1785.

PROCEEDINGS OF THE CELEBRATION

· BY THE

DAUPHIN COUNTY HISTORICAL SOCIETY,

Tuesday, April 14th, 1885.

PROGRAMME.

President of the Meeting, ... DAVID MUMMA

Introductory Address, ... A. BOYD HAMILTON

Centenary Poem, ... BENJAMIN M. NEAD

The First Officers of the County, ...

The Commissioners to Lay Out the Town, WILLIAM H. EGLE, M. D

THE FOUNDING OF THE TOWN.

On the 15th of September, 1783, the General Assembly passed a resolution directing the appointment of commissioners for the purpose of receiving "proposals of such person or persons as may offer lands to the public, for the purpose of building a town or towns on the east bank of the Susquehanna." What the ulterior object was we of the present day can readily see. They had far-seeing men in those days—but other legislators were as obtuse as some of the present. On the 20th of September following, the House proceeded to elect commissioners for the purpose expressed in the resolution of the 15th, "and the ballots being taken it appeared that David Rittenhouse, Thomas Hutchins and Nathan Sellers, Esquires, were duly elected." Every Pennsylvanian knows about the famous astronomer Rittenhouse. Thomas Hutchins was prior to the Revolution in the British service, and was a geographer of much prominence in that era of American history. On the 4th of March, 1784, they made their report. Those famous men were correct in their opinion of this locality, which time has verified, notwithstanding the malignity of the enemies of our town or the stupidity of croakers. Here is their report:

PHILADELPHIA, March 4, 1784.

To the Honorable, the Representatives of the Freemen of the Commonwealth of Pennsylvania, in General Assembly Convened:

In consequence of instructions which we, the subscribers, were honored with on the 20th of September last, we have this day received the inclosed proposals from Mr. John Harris, setting forth his desire of granting lands on the east side of the Susquehanna for the purpose of building a town thereon; and though the inclemency of the season has hitherto prevented our viewing the ground, as we intended doing, yet from a competent knowledge, long since acquired, we are well acquainted with the situation. At the particular instance of Mr. Harris, we respectfully report to the Honorable House, that it is our humble opinion the place mentioned in the enclosed proposal is preferable to any that we as yet know of, on or near the Susquehanna, and for the following reasons: The situation is high, airy, healthy and pleasant; the soil rich and water wholesome; there is clay proper for brick, stone for building, and fuel in the greatest abundance; it confines on the great road leading from one end of the Continent to the other; the river at the ferry is commonly fordable the greater part of the summer season; and its situation is very convenient for receiving the produce of the upper parts of the river.

DAVID RITTENHOUSE,
THOMAS HUTCHINS.

Whether at the outset a new county was contemplated to be formed we know not, but the proposals of John Harris looked to that end. The facts are that no sooner was the struggle for independence brought to a close than from nearly every county in the State came applications for a division and the erection of a new county. The inhabitants of the northern part of Lancaster county found it inconvenient and expensive to go to the then county town, but no sooner was there a prospect of the erection of a new county, than efforts were made to secure the location of the county town. John Harris, with his project for laying out a town at Harris' Ferry, in accordance with the resolution of the General Assembly, on the 4th day of March 1784, made "Proposals" to the General Assembly which were read and referred. These are as follows:

"Proposals of John Harris for the Laying out of a Town on his Land on the River Susquehanna.

"That the said John Harris will immediately (if encouraged by Government) lay out a Town of Two Hundred Lots, on high ground above his dwelling house, the lots about the Quantity of a Quarter of an acre each, in such form, with respect to streets, lanes and alleys as the Commissioners may approve, a large street to be left for publick landings along the River side. That the said John Harris agrees that the Honourable Assembly of this Commonwealth shall appoint commissioners to value his said lots. after reserving Twenty lots for his own use; That the said John Harris will convey all the streets. lanes and alleys to the inhabitants of said Town, and will convey to proper Commissioners a lot for a Court

House and Goal, and a Square of four Acres to the
State of Pennsylvania, for such purposes as the Government may apply the same; the applyers to have
it as their choice to take the lots on a reasonable
Ground Rent, or to purchase the Fee Simple of the
same; The commissioners in both cases to be the
judges; that as soon as the said Two Hundred Lots
are built on or disposed of, should there be further demand for lots, the said John Harris engages, that the
Publick shall be accommodated at a reasonable rate.

John Harris."

As these proposals are dated "Philadelphia, March
3d, 1784," it is probable the proprietor was in that
city looking after his interests. The committee to
whom they were referred made report on the 6th of
March :

"That they find, on the strictest examination, that
a division of the said county is necessary, and that
the fixing of the county town at Harris' Ferry will
not only be highly acceptable to a great number of
the petitioners, but would be attended with beneficial
consequences to the commerce of this State. Your
committee are convinced of the propriety of the Commissioners' report, and fully satisfied with the proposals offered by Mr. Harris."

Then follow the bounds of the proposed new
county, and this additional resolution :

"Resolved, That the proposals of John Harris be
accepted of, for the laying out of the county town and
entered on the minutes of this House for the future
government of the Commissioners ; and that Joseph

Montgomery, Jonathan Hoge and Moses Maclean be the Commissioners for carrying into effect the proposals of the said John Harris."

When the act erecting the county of Dauphin was passed, five gentlemen, residents of the locality, were named as commissioners to carry into effect the proposals of John Harris. They made their report on the 14th of April, 1785, one hundred years ago this day, and as that report was the act which permanently fixed the county seat at Harris' Ferry, it was the proper thing for not only the Historical Society, but the citizens generally to celebrate the event.

The One Hundredth Anniversary of this event occurring on Tuesday, April 14, 1885, the Dauphin county Historical Society celebrated the same by appropriate services. The exercises were held in the Grand Jury room on the upper floor of the Court House. Around the walls, neatly arranged, were some rare old relics, maps, views, and portraits. These gave interest to the occasion.

David Mumma presided, and on calling the assemblage to order said that they were gathered together to celebrate the laying out of a village, later a borough and now the city of Harrisburg, the Capital of the great State of Pennsylvania. This was a sort of introduction to the regular Centennial celebration which was to follow. There were many events concerning the establishment of the city of Harrisburg and the county of Dauphin, which to many residents were unknown, and it was eminently proper that some action be taken looking to a preservation of the records and enlightenment of the present generation. The celebration proposed was not designed merely for amusement, but to assist in informing the children with respect to the deeds of their ancestors, and how they lived an hundred years ago. In view of the celebration in September, 1885, it was important that the citizens start with the matter well in hand, to the end that the celebration might in every way be complete in every particular, in fact, the greatest ever witnessed in this section. He hoped everybody would assist in making it a success. The firemen of the city were straining every nerve to make a creditable display, and he praised them for the efforts they had already made.

ADDRESS BY A. BOYD HAMILTON.

Mr. Chairman, Ladies and Gentlemen:—This imperfect sketch of very early Harrisburg has for its purpose the preservation of certain portions of its history not generally known. They are of interest, and I hope will awaken a desire to make our Centennial, that which it promises to be, an event of first rate magnitude and good feeling.

There is no one now within the borders of Dauphin county who will live to celebrate a second event, such as we have met to commemorate this moment. Certainly, no one lives in the county that lived in it at its formation, and all the original men and women, making up the small village of Harrisburg, on the 14th of April, 1785, have passed to their fathers.

The story of the county we do not propose to detail, particularly as there are so many interesting

incidents relating to the early days of Harrisburg
that remain to be told. Some of these, traditional,
are especially attractive in their narration. But as
this commemorates an historic event, the details
should be, and we hope are real facts, for the proof
of which written evidences have been preserved.
They are from dusty records, and therefore do not
possess the romantic interest that clings to the "shad
fisherman, deer slayer, or Indian scout of one hundred years ago," but not the less worthy, in spite of
that, of preservation.

The first John Harris was at this point about 25
years after the landing of Penn. He obtained a
trader's license, which assumed to give a right to
erect a house, palisaded, and loopholed for defense. Harris took under this right all his land and
held it until his death in December, 1748. His eldest
son, also a John Harris, succeeded, purchasing, before the Revolution, the rights of his brothers and
sisters to the land held by the father. This comprised 800 acres.

We pause to glance at a transaction on this frontier of the Province of Pennsylvania, thus described
in an advertisement in the "Philadelphia Advertiser," July, 1794:

"Whereas, on or about the 20th of May last, there
came to the House of John Harris, on the Susquehanna, a Man who said he lived near the Great
Swamp in Bucks County, and brought Two Horses
with him, one a Black, the other a Dun with one eye,
which Person took a walk from the said Harris's in

the Evening and has not since been heard of; These
are therefore to desire the owner to fetch the Horses
away.   JOHN HARRIS.

"June 22d, 1749."

The foregoing is among the earliest account authen-
ticated by names and dates, that we have of the
Harris settlement; the first relation of one of its incidents. The poor fellow who probably lost his life on
that pleasant May evening, who so utterly disappears,
to those who will have read and now read this notice,
how sad his fate! At this moment, so long after the
occurrence, we may fancy the search Harris and his
ferrymen made for the missing stranger, and what
trouble they took to make his fate known. Then
there was but one road to Philadelphia from Harrisburg. no mail, and it was not often travelers presented
themselves at "the ferry," to whom it would be safe
to entrust a letter. The busy activities of the present
about the old "Ferry" were not even thought of by
the most inveterate guesser.

As early as 1775, Harris purchased and prepared a
book for his projected town. This book became the
"Lot Book." No name was given the town. In
1784 he made a proposal to the Legislature to lay
out a town, which is of so much interest that we
quote it in full :

PHILADELPHIA, March 3, 1784.

"Proposals of John Harris for the laying out of a
town on his land, on the River Susquehanna:

"That the said John Harris will immediately (if
encouraged by government) lay out a town of two

hundred lots, on the high grounds above his present house, the lots of about the quantity of a quarter of an acre each, in such form, with respect to streets, lanes and alleys, as the commissioners may approve, a large street to be left for public landings along the river side. That the said John Harris agrees that the honorable Assembly of this Commonwealth shall appoint commissioners to value his said lots, after reserving twenty lots for his own use: That the s'd John Harris will convey all the streets, lanes and alleys, to the inhabitants of s'd town, and will convey to the proper commissioners a lot for a court house and jail, and a square of four acres for the State of Pennsylvania, for such purposes as the government may apply the same; the applyers to have it at their choice to take the lots on a reasonable ground rent, or to purchase the fee simple of the same: The commissioners in both cases to judge: That as soon as the s'd two hundred lots are built on or disposed of, should there be a further demand for lots the s'd John Harris engages, that the publick shall be accommodated at a reasonable rate."

These considerations were faithfully complied with in the next year, 1785, as we learn from the report of the commissioners named in the act of Assembly, which is as follows:

"We the subscribed commissioners appointed to carry into effect the proposals of John Harris respecting the laying out of the county town of the county of Dauphin, do hereby make known that the said town, with respect to the size of the lots, disposition of the streets, lanes and alleys, and the choice of the public grounds, was laid out under our direction and inspection, agreeably to the adjoining plan of the said town; the said lots, in general, containing about one-quarter of an acre each, and extending from 52½ feet, with a depth of 210 feet, with some unavoidable variations in particular courses, as may easily be seen by inspection; the whole been laid down from a scale of 200 feet to the inch.

Witness our hands the 14th day of April, 1785,

JACOB AWL,   JOSHUA ELDER,

ANDREW STEWART,   JAMES COWDEN,

WILLIAM BROWN."

In 1786 the Supreme Executive Council changed the name from Harrisburg to Louisburg, "for the sake of euphony," as Governor McKean expressed it, so that the name of the town might agree with the compliment to the French king in the name of the county. In 1791 we returned to Harrisburg by an act of assembly, and have rejoiced in that name since.

The land surveyed for the new town absorbed nearly 600 acres of the 800 owned by the founder.

In the lot book of John Harris are found autographs of many of the very earliest inhabitants of this town. The fashionable way, one hundred years ago, of settling a money transaction was for both parties to sign receipts, or acquittances. As an example, Thomas Elder purchased lot 75 for £56, and owed for ground rent, &c., at the time of the death of Harris, £85 6, which he paid, and so states the account on the lot book, signing his name in the exact form, without the flourish, that it is found fifty years after on the issues of the Harrisburg bank.

Harris wrote a good hand, so with Maclay and the Harris sons. Jacob Stayley signed in German, as did Christopher Hocker, in a miserable scratch, whilst his brothers, John and Adam, signed in fair characters. These are followed by Samuel Weir, Samuel Hill, Samuel Berryhill, Tobias Seyboth, Robert Barr, Thomas Murray and Peter Graybill. To these must be added the autographs of John Elder, jr., William Wilson, John Miller, Frederick Youse, Frederick Girt, (in German); James Clunie, very clean and neat; John Comfort, Mathias Hutman, Michael Peters, John Chambers, Andrew Newman and George Hotz; the two last in German and not very well done; followed by James McNamara, John Ebert, James Beatty, John Zinn (German), Samuel Barnes Davis, Jacob Earnest, Peter Unger, George Reddick, (the last three in German;) James Mitchel, Samuel Grimes, John Cremer, (German;) John Hoge, (the signature of an aged or nervous person). Thus we have preserved in the library of the Historical Society a valuable collection of the autographs of many of the original settlers of the city.

The names of the purchasers of lots appear upon this Lot Book, as follows:

1. John A. Hanna.	110. Hugh Boden.
2. Mary Harris.	113. William Glass.
5. Jacob Weidman.	115. Archibald McAllister.
6. Francis Johnston.	117. Moses Gilmor.
8. Jacob Ebright.	118. Andrew Stephens.
10. John Hoys [Hice.]	119. Wm. Mitchell, esq.
11. Mrs. Lincoln.	120—121 JAIL.

13. William Brown.
17. Thos. Hartley, York.
18. Alexander Greaden,
20. Henry Fulton.
21. John Hamilton.
23. William Bailey, York.
24. John Maclay, jr.
25. Christian Kunkle.
26. George Hoyer.
27. Henry Hepsman.
28. Clem. Stewdebacker.
29. John Joseph Henry.
32. Lawrence Keen.
33. David Harris.
34. John Crocket.
35. George Irvin.
36. George Ziegler.
37. ⎧ Mary Hanna.
37. ⎪ Robert Harris.
38. ⎨ James Harris.
⎩ All by will.
40. John Hoge.
42. George Fridley.
43. Thomas Paine.
44. Robert Whitehill.
45. Abraham Huston.
47. Thomas Burling.
48. Benjamin Crockett.
49. James Clunie.
50. Abdiel McAlister.
52. Alexander Power.
54. David McGumery.
56. Frederick Youse.
57. Conrad Bombaugh.
59. Galbraith Patterson.
·64. Wendle Hepsman.
68. Frederick Smith.
70. Samuel Awl.
76. Thomas Fider.

122. Michael Stoner.
123. Andrew Stewart.
127. Alexander Barr.
129. John Watson.
134. Thomas Morrow.
135. Gawin Irwin,
136. Charles Stewart.
137. Samuel Martin.
138. Andrew Gregg.
139. George Firestone.
140. George Buyer.
141. John Harsha.
142—148. COURT HOUSE.
144. Samuel Grimes.
145. Peter Lice.
146. Christopher Hocker.
147. Andrew Copp.
148. Michael Copp,
149.   do.
151. John Carson.
152. James Cavitt.
153. John Gilchrist, jr.
154. Isaac Deardough.
157. John Norton.
161. Melchar Rham.
171. Joshua Elder.
172. James Cowden.
175. John Gillard.
176. Dr. Joseph McCumercy.
177. John Ebert.
179. John Millar.
180. Robert Whitehill, jr.
184. Henry Markley.
187. Benjamin Speaker.
189. Rachel Guygar.
192. Philip Eppright.
193—194. James Duncan.
195. Jacob Awl.
196. Valentine Wineland.

78. Anthony Waine.
81. Howard Moore.
87. Alex. Berryhill.
88. John Zinn.
93. James Wetherspoon.
94. Roree Frazer.
96. Samuel Berryhill.
97. James McDonnel.
98. James Sawyers.
99. James Elder.
100. Charlott Baker.
101. George Frey.
102. George Bruner.
103. William Baily, York.
104. Thomas Hartley, York.
107. John File.
108. Thomas Forster.
109. James Beatty.

200. John Boyd.
201. George Allen.
202. John Chambers.
203. Robert Henry.
204. Thomas McArther.
205. Robert Armstrong.
206. Jonathan Wallace.
207. George Ziegler.
208. Jacob Peiffer.
210. Stoner & Bennett.
212. Adam Boyd.
213. Philip Rymout.
214. Robert Stevenson.
215. Henry Peter.
216. James Michell.
217. Mrs. Fulsom & Sons.
218. Valentine Hurter.
219. A. and M. Smith.

After the death of the founder, his executors laid out 114 additional lots, as is shown upon the town plot recorded in the office at Harrisburg.

It was not until April 14, 1785, the date upon which the first deeds were executed, that the name of the town was fixed as HARRISBURG. It then contained nearly 300 persons, including fishermen, ferrymen and slaves. There were about 50 dwelling houses on the town plot.

One of the very earliest conveyances of 1785, by Harris, is No. 149, bounded "on Market place." This lot is on South Market Square, east side. The deed is very specific, is written by John Joseph Henry. witnessed by him and Joseph Montgomery. The lots on the Market Place are 52½ feet shorter than the lots in other parts of the town, or 158½ feet in depth. A full lot is 210 feet deep.

In 1792 William Maclay "leveled the water from the bridge in the town to McAllister's three locust trees," and found the "face of the water to the face of the stone work on the N. E. corner of the market to be 33½ feet" above. So that a market house was in the square on July 17 and 18, 1792, and at no time since has it been without one.

Another interesting paper has been preserved. It is found in a note-book of John Kean, esq., one of the first commissioners, a long time senator in the Berks and Dauphin district, and registrar-general of Pennsylvania. His note reads:

"I removed to Harrisburg, the twenty-second day of April, 1785, where from the vast number of people crowding to this new place, and no houses being yet erected, I was compelled to take lodgings with a Dr. Sterling, a mile above the town. [South street was then the upper town boundary.] In the beginning of June, 1785, I entered into partnership with Mr. James Clunie [afterwards high sheriff] in store-keeping at Harrisburg. We erected a house and in August opened a shop. Our sales quite equalled our expectations. In the beginning of May, 1786, my fellow-townsmen were about forming a system of police for the rising town. They elected me the justice of the peace without dissent, and I was not aware of the affair until the election was over."

I have not been able to discover further particulars of this unauthorized election or what view the Executive Council took of it. We have every reason to believe that police regulation was a real want, which the people were determined to fill, for the protection of their lives and property. Kean served about a year, by which time the executive power had provided regular "squires" for the bustling community. In 1791, they were empowered to elect burgesses, and the citizens chose George Hoyer and Adam Boyd. They were the fathers of our present municipal administrators.

This paper presumes to deal only with the earliest history of the town. To enlarge upon or criticise its subsequent history would be unjust to those who have prepared the many excellent and reliable publications printed in relation to it. Yet I cannot refrain from quoting what Cutler says of us in 1787, and Penn in the following year.

Cutler writes of a Sunday he stopped at Harris' Ferry: "The town contains about 100 houses, many of them brick, and a large number of taverns. About one half the people are English. People were going to church; they meet in private houses; no churches yet." He tells us also that the people were very well and gayly dressed. This town still keeps its early reputation in that respect.

Penn, in 1788, writes: "The situation of this place is the finest I ever saw." He lodged at the "Compass," which we judge to be the stone house erected by the founder in 1766. Penn says the room he occupied was "22 feet square and high in proportion." It is the southeast room of the second story of General Cameron's present residence.

Another writer of the same period speaks of the "fine looking, healthy women." While still another traveler on his way westward, is delighted with the excellent accommodations, the fine market, abundance of fish and the Philadelphia looking houses and streets. Unfortunately for too many years, we have been a copy of that city in more particulars than one.

The ground upon which we tread of the original town plot, was neither a wild or a forest in 1785. It was a well cultivated and productive tract divided into three farms, under intelligent culture for more than fifty years previously. Its mansion orchard extended from the stone house to Mulberry street in one direction, and below that street to Paxtang or the great road, on the other; about forty acres. Its meadows along the valley of the Paxtang creek, and its best wheat fields above Mulberry, as far up the Susquehanna as Walnut street.

The quarries below the great road, now Paxtang street, were in constant use. A brick yard along this "great road to the ferry" had been in use for "three or four years." There was "a hickory log house for the upper farm," above the present Harrisburg academy. This house was occupied by Governor McKean and his colleagues, the judges, during the occupancy of Philadelphia by the British army in the Revolution. The open fields about this point, Governor McKean stated to my Grandfather Boyd, "were the best cultivated, most charming he had ever seen."

The outer farm on the "great road," this side of the poor house farm, had an orchard upon it, and produced "fine fruit and large walnuts" in the youth of the late Gen. John Forster, who died twenty years ago, eighty-six years of age. The house on this

farm, erected before 1765, is still standing, and is
occupied as a farm dwelling by a tenant of the
speaker. It is constructed of poplar logs, and its
interior partitioned with yellow pine boards.

> " In these green fields life flowed afresh,
> And young-eyed Health exulted."

I have conversed with many persons who knew
Mr. Harris before 1785, and from that date to the
period of his death in 1791, had much social and
business intercourse with him. He is described as a
tall, well proportioned, sturdy man, with good teeth,
smooth shaven, healthy appearance, and hair inclined
to turn gray from an original rich brown. This he
wore in the fashion of his time, long, and upon the
Fourth of July had it powdered. His dress was
"leather breeches," in the fit of which he took great
pride; brown coat and vest, long white woolen stockings, silver buckles and heavy low-cut shoes; fond of
his gun, rod and dog; and equally fond of fishing or
of a shooting-match : quite an adept at " long bullets,"
or shuffle-board. He did not hesitate about expressing an opinion upon any subject of discussion, and
was most emphatic in his admiration of Washington
and those who had served under him. He lived long
enough to see his town well started on the way to its
present proportions.

The valor of our forefathers gave us our liberty :
the founder of Harrisburg gave us a precious dwelling place; may our sons be the pillars of it, our
daughters its corner stones, "and that there be no
complaining in our streets. Happy is that people
that is in such a case."

POEM BY BENJAMIN M. NEAD.

Since Chaos took form in God's primal thought,
Unsatisfied man first causes has sought.
The springs of the action of the planets on high,
The course of the sun and the moon in the sky,
The source whence the lightning derives its dread power,
The agents which cause the storm clouds to lower,
Whence cometh the wind and the rate of its blowing,
Why summer is hot, and the cause of the snowing,
Cosmographically noting the bounds Oceanic,
And the orders of creatures in the Era Organic.
And then rising higher to a worthier thought,
His own matchless self into judgment is brought.
How came he to live, and what of his soul?
And when living is ended the ultimate goal
Of the part called immortal, and what is in store?
Whether joy everlasting or pain evermore.
Concerning these things do men scientific
Profound grow in research, in discourse prolific;
With men theologic wax warm in dispute
Creeds new to establish and old ones refute.

But enough in this deep metaphysical strain;
We are busied to-night in another domain.
When Adam first ate of the fruit of the Tree,
Though forbidden to do so by God's own decree,
The desire fell upon him to wander abroad,
That he might never more see the face of his God.
And those who came of him, his own sons and daughters,
In turn wandered forth through lands and o'er waters,
To regions remote from the place of their birth,
Till the children of Adam had peopled the earth,
Scattering hither and thither as they ceased not to roam,
The traditions and memories of Eden their home.
And the seed of all nations wise men may now trace
Through the changes of centuries to the first of our race.
In the dubious reflections of ages unknown,
In the legends transmitted from the northermost zone,
In the tales Atlantean, by many esteemed,
But myths of the night by philosopher dreamed.

In the culture and art of the race called Aryan,
In the skillful achievements of the people Barbarian,
In the rune of the Norseman, the tale of the Dane,
In the monuments marking the American plain,
A few of the proofs may be found in array,
That presagements of Eden are facts of to-day,
And a nation of millions on Columbia's shore,
All the prophecies prove of the sages of yore.

   Slept our vales and slept our mountains,
     And in stillness swept our streams;
   Brave nomads drank at our fountains,
     And basked in our bright sun's beams;
   Till God, in His own good pleasure,
     Taught men t'interpret aright
   The signs of the wondrous Treasure
     Concealed so long from their sight.

   Spare we time, a little measure,
     From our present busy life,
   From our thoughts of gain and pleasure,
     From our never ending strife,
   From the never ceasing worry,
     From the grief and from the care,
   From the bustle and the hurry
     Of our life, the larger share.
   Turn for once, from present duty
     To the half forgotten past
   To admire the scenes of beauty
     Which adorn its vistas vast.

   Inspired poet writing neatly
     Of pictures on Memory's wall,
   Of the dim old Forest, sings sweetly,
     "It seemeth the best of all."
   The dim old Forest primeval
     Has part in our thoughts to-night,
   And scenes with the Forest coeval
     Our minds and fancies delight.
   A noble, an inland River,
     Sweeping outward to the Sea,

On its bosom sunbeams quiver,
   Shadows fall from forest tree,
Glassy surface still unbroken
   By the keel of white-winged ship,
Bearing name yet never spoken
   Save by swarthy Native's lip;
Nestling now by base of mountain
   Rippling now through flow'ry vale
Drinking in from shaded fountain,
   Crystal springs which never fail.
Flow'ry meads awaiting tillage
   From the coming white man's hands
Curling smoke from Native's village
   Resting place of Indian bands,
Where the sound of warrior's rifle
   Wakes a thousand friends to war
If a neighbor dares to trifle
   With Shawanese or Delaware,
Tribes which dwell by bright Swatara
   And by rippling Paxtang's side,
O'er whose water swift as arrow
   In their birchen boats they glide.

Precious as the ancient manna
   Dropped in desert from on high
Was the sight of Susquehanna
   To that white man's hungry eye.
From the hills he looked in wonder
   And to him there came a dream
Of a city founded yonder,
   Looking out upon the stream;
By no narrow limits bounded,
   But embracing landscape fair,
Like city which Penn founded
   On the sparkling Delaware.
So he planted and he founded
   Better far than he then knew,
By dangers thick surrounded,
   This home for me and you.
Savage Natives kind, but wary,

Brooked the white men's presence there,
Until the busy Ferry,
Was heard of everywhere.
Still the old world knew oppression,
None in thought nor act were free,
If opinion found expression,
'Twas at risk of liberty.
So men came from homes of childhood
From the land which gave them birth,
And sought in our western wildwood
For this garden spot of earth.
And they settled round our Ferry,
Men from distant Donegal,
From old Antrim, and from Derry,
And from spots beyond recall;
Dwelt in peace with selves and neighbor,
Placed their faith and trust in God,
Spent their lives in honest labor,
Slept at length beneath the sod.

Thus was founded, thus was builded,
City proud as regal Rome;
City free as ancient Athens,
Of thousands now the home.
Stand now upon the hill-top
And gaze toward yonder stream
And note the grand fulfillment
Of the settler's wildest dream.
No sign of waving Forest
Where Forest used to be,
Save one token, fragile, broken
Trunk of ancient forest tree.
Tree with age far past the noting
Of any white man's ken,
But the legends say it blossomed
In the days of William Penn.
Now preserved as fitting relic
To mark the noted spot,
Where settler seized by savage Clan,
And bound to stake with fiendish plan,

Escaped by chance the plot.
  Gone is the busy Ferry
Linking river shore to shore,
  The boatman brave hath lain in grave,
A hundred years or more.
  Grand bridges span the river,
Which bear on pier and arch
  The freighted wains, the lengthened trains
Of Traffic's onward march.
  Look now adown the river
Through smoke the red fires gleam,
  And the furnace light, at dead of night
Makes bright the silent stream—
  Turn to the noble City,
Spread out like picture grand,
  Its towering spires, its mosque-like domes,
Its buildings tall, its palace homes
  Majestically stand.
No prouder State in the Union
  Than the Keystone of the arch;
Note her grand achievements
  In time's progressive march,
And this her chiefest city,
  What greater word of praise,
Could advocate of actions great
  Of sister city raise.
'Tis fitting we should celebrate
  Our City's hundredth year
And all take part with gladsome heart
  In wishing her good cheer.
God rule this rising city,
  A Ruler safe is He,
And grant that as its Past has been,
  So may its Future be.

THE FIRST OFFICERS OF THE COUNTY.

In the absence of the gentleman to whom was assigned the "First Officers of the County," James M.

Lamberton, esq., read the paper prepared by Dr. Egle.

One hundred years ago office-seekers were abundant as now. The cause of this was partly due to the fact that an eight years war had left many good men without business and without means. The exposures incident to the prolonged struggle for independence also rendered many of the patriots unfit for manual labor, and hence when all over the State the rage came for division of counties, and the formation of new ones; applications without number were made to the Supreme Executive Council, the appointing power of the State under the Constitution of 1776, for official positions.

No sooner was it certain that the act for the erection of the County of Dauphin would pass the Assembly, than memorials were presented to the Council from Capt. Alexander Graydon and the Rev. Joseph Montgomery requesting the appointment of Prothonotary of the proposed new county—that office being considered the most lucrative. The result is well told in Mr. Graydon's delightful " Memoirs :"

"Among the newly introduced maxims of republicanism it was an highly favored one in Pennsylvania, to bring justice home to every man's door. In the spirit of this principle several new counties had been erected ; and in the year of 1785 I had the good fortune, through the warm exertions of an influential friend, to obtain an appointment to the prothonotaryship of Dauphin county. By a combination of small circumstances working together for my advan-

tage, I obtained, contrary to expectation, the suffrage
of the Supreme Executive Council of which Mr.
Dickinson was then president. The republican party
possessed a majority in the Council, and Col. Atlee,
who belonged to it, was designated for the office.
He was conspicuous as a party man, and if I mis-
take not, at the time a member of the Legislature;
and on the score of services and character, no one
had better claims. But on this occasion the nega-
tive character of my politics, contrary to the usual
course of things, probably gave me the advantage.
To keep out Atlee, the Constitutionalists were disposed to give their votes to any of his competitors.
Of course I had all their strength; and by adding to
it two or three Republican votes, I acquired a greater
number than any in nomination. As the rule was
to vote for the candidate individually, there was no
physical or, perhaps, moral impediment to each of
them receiving the vote of every member. A promise to one was not broken by voting also for another,
unless it was exclusively made. The president had
probably given a promise to Col. Atlee as well as to
myself, and considering me too weak to endanger
his success, thought he might safely gratify my
friend, who pinned him to the vote, which on coming to the box he seemed half inclined to withhold.
Or, where was his crime if he really thought our pre-
tentions equal, and, therefore, determined not to decide between us? Such were the accidents which
procured my unlooked for appointment."

Of this first officer, the prothonotary, appointed on
the 9th of March 1785, we have the following account:

Capt.ALEXANDER GRAYDON, son of Alexander Graydon and Rachel Marks, was born April 10, 1752 (N. S.,) at Bristol, Bucks Co., Pa. At the age of six years he was sent to Philadelphia to the care of his maternal grandfather, and put to the school of David James Dove, an Englishman, and much celebrated in his day as a teacher. He was afterwards entered at the academy now the University of Pennsylvania, where he was placed in charge of the Rev. Mr. Kinnesley, teacher of English and Professor of Oratory. In 1761 he entered the Latin school of John Beverage. At the age of sixteen he left college, and some eighteen months after commenced the study of law with his uncle, Edward Biddle of Philadelphia. In 1773 he was, on account of impaired health, sent by the latter to York, to the care of Samuel Johnson, prothonotary of that county and a lawyer of some prominence, where he remained about six months, when he returned to his home at Philadelphia. The study of law was continued, at the suggestion of his uncle, with James Allen, a second son of William Allen, then chief Justice of Pennsylvania. About the time when he should have been admitted to the bar the war of the Revolution opened, and, imbued with the military ardor and patriotic spirit of the hour, he received the appointment and was commissioned captain, Jan. 5, 1776, of Col. John Shee's (Third Pennsylvania) battalion. Of his services, his being taken prisoner at the capture of Fort Washington, on the Hudson, Nov. 16, 1776, and of his being released on parole, we can only refer to his "Memoirs." He was exchanged in April, 1778. Having lost his rank by reason of his capture and parole, he did not again enter the service. His mother having removed to Reading during the occupancy of Philadelphia by the British, thither Alexander went, and being admitted to the bar of Berks county, began the practice of his profession. Upon the organization of the new county of Dauphin in 1785, through the influence of Gen. Mifflin, Mr. Graydon was appointed by the Supreme Executive Council of Pennsylvania, prothonotary of the county. He removed there, and performed the duties of his office in a manner alike creditable to himself and advantageous to the public.

During the Whiskey Insurrection of 1794, when Gen. Washington reached Harrisburg, the address of the burgesses was from the facile pen of Mr. Graydon, while upon the accession of John Adams to the Presidency, the letter of the citizens of the county to that functionary shows his elegant diction. Upon the election of Governor Thomas McKean, he was suddenly displaced from office. He then retired to a small farm near the borough, where he continued to reside until the year 1816, when he removed to Philadelphia with the intention of engaging in literary persuits, and, with a view to the increase of a very restricted income, of entering upon the business of a publisher. Ere he could mature the plans, however, he yielded to the mandate which all must obey, and closed his life on the 2d day of May, 1818. Mr. Graydon was ardently attached to literature and literary pursuits. He was a frequent and acceptable contributor to the Port-Folio in its palmiest days of popularity and influence. These contributions, which for the most part, were modestly denominated "Notes of a Desultory Reader," contain his opinions of the authors whose works he had read, accompanied with occasional critiques upon their style, and all invariably written in a strain of candor and ease, affording indubitable evidence of the elevation and purity of his own sentiments, and of an enlarged, well-disciplined, and highly cultivated mind. These articles, with others written from time to time for the press, of which a memoranda list is in existence, deserve to be collected in a volume and printed. In 1811 he published at Harrisburg "Memoirs of a Life chiefly passed in Pennsylvania within the last Sixty Years, with Occasional Remarks upon the General Occurrences, Character, and Spirit of that Eventful Period." In 1822, John Galt, of Edinburgh, well known for his valuable contributions to English literature, caused its republication in that city, to which he prefixed a dedication to the American envoy then resident near the court of St. James. In this dedication he says of the "Memoirs:" "It is remarkable that a production so rich in the various excellencies of style, description, and impartiality should not have been known to the collectors of American books in this country, especially as it is, perhaps, the best personal narrative that has yet appeared relative to the history of that great conflict which terminated in establishing the independence of the United States. The candor with respect to public occurrences which it displays, the views of manners in Pennsylvania prior to the memorable era of 1776, and the inci-

dental sketches of historical characters with which it
is enriched, cannot fail to render the volume a valuable addition to the stock of general knowledge, and
will probably obtain for the author no mean place
among those who have added permanent lustre to
the English language." In 1846, John S. Littell, of
Philadelphia, edited the work, with notes, index, etc.,
which was printed in an octavo of five hundred
pages, changing the title to "Memoirs of His Own
Times, with Reminiscences of the Men and Events
of the Revolution, by Alexander Graydon." Of this
edition many copies were issued, and it too has be-
come rare.

On the 11th of March, the Rev. JOSEPH MONT-
GOMERY was appointed "Recorder of Deeds and Register of the Probate of Wills" "in and for the county
of Dauphin." He was Capt. Graydon's opponent for
the Prothonotaryship and resided in the county. It
is doubtful if he was an applicant for this office, and
although Graydon secured his position through
strong political influence that especially of Gen.
Thomas Mifflin, who was his full cousin, Mr. Montgomery's claims as set forth in his memorial were
sufficient to secure to him the office of Register without opposition. Of him the only officer of the county
during the first year of its existence, who was born
within its limits, we shall briefly refer to.

Joseph Montgomery, was the son of John and
Martha Montgomery, emigrants from the North of
Ireland, and born Sept. 23, 1733 (old style) in Pax-
tang township, Lancaster now Dauphin County,
Penn'a. His father was one of the earliest settlers

having emigrated to America prior to 1730. The son was educated at the College of New Jersey (now Princeton College) from which he graduated in 1755; and was afterwards appointed master of the grammar school connected with that institution. In 1760 the College of Philadelphia (now University of Penn'a) and also Yale College, conferred upon him the Master's degree. About this time he was licensed to preach by the Presbytery of Philadelphia and soon after by request entered the bounds of the Presbytery of Lewes from which he was transferred to that of New Castle, accepting a call from the Congregation at Georgetown, over which he was settled from 1767 to 1769. He was installed pastor of the Congregations at Christiana Bridge and New Castle, Delaware, on the 16th of August, 1769, remaining there until the autumn of 1777, when he resigned, having been commissioned chaplain of Col. Smallwood's (Maryland) regiment of the Continental Line. During the war his home was with his relatives in Paxtang. On the 23d day of November, 1780, he was chosen by the General Assembly of Pennsylvania one of the delegates in Congress, and re-elected the following year. He was elected a member of the General Assembly of the State in 1782 serving during the sessions following. He was chosen by that body on the 25th of February, 1783, one of the Commissioners to settle the difficulties between the State and the Connecticut settlers at Wyoming. When the new county of Dauphin was erected, as previously mentioned, the Supreme Executive Council appointed him Register and Recorder which office he held from March 11, 1785 to October 14, 1794, the date of his death. "Mr. Montgomery filled conspicuous and honorable positions in Church and State in the most trying period of the early history of the country. In the Church he was the friend and associate of men like Witherspoon, Rodgers and Spencer, and his bold utterances in the cause of Independence, stamp him as a man of no ordinary courage and decision. .

. . . He enjoyed to an unusual degree the respect and confidence of the men of his generation." As one of the men of mark at the beginning of our history as a county it is but proper that his name and the leading actions of his life be made familiar to the citizen of To-Day.

THE COMMISSIONERS TO LAY OUT THE TOWN.

The "Act for erecting part of the county of Lancaster into a separate county," "to be henceforth known and called by the name of Dauphin county," recited in section seven of said act:

" That it shall and may be lawful to and for Jacob Awl, Joshua Elder, Andrew Stewart, James Cowden, and William Brown of Paxtang, or any three of them, to take assurance to them and their heirs of such lot or piece of ground as shall be laid out and approved of by the said Commissioners or any three of them, for the erecting a Court House and Goal thereupon, in trust for the use of the inhabitants of the said County of Dauphin, and thereupon to erect a Court house and prison sufficient to accommodate the publick service of the said county."

It is of these men, thus specially named, to whom
our references shall be confined. They were all men
of mark in the early days of Paxtang settlement, and
became more prominent in the beginnings of our
county's history in 1785. Apart from this, they were
warm personal friends of the proprietor of the New
Town and earnest advocates in the locating of the
county seat at Harris' Ferry.

The first named. JACOB AWL, was a native of the
north of Ireland, where he was born on the 6th of
August, 1727. He learned the trade of a tanner, and
was an early settler in Paxtang, where he took up a
large tract of land, which he improved, erected a tan-
nery and on which he lived to the time of his death.
During the disastrous Indian war which brought
terror to our ancestors in this beautiful Kittochtinny
Valley, he did valiant service for their protection.
He was an ensign and afterwards a lieutenant in the
Rev. John Elder's battalion of Rangers in the frontier
wars from 1755 to 1764; and at the breaking out of
the war for Independence, aided by his counsel and
his purse in organizing the associated battalions of
Lancaster county, which did such effective service in
the Revolution. Although never holding an office
of profit, yet he was a representative man, influential
and potential in the county. At one time he was
offered the nomination as member of the Assembly
but positively declined. He died on the 26th of
September, 1793, and his remains rest within the
shadow of old Paxtang Church, of which he was in
life a consistent member. He married Sarah, daughter of Jeremiah Sturgeon, and their descendants to

4

the fourth and fifth generation occupy prominent positions in life. Especially have they been distinguished in the profession of medicine.

JOSHUA ELDER, was a very important personage. He was a son of Rev. John Elder of pious memory, and his wife Mary Baker, and was "to the manor born." In Paxtang, on the 9th of March 1744–5 he first saw the light and for three-quarters of a century thereafter his influence was felt in that neighborhood. He was brought up on his father's farm; but when the marauding Indian began to desolate the homes of the pioneers, he became imbued with a martial spirit and served in the ranks as a private soldier. In the Revolutionary struggle he was no idle spectator. In common with his friends and neighbors his sympathies were with the people, and he became a leader on the patriot side. He was appointed a sublieutenant of the county and was also a justice of the peace, serving his country faithfully until the close of the war. He was, as already stated, a prominent advocate for the formation of the county of Dauphin, and under the Constitution of 1790 was commissioned by Gov. Mifflin one of the Associate Judges of the Courts, August 17, 1791. The appointment, however of ex-sheriff Clunie to the bench on the resignation of David Harris, a son of the founder, who had removed to Baltimore, so incensed him that he peremptorily resigned. The correspondence between the Governor's Secretary of the Commonwealth and Col. Elder is very spicy. Upon the election of Gov. McKean, a warm personal friend, that functionary appointed Mr. Elder, on the 5th of January 1800, prothonotary, which position he filled by re-appointment until the 6th of February 1809, when he was retired by Gov. Snyder. In March, 1810, Mr. Elder was elected Burgess of the Borough of Harrisburg. It is probable he removed to his farm in Paxtang a year or two after. He died there on the 5th of December, 1820, in the seventy-sixth year of his age. In many respects he was a remarkable man. He was imbued with all the fire of a Scotch-Irish Presbyterian—was firm and decided, and yet generous to a fault. Although twice married, he left no children, but there are of the family of Elder many who bear the name of Col. Joshua Elder of Paxtang.

ANDREW STEWART resided in Lower Paxtang. He was the son of Andrew Stewart and Mary Dinwiddie, whose remains lie in old Paxtang Church yard. The first Andrew Stewart with his brother Archibald Stewart came to America prior to 1733 and settled in Paxtang township, then Lancaster county, Pa. The former remained there, while Archibald drifted down the Kittochtinny Valley into the Valley of Virginia, and settled in Augusta county that State. He was the head of a large family and whose descendants have been represented in the recent history of our country by the rebel chieftain, Gen. James E. B. Stuart, "the Murat of the Confederacy," and by the Hon. A. H. H. Stuart a prominent Virginia statesman of the old *regime*. The youngest son of Andrew Stewart, senior, was the subject of our sketch, also named Andrew. He was born in Paxtang in 1748, and was a farmer by occupation. He was one of the leaders in the movement for the erection of the new County of Dauphin, and hence was named as one of the Commissioners. In 1792 Mr. Stewart sold his plantation in Paxtang, and removed to western Pennsylvania. He died in Allegheny county about the year 1827, the date of his will being the 14th day of June that year. Capt. John Rutherford and Thomas Brown, of the county of Dauphin, were the executors named in his will, but the former passed away before the settlement of the estate. We have no information as to any descendants.

JAMES COWDEN was another of the "Paxtang Boys." His father, Matthew Cowden came from the North of Ireland to Pennsylvania prior to 1729, and took up a tract of land in afterwards Paxtang township, Dauphin county. Here the son James was born on the 16th of June 1737, and here he died on the 10th of October 1810. Brought up on his father's farm, he nevertheless enjoyed the advantages of that early education of pioneer times which among the Scotch-Irish settlers was remarkably comprehensive and ample. Apart from this he was well-grounded in the tenets of the Westminster Confession, which among that class of people formed a part of the instruction given to all. Until the thunders of the Revolution rolled toward the Susquehanna, Mr. Cowden remained on the paternal acres, busily engaged in farming. At the outset he was a strong advocate for active defensive measures and in favor of independence. He was one of the leading spirits at the meeting at Middletown June 9, 1774, of which Col. James Burd was chairman, and whose action, in conjunction with those of Hanover, nerved the people of Lancaster in

their patriotic resolves. Suiting the action to the
word, Mr. Cowden and the young men of his neighborhood took measures toward raising a battalion of
associators, of which Col. James Burd was in com-
command, and a company of which was intrusted to
Captain Cowden. His company, although not belonging to the Pennsylvania Line, was nevertheless, in several campaigns, and did faithful service at
Fort Washington, in the Jerseys, at Brandywine
and Germantown; and in the war on the Northern
and Western frontiers of the State, defending them
from the attack of the savage Indian and the no less
treacherous Tory. The war over, the patriot Captain
returned to his farm. He was appointed one of the
Commissioners to lay out the county seat, and under
the Constitution of 1790 was appointed the justice of
the peace for the district of Lower Paxtang township.
On the 2nd of October, 1795, he was commissioned by
Gov. Mifflin one of the associate judges of the county,
an office he filled acceptably and creditably. In 1809
he was chosen a Presidential elector and was an ardent supporter of Madison. He lived a long and
useful life. He was a decided patriot, a faithful officer, an honored citizen and an unflinching Presbyterian. His descendants remain with us to-day filling positions of trust, and have the respect of the community.

"WILLIAM BROWN, of Paxtang," thus designated
in the act to distinguish him from Captain William
Brown, of Hanover, a cousin. Of the ancestry of
this prominent man and citizen we have the following: John Brown, "the pious carrier" of Muirkirk

parish, Ayrshire, Scotland, was captured by Graham
of Claverhouse and his troops on the first of May,
1685, and ordered to take the oath of conformity,
which he refused to do. Claverhouse bid him go to
his prayers, because he had but a few minutes to live.
He did pray with such power that when Claverhouse
ordered his men to fire upon him they refused, and
with a pistol and an oath he blew his brains out, and
then turned to the widow and said, "What thinkest
thou of thy husband now?" She answered, "I ever
thought meikle of him, but never so meikle as I do
this day." He said, "It were but justice to lay thee
beside him." She answered, "If you were permitted,
I doubt not but your cruelty would go that length;
but how will you answer for this morning's work?"
"To man I can be answerable, and as for God I will
take Him into my own hand," he replied and rode
away. She laid down her child, tied up her husband's head with her apron, stretched out his limbs,
covered him with her plaid, and sat down and wept
long and bitterly. Without means, without a friend
to help, and liable to be persecuted, she was at her
wit's end. But God cared for her and removed her
to Ireland, where she found friends, and where she
married again. From this second marriage sprung
the Weir family of our county. John Brown's sons
were James and John, both of whom came to America
about 1720, the former settling on the Swatara, the
latter in Paxtang. A son of John, born 30th of
June, 1720, was William Brown of Paxtang. He
was a prominent actor in Provincial and Revolutionary times, a representative man on the frontier, and

as might be supposed a zealous Covenanter. At his own expense he visited Ireland and Scotland on behalf of his religious brethren, to procure a supply of ministers, and brought over the celebrated divines, Lind and Dobbins. He was a member of the Pennsylvania Assembly in 1776, and during its sessions proposed the gradual emancipation of slaves within the Commonwealth, a measure not very favorably received at the time, but which four years afterwards was enacted into a law. He served again in the Assembly in 1784, and was a member of the Board of Property Dec. 5, 1785. He was afterwards, October 2, 1786, appointed one of the Commissioners to superintend the drawing of the Donation Land Lottery. Mr. Brown died on the 10th of October, 1787, and is buried in Paxtang Church grave-yard. He was not only an active, earnest and public-spirited Christian, of unquestioned piety of heart, but as a neighbor and citizen generous and kind-hearted, which insured respect and won friendship. He had no children, but to his paternal and loving care are we indebted for the education of his distinguished nephew, Rev. Matthew Brown, LL. D., President of Washington and Jefferson College.

These were the men who a century ago fulfilled the trust confided to them. They were all Scotch-Irish Presbyterians—all save one born in the Paxtang of old—and all save one rest beneath the hallowed God's acre which lies within the shadow of that historic land-mark, Paxtang Church. The founder and his friends (for they were his warm personal friends) lie within the same enclosure. They were but human, it is true, yet they were men who never shrunk from the fulfillment of duty, and we of to-day in calling up their names and honoring their memories will do well to follow their example.

THE FIRST COUNTY COURT.

Third Tuesday of May, 1785.

Tuesday, May 19, 1885.

ACTION OF THE COURT.

On the 7th of April, 1885, Joseph B. Ewing, Esq., presented to the Court the following:

The undersigned, a committee on behalf of the General Committee to make arrangements for celebrating the Centennial of the erection of Dauphin county, respectfully request that you will convene an informal meeting of the bar at as early a moment as convenient, for the purpose of appointing a committee to confer with us relative to a commemorative celebration of the opening of the first court held in Dauphin county, on the third Tuesday of May, 1785, which will fall upon Tuesday, May 19, 1885. Your attention will oblige yours with respect.

A. Boyd Hamilton,
George Wolf Buehler,
Joseph B. Ewing.

In accordance with the foregoing suggestion, Judge McPherson requested the Bar to meet on Thursday, April 9th, to take such action as seemed desirable.

On the day designated, a meeting was organized by the election of Hon. David Fleming as chairman and Frederick M. Ott, Esq., secretary. A committee of five was then appointed to arrange a programme as follows: Joshua M. Wiestling, David Mumma, Levi B. Alricks, Charles H. Bergner, and Benjamin M. Nead. The committee, however, never acted, owing to the duties of most of the members in connection with the Supreme Court of the State. One of the papers prepared for the occasion is given.

THE FIRST COURTS.

The record of the first court appearance docket reads as follows:

"At a Court of Common Pleas holden near Harris' Ferry in and for the county of Dauphin, the third Tuesday in May, in the year of our Lord one thousand seven hundred and eighty-five, by virtue of an act of General Assembly of the Commonwealth of Pennsylvania, entitled "An act for erecting Part of the County of Lancaster into a separate county."

"Present—Timothy Green, Esquire, president; Samuel Jones and Jonathan McClure, Esquires, justices, &c.

"On motion of Stephen Chambers, Esquire, on his own behalf, the said Stephen Chambers, Esq., is admitted an attorney of this court, having taken by oath the Qualification prescribed by law.

"On motion of Stephen Chambers, Esquire, in behalf of John Wilkes Kittera, John Clark, Joseph Hubley, John Andre Hanna, James Riddle, John Joseph Henry, Peter Hoofnagle and Jacob Hubley Esquires, the said John Wilkes Kittera, John Clark, Joseph Hubley, John Andre Hanna, James Riddle, John Joseph Henry, Peter Hoofnagle and Jacob Hubley, Esquires, are admitted attorneys by this court, having severally taken by oath the Qualification prescribed by law.

"On motion of Stephen Chambers, Esquire, James Biddle and Collinson Reed, Esquires, are admitted attornies of this court, having severally taken by oath the Qualification prescribed by law.

"On motion of John Joseph Henry, Esquire, George Ross, Esquire, is admitted an attorney of this court, having taken by oath the Qualification prescribed by law.

"On motion of John Wilkes Kittera, Esquire, John Reily, Esquire, is admitted an attorney of this court, having taken by oath the Qualification prescribed by law.

"On motion of Stephen Chambers, Esquire, '*Rule*', that the admission of attorneys in this court shall be regulated by the same rules as have been adopted in this respect in the county of Lancaster.

"MAY TERM, 1785, ⎫
"1. JOHN BICKLE, ⎪ *Debt sans Bred,* - - - £50
        vs.   ⎪ *Costs,* - - - - - 2.12:3
NICHOLAS GEBHART. ⎭

"And now to wit, May the seventeenth, A. D. 1785, Peter Hoofnagle, Esquire, attorney for the Defendant by warrant of attorney specially constituted, appears for the above named, Nicholas Gebhart, and confesses judgment against him to the Plaintiff, John Bickle, for the sum of Fifty Pounds in Gold or Silver Debt, besides costs of suit, &c.

"Eod. Die Ex't. Fi. Fa.   Coram me,

                                    "ALEX. GRAYDON."

The proceedings of the first Court of Quarter Sessions, after a similar statement to the record on the appearance docket, are as follows:

"The sheriff of the county of Lancaster, being by the said act of Assembly authorized and required to exercise for a time therein specified the duties of his office within the county of Dauphin, having returned the precept to him directed, with the panel thereunto annexed, the following persons were respectively sworn and affirmed a Grand Inquest for the body of the said county of Dauphin, to wit:

"James Cowden, foreman. Robert Montgomery, Barefoot Brunson, Rowan McClure, John Wilson, Archibald McCallister, John Pattimore, Jacob Awl, Andrew Stewart, Samuel Stewart, John Gilchrist, John Clark, John Carson, William Crain, Richard Dixon, James Crouch, William Brown, James Rogers, John Cooper, Alexander Berryhill.

"*Townships.*					*New Constables.*
Heidelberg,	-	-	-	-	——————
Lebanon,		-	-	-	Rudolph Kelker.
Derry,	-	-	-	-	Peter Fridley.
London Derry,	-	-	-	-	James Kelly.
Upper Paxton,	-	-	-	-	Peter Eckert.
Lower Paxton,	-	-	-	David Montgomery.
East Hanover,	-	-	-	-	John Winter.
West Hanover,	-	-	-	Robert McCord.
Bethel,	-	-	-	-	Abraham Sebolt.

"May Session, 1785.

REPUBLICA   }   *Larceny in stealing a Roan*
      vs.   } *mare, the property of Peter Lan-*
GEORGE FOULKE.   } *dis.*

"George Foulke being three times solemnly called appeared not. Ideo recognizance forfeited.

"John Cearman being three times solemnly called to bring forth the Body of George Foulke appeared not. Ideo recognizance forfeited and respited until next sessions.

"August session, 1785. The court, on motion, further respite this recognizance until next sessions."

The foregoing are exact transcripts from the first courts. Of the individuals to whom were confided the duties of sitting in judgment, we have the following information:

TIMOTHY GREEN, the presiding justice, was born about 1733, in Hanover township, Lancaster now Dauphin county, Pennsylvania. His father, Robert Green, of Scotch ancestry, came from the north of Ireland about 1725, locating near the Kittochtinny mountains, on Manada creek. The first record we have of the son is subsequent to Braddock's defeat, when the frontier settlers were threatened with extermination by the marauding savages. Timothy Green assisted in organizing a company, and for at least seven years was chiefly in active military service in protecting the settlers from the fury of the blood-thirsty Indian. In the Bouquet expeditions of 1763 and 1764 he commanded a company of Provincial troops. For his services at this time the Proprietaries granted him large tracts of land in Buffalo valley, and on Bald Eagle creek. At the outset of the Revolution Captain Green became an earnest advocate for independence, and the celebrated Hanover resolutions of June 4, 1774, passed unanimously by the meeting, of which he was chairman, show that he was intensely patriotic. He was one of the Committee of Safety of the Province, which met Nov. 22, 1774, in Lancaster, and issued hand-bills to the import that "agreeable to the resolves and recommendations of the American Continental Congress, that

the freeholders and others qualified to vote for representatives in Assembly, choose, by ballot, sixty persons for a Committee of Observation, to observe the
conduct of all persons towards the actions of the
General Congress; the committee, when elected, to
divide the country into districts and appoint members of the committee to superintend each district,
and any six so appointed to be a quorum, etc." The
election was held on Thursday, 15th December, 1774,
and among others Timothy Green was elected from
Hanover. This body of men were in correspondence
with Joseph Reed, Charles Thompson, George Cly-
mer, John Benezet, Samuel Meredith, and Thomas
Mifflin, of Philadelphia, and others. They met at
Lancaster again, April 27, 1775, when notice was
taken of Gen. Gage's attack upon the inhabitants of
Massachusetts Bay, and a general meeting called for
the first of May at Lancaster. During the progress
of the Revolution he commanded the Tenth Battalion of Lancaster Associators, and was in active service in the Jersey campaign of 1776. Before the
erection of the county of Dauphin, Col. Green, being
the oldest justice of the peace in commission, and
under the constitution of 1776, became president of
the courts. He continued therein until under the
constitution of 1790, which required the presiding
judge "to be learned in the law," Judge Atlee, of
Lancaster, was appointed. After his retirement,
Judge Green returned to his quiet farm at the mouth
of Stony Creek, where he had erected a mill and
other improvements. He died there on the 27th of
February, 1812, and is buried in the old grave-yard

back of Dauphin. His legal knowledge was not of
the highest order, but he was surrounded by as brilliant a bar as has since illumined our county courts,
and hence said little and acted wisely.

SAMUEL JONES, associate justice, was from Bethel
township, now in Lebanon county, where he was
born about the year 1750. His father, William
Jones, laid out Jonestown, dying in November, 1771,
the son coming into possession of the greater portion
of the estate. He was in active service during the
struggle for independence, and November 8, 1777,
was appointed by the Supreme Executive Council
one of the commissioners to collect clothing, blankets, etc., for the half-clad army at Valley Forge.
This service was well performed. On the 15th of
August, 1784, he was appointed one of the justices of
the peace for Lancaster county, and judge of the
court of common pleas January 3, 1785. He was the
next oldest in commission when the new county of
Dauphin was formed. Of Judge Jones' subsequent
life we have little knowledge. It has been stated that
he removed to Pittsburgh towards the close of the
century, but even that is not certain.

Of JONATHAN McCLURE, the remaining associate
justice, we have better information. He was the son
of Richard McClure, born about 1745 in Paxtang
township, Lancaster, now Dauphin county. He was
one of Joseph Hutchinson's pupils, received a good
English education, and was brought up to mercantile pursuits. When the war of the Revolution
needed his support, he became a lieutenant in Capt.
John Rutherford's company and did valiant service

during the New Jersey campaign of 1776, and that
around Philadelphia the year following. Towards
the close of the war he commanded a company of
militia raised in Paxtang for the defense of the
frontiers. He was commissioned by the Supreme
Executive Council a justice of the peace September
8, 1784, and on the 17th of November following one
of the judges of the court of common pleas. When
the county of Dauphin was organized the spring following he came to be one of the first judges of the
courts. He died at Middletown on Wednesday, December 11, 1799, aged about fifty-four years. Of the
three persons who illumined the judicial bench one
hundred years ago, Judge McClure was the most intelligent. He was one of the men of mark of this
locality, and it is proper that his memory, with those
of the other two worthies, his colleagues, be preserved.

INVITATION BY COUNTY OFFICIALS.

DAUPHIN COUNTY CENTENNIAL.
1885
September 15th, 16th and 17th.

We, the Commissioners of Dauphin County, Pennsylvania, respectfully and cordially invite you to participate at our Centennial Celebration.

Opening Day, 14th Sept.   Industrial Display, 16th Sept.
Military Display, 15th Sept.   Firemen's Display, 17th Sept.
Antiquarian Exhibition, open from Sept. 10th to 17th.

We will be pleased to meet you on the 15th, 16th and 17th of September, at the Commissioners' Office, Court House, Harrisburg, Pa., at 2. P. M., on either, or all of these days. If convenient, advise us if we shall have the pleasure of your presence.

Very respectfully,

CHAS. E. RIEGEL,   CHRISTIAN L. GINGRICH,
Clerk.   CORNELIUS BIXLER,
JNO. M. STRICKLER,   JOHN W. STOBER,
Ass't Clerk.   *Commissioners.*

INVITATION TO BOROUGHS.

COMMITTEE.

S. C. WILSON, Mayor, *Chairman.*

WILLIAM K. VERBEKE, Ex-Mayor,

JACOB D. BOAS, Ex-Mayor,

JOHN D. PATTERSON, Ex-Mayor,

JOHN C. HERMAN, Ex-Mayor,

WILLIAM L. GORGAS, President Select Council,

JOHN C. HUTTON, President Common Council.

INVITATION OF THE COMMITTEE.

The citizens of Harrisburg request the honor of the presence of the burgess of ——— at the celebration of the One Hundredth Anniversary of the erection of the County of Dauphin and the founding of the City of Harrisburg, September 14th, 15th, 16th and 17th, 1885.

S. C. WILSON, *Chairman.*

J. D. BOAS.   JOHN C. HERMAN,
W. K. VERBEKE,   W. L. GORGAS,
JOHN D. PATTERSON.   J. C. HUTTON.

Committee on Invitation.

THE CITY'S CONTRIBUTION.—The City Councils of the city of Harrisburg. Dauphin county, Pa., appropriated of the funds of the city treasury the sum of $1,000 to the Centennial celebration of the county of Dauphin. and disbursed the same as follows:

T. D. Greenawalt, Centennial Treasurer . .	$100 00
F. U. Bergner & Bro., stationery, stamps, &c . . .	69 94
A. B. Hamilton and Dr. W. H. Egle, stamps, &c . .	14 04
A. F. Fry, furnituJe for office	19 55
C. O. Zimmerman, rent	80 00
G. C. B. Swartz and Wilson Elder, secretary and clerk . .	118 00
Adams Express Co., and others, badges, medals and flags .	108 47
J. S. Sible, Market square arch	40 00
I. S. Trostle, supplies	150 00
Calder, Lauer and others, horses and carriages. . . .	300 00
Total appropriation	$1,000 00

INVITATION TO LEBANON.

COMMITTEE.

JOHN J. PEARSON, *Chairman.*

FRANCIS WYETH,	HENRY OMIT.
JACOB C. BOMBERGER,	WILLIAM K. COWDEN.
JOHN B. RUTHERFORD.	WILLIAM R. GORGAS,
JOSIAH ESPY,	ALEXANDER F. THOMPSON.

OFFICIAL INVITATION.

To the Citizens of Lebanon County:

The undersigned having been appointed a committee to extend to the citizens of the county of Lebanon an invitation to participate in the celebration of the One Hundredth Anniversary of the erection of the county of Dauphin, now undertake the performance of that pleasant duty.

On the 4th of March, 1785, when the act was passed forming the county of Dauphin, the scope of country now comprising the flourishing and progressive county of Lebanon was a part of the territory of the new county. On putting into motion the political machinery, the elective offices were divided between the eastern and western portions of the county. From 1785 until the year 1813 when Lebanon was set apart as a distinct county, we have a long list of worthies resident in that locality who filled honorable positions in the new county. In the Senate of the Commonwealth were Gloninger, Kean, and Orth; while Meily, Kelker, Shouffler, Weirick, Krause, Ley, Shulze and Shindel represented Dauphin in the popular branch of the General Assembly. And so in all the various county offices, the representative men of now Lebanon county served the new county well and faithfully. It is fitting, therefore, that the descendants of those early citizens, or those who honor and revere their memories, take a deep interest in the celebration of the event which they assisted

in forming one hundred years ago. In all the years
which have since elapsed, the interest of the two
counties have been in accord, and politically they
have never been disunited.

It is very appropriate that in the celebration of the
coming Centennial the county of Lebanon participate. We extend to her citizens a hearty and cordial invitation so to do. We desire that they will
unite with us in the inaugural ceremonies incident
to the occasion, when their fellow-citizen, Hon. John
B. McPherson, will deliver the oration; that in the
military and civic parade they will not be absent;
that their industries, of which they may be justly
proud, will largely swell the trades' display procession; and their brave volunteer firemen will honor
the closing ceremonies. In addition, your citizens
can greatly aid in the antiquarian exhibition, adding to its list of old, rare and curious articles.

In this participation we fondly hope Lebanon will
show that neighborly and fraternal spirit which has
ever actuated her in the past one hundred years of
her magnificent history.

> JOHN J. PEARSON,
> FRANCIS WYETH,
> JOHN B. RUTHERFORD,
> JOSIAH ESPY,
> HENRY OMIT,
> WILLIAM K. COWDEN,
> WILLIAM R. GORGAS,
> ALEXANDER F. THOMPSON,
> JACOB C. BOMBERGER.

COMMEMORATIVE MEDAL.

COMMITTEE.

JOHN W. SIMONTON, *Chairman.*

HAMILTON ALRICKS,   JOHN B. McPHERSON,

BENJAMIN F. MEYERS,   M. WILSON McALARNEY.

THE CENTENNIAL MEDAL.

DESCRIPTION.—The medal adopted by the committee, as produced in white metal, bronze and silver, represents on one side the log cabin of the pioneer John Harris, with the motto "E Feritate Cultus, pro Solitudine Multitudo," that is, "Out of barbarism civilization, for solitude a multitude." On the obverse, a scene representing the three great industries of the county, mining, manufactures and agriculture; on the other border, "1785-1885—Dauphin County Centennial."

THE MEDAL ACCOUNT, as audited by the Centennial Auditor, George J. Shoemaker, is as follows :

The General Committee of the Dauphin County Centennial in account for official medals—Debtor : September 1, 1885 :

For die of official medal	$75 00
For 2,000 white metal medals.	200 00
For 2,000 white metal medals.	180 00
For 200 bronze metal medals	100 00
For 50 silver metal medals	100 00
For J. J. Maguire, drilling medals	21 45
For W. O. Hickok, drilling medals	1 80
For incidental expenses	21 75
Total cost of medals.	$700 00

Samuel W. Fleming, on account Centennial medals—Debtor :

White metal medals sold	$509 50
Bronze metal medals sold	38 00
Silver metal medals sold	27 00
	$569 50

Credit :—

By order No. 4, paid to T. D. Greenawalt	$260 30
By order No. 15, paid to J. J. Maguire	15 00
By order No. 23, paid to William O. Hickok	1 80
By order No. 39, paid to Peter L. Krider	219 70
By order No. 54, paid to J. J. Maguire	6 45
March 11, 1886, balance	66 25
	$569 50

COMMITTEES FROM ELECTION DISTRICTS.

GENERAL COMMITTEE.

JOHN H. WEISS, *Chairman.*
AUGUSTUS REEL,
MICHAEL B. MOYER, Derry Church.
NELSON ENDERS, Enders,
PHILIP C. SWAB, Lykens,
ELIAS HOLLINGER,
WILLIAM SHEESLEY,
JOHN D. SNYDER, Berrysburg,
SAMUEL W. FLEMING, *Secretary.*

SPECIAL COMMITTEES.

The committee to whom was delegated the subject, formed the following special committees for each district of the county; whereupon the Secretary was authorized to forward a copy of the list to each person chosen, with the earnest wish of the whole committee that he would give his hearty support to the efforts forming to make the commemoration of the first hundred years of the life of Dauphin county memorable by a grand celebration of the interesting event. The committee aided in organizing clubs to join the general and particular displays upon the occasion; ascertained and sent information of the Household and other Historical Relics in their districts and obtained them for exhibition.

HARRISBURG.

FIRST WARD.

George Frank,
L. O. Phillips,
Abraham Anderson,
John Keil,
Edward Sparrow.

SECOND WARD.

Amos F. Fry,
William J. Bergstresser,
William K. Cowden,
John A. Reily,
Henry S. Sourbeer.

THIRD WARD.

Jacob A. Miller,
Jacob F. Haehnlen,
J. Brisben Boyd,
Weidner W. Boyer,
Frank A. Boehmer.

FOURTH WARD.

Jacob F. Seiler,
William P. Smull,
John W. Glover,
Charles B. Fager,
Andrew K. Black.

FIFTH WARD.

David Maeyer,
H. B. Mitchell,
Albert B. Tack,
John S. Sible,
Andrew Schlayer.

SIXTH WARD.

George W. Porter,
Josiah Higgins,
Perry Adams,
William O. Bishop,
George H. Sourbeer.

SEVENTH WARD.

Frank Darby,
David C. Burnite.
John A. Graham,
Harry C. Demming,
A. Hockley.

EIGHTH WARD.

W. Howard Day,
John W. Simpson,
Charles A. Miller,
John Young,
Andrew R. Kieffer.

NINTH WARD.

Simon Duey,
Daniel Leedy,
Jacob Zarger, Sr.,
Joseph Kahnweiler,
John Beatty,
M. McCloskey.

WILLIAMSTOWN.

J. R. Carl,
G. W. Hain,
J. W. Parks,
William D. Mason,
James T. Waters.

LYKENS.

Alfred G. Stanley,
Edward Miller,
H. W. Snyder,
Hiram Bueck,
Samuel M. Fenn

JACKSON.

L. J. Enders,
James Seiders.

FISHERVILLE.

Cornelius Bixler,
George W. D. Enders,
Valentine E. Eisenhower,
Charles Coleman.

SUSQUEHANNA.

NORTH DISTRICT.

Gabriel Hiester,
Fred M. Ott,
John Saul,
George Garman,
James H. McAllister.

SOUTH DISTRICT.

William A. Haverstick,
John M. Major,
J. A. Fisher,
Charles E. H. Brelsford.
J. Z. Gerhard.

SWATARA.

FIRST DISTRICT.

Michael A. Frantz,
George Cumbler,
Jacob Livingston,
Jacob Boyer, Jr.,
John Parthemore.

SECOND DISTRICT.

Abner Rutherford,
John Roop,
Harry G. Eshenour,
George T. Richer,
John Peifer.

LOWER SWATARA.

Elijah Balsbaugh,
Samuel Poorman,
Frank Wolf,
Henry Roop,
Isaac B. Nissley.

HUMMELSTOWN.

Thomas G. Fox,
William C. Baker,
E. M. Hoffer,
U. L. Balsbaugh,
Frank Hummel,
Josiah Burkholder.

MIDDLETOWN.

SOUTH WARD.

Benjamin S. Peters,
Frank Nissley,
Elijah McCreary.
Daniel J. Hake,
Charles Harline.

MIDDLE WARD.

James Young,
William D. Hendrickson.
Dr. John Ringland,
E. B. Cobaugh,
Joseph Campbell.

NORTH WARD.

John L. Nissley,
Frederick R. Wagner,
William A. Hill,
Joseph H. Nissley,
William A. Croll.

HALIFAX.

Frank Loomis,
James Fetterhoff,
Isaac Bechtel,
David B. A. Mahargue,
William Kline,
Abram Fortenbaugh,
Thomas B. Liebrich,
Samuel B. Potteiger,
William B. Gray.

MILLERSBURG.

William B. Meetch,
James Michaels,
Frank S. Bowman,
John B. Seal,
Edward H. Leffler.

WASHINGTON.

James Miller,
Peter B. Lyter,
Frederick Weaver.

STEELTON.

FIRST WARD.

L. E. McGinnis,
E. C. Felton,
A. Y. Knisely,
Joseph M. Metzger,
Martin H. Grunden.

SECOND WARD.

D. B. Traver,
John B. Litch.
A. B. Dunkle,
James F. Newlin,
John W. Grove.

THIRD WARD.

William M. James,
Samuel F. Dunkle,
James Dickinson,
Henry F. Koesel,
John Hess.

BERRYSBURG.

Jonathan Moyer,
Joseph Romberger,
Cornelius Swab,
Valentine Lenker,
Edward Holtzman,

RUSH.

Tobias Shadle,
Frank Reiner,
Alexander McAllister,
Paul Kessler,
Philip Dietrich.

REED.

Henry Lower,
Samuel Newbaker,
James Carpenter,
Henry Heikle,
David Hoffman.

CURTIN.

Charles S. Zimmerman.

JEFFERSON.

Jonathan Spayd,
Alexander McLaughlin
Martin Etzweiler,
John Sheetz,
A. D. Zimmerman.

MIFFLIN.

John W. Deibler,
Emanuel Shoop,
George W. Wade,
Samuel Clark,
Isaac Kebauch.

UNIONTOWN.

George D. Boyer,
William Hoffman,
Dr. W. C. Raker,
Uriah Bowman,
D. B. Klinger.

UPPER PAXTON.

Philip Moyer,
D. Y. Lenker,
James Holtzman,
Charles Miller,
Samuel Gilbert.

LOWER PAXTANG.

Dr. C. H. Smith,
E. H. Shaner,
Jacob Widmoyer,
David Cassel,
John Ebersole.

MIDDLE PAXTANG.

L. W. Clemson,
Bailey Kennedy,
George R. Dennison,
I. M. Bayard,
John Shepler.

SOUTH HANOVER.

Dr. David C. Keller,
Simon P. Rhoads,
Samuel R. Miller,
John H. Cassel,
Daniel Shaffner.

EAST HANOVER.

Amos Early,
William Kline,
Charles V. Thome,
John Rauch,
D. A. Boyer.

WEST HANOVER.

George W. Fox,
John Kramer,
David Brightbill,
John Bomgardner,
Christian Cassel.

CONEWAGO.

Cyrus G. Shenk,
Jacob E. Shenk,
S. H. Hoffer,
Alfred Felty,
George Redsecker.

DERRY.

James G. Fox,
Christopher Moyer,
Martin L. Hershey,
George H. Seiler,
Joseph S. Strickler.

DAUPHIN.

Alfred F. Stees,
Charles Rodearmel,
Dr. A. T. Poffenberger,
J. B. Krause,
Dr. John R. Umberger.

LONDONDERRY.

Charles L. Gingrich,
John S. Longenecker,
John H. Epler,
H. Techtmeyer,
Edward S. Kerper.

WEST LONDONDERRY.

David Metzger,
Jonathan Kope,
William Shireman,
John N. Rife,
Samuel Kinsey.

WAYNE.

J. A. Lebo,
Samuel V. Enders,
S. H. Gripple,
H. E. Welker,
A. Bowerman.

WICONISCO.

George A. Pinkerton,
Daniel Israel,
A. F. Kimmel,
L. M. Neiffer,
James Fennel.

LYKENS.

Joseph Gise,
Preston Artz,
John W. Hoffman,
Frank Ferrel,
Jacob Shade.

GRATZ.

John Moyer,
Dr. I. S. Schminkey,
Daniel Blyler,
Henry W. Good,
J. B. Gise.

LOYALTON.

David K. McClure.

CENTENNIAL FINANCES.

GENERAL COMMITTEE.

SIMON CAMERON, *President.*

WILLIAM W. JENNINGS,   DAVID FLEMING,

JACOB S. HALDEMAN,   JOSEPH B. EWING.

SPECIAL COMMITTEES.

The following persons were appointed by the General Finance Committee sub-committees to solicit contributions :

HARRISBURG—BY DISTRICTS.

First—Poplar street to Manada, from Eighteenth to Pennsylvania canal, Charles P. Mason, DeWitt C. Denny, H. L. Champlain.

Second—Pennsylvania canal to Front street, from Dock street to southern city limits, J. A. Fromm, Edward Fogarty.

Third—Front street to Eighteenth, from Paxton to Dock, and Manada streets, Edward Drinkwater, John Kiel, Frederick W. Liesman.

Fourth—Paxton street to Mulberry, from Pennsylvania canal to Front street, Hugh Hamilton, George Dunn, Richard Hogan.

Fifth—Mulberry street to Chestnut, from Pennsylvania canal to Front street, Thomas Elder, Joseph Pilkay, J. Bucher Hummel.

Sixth—Chestnut street to Market, from Front street to Third, William A. Kelker, Warren A. Zollinger, Edward R. Bergstresser.

Seventh—Chestnut street to Market, from Third street to Pennsylvania canal, John C. Hutton, Henry E. Hershey, George K. King.

Eighth—Market street to Walnut, from Front street to Third, Daniel C. Herr, Edward M. Haldeman, Richard Fox.

Ninth—Market street to Walnut, from Third street to Pennsylvania canal, Samuel A. Hummel, Naudain Hamilton, Elias Z. Wallower.

Tenth—Walnut street to Pine, from Front street to Third, Henry J. Beatty, Casper Dull, S. Bethel Boude.

Eleventh—Pine street to State, from Front street to Third, Samuel W. Fleming, Thomas T. Wierman, Jr., Dr. J. Ross Swartz.

Twelfth—State street to North, from Front street to Third, Harry D. Boas, William Rodearmel, Dr. Hiram McGowan.

Thirteenth—Walnut street to State, from Fourth street to Pennsylvania canal, William Wolfinger, John A. Krause, John W. Simpson

Fourteenth—State street to North, from Fourth street to Pennsylvania canal, Callaughen McCarty, William M. Gastrock, David S. Herr.

Fifteenth—North street to Forster, from Front street to Third, William J. McFadden, Christian W. Lynch, Chambers Dubbs.

Sixteenth—North street to Forster, from Third street to Pennsylvania canal, Edwin S. Herman, James Nalen, O. S. Houtz.

Seventeenth—Forster street to Boas, from Front street to Third, W. Luther Gorgas, Louis Dellone, John R. Shoemaker.

Eighteenth—Forster street to Boas, from Third street to Sixth, Horace B. Mitchell, Dr. A. E. Eyster, William C. Kirby.

Nineteenth—Forster street to Boas, from Sixth street to Pennsylvania canal, Aaron M. Steever, Robert Sites, Charles A. Wilhelm.

Twentieth—Boas street to Cumberland, from Front street to Third, William H. Smith, David Meyer, George F. Rohrer.

Twenty-first—Boas street to Cumberland, from Third street to Sixth William E. Machlin, John S. Sible, Howard D. Potts.

Twenty-second—Boas street to Cumberland, from Sixth street to Pennsylvania canal, John A. Gramm, Isaac J. Wilcox, Samuel S. Hall.

Twenty-third—Cumberland street to Verbeke, from Front street to Third, Albert B. Tack, Henry Fraley, George C. B. Swartz.

Twenty-fourth—Cumberland street to Verbeke, from Third street to Sixth, Leonard H. Kinnard, Frank J. Hess, James D. Hawkins.

Twenty-fifth—Cumberland street to Verbeke, from Sixth street to Pennsylvania canal, William H. Sible, Luther F. Cripple, John B. Foltz.

Twenty-sixth—Verbeke street to Reily, from Front street to Third, Charles T. George, B. Reily Wilson, Adam Reel.

Twenty-seventh—Verbeke street to Reily, from Third street to Sixth, Conrad Dapp, Hiram Starr, William O. Bishop.

Twenty-eighth—Verbeke street to Reily, from Sixth street to Pennsylvania canal, Henry Sourbeer, Jacob H. Santo, Samuel W. Fitzgerald.

Twenty-ninth—Reily street to Hamilton, from Front street to Fourth, George W. Wolford, Levi Kauffman, John W. Hœrner.

Thirtieth—Reily street to Hamilton, from Fourth street to Pennsylvania canal, Milton G. Potts, Charles Wollerton, Harry Ebersole.

Thirty-first—Hamilton street to Maclay, from Front street to Fourth, Daniel S. Early, Harry Reily, Henry Schuddemage.

Thirty-second—Hamilton street to Maclay, from Fourth street to Pennsylvania canal, Ellis W. Ford, Thomas Fitzsimmons, John Oenslager.

Thirty-third—Paxton street to Market, from Pennsylvania canal to Thirteenth street, Bartholomew Devout, Simon Duey, Ed. Heffelfinger.

Thirty-fourth—Paxton street to Market, from Thirteenth street to Eighteenth, Henry M. Kelley, John C. Forney, Conrad Blumenstine.

Thirty-fifth—Market street to Maclay, from Pennsylvania canal to Eighteenth, James McCleaster, David Leighton, George Bomgardner.

DAUPHIN COUNTY—BY TOWNSHIPS, DISTRICTS AND
WARDS.

Williams—Charles Curtis, G. F. Matter, Jacob Collyer.

Hummelstown—John J. Nissley, Thomas G. Fox, Edward Hoffer.

Lykens—Alexander F. Thompson, Henry K. Myers, H. W. Snyder.

Susquehanna, North—James McAllister, Jr., Harry Reicard, Frederick M. Ott.

Susquehanna, South—Simon Pretz, Jacob Boozer, Amos Enders.

Swatara, First—John Peiffer,W. Franklin Rutherford, Christian Hess.

Swatara, Second—Michael Frantz, John Livingston, G. W. Cumbler.

Lower Swatara—Frank Wolf, Eli Balsbach, J. F. Klugh.

Berrysburg—Valentine Lenker, Benjamin Bordner, Benjamin Romberger.

Middletown, South ward—John McCreery, John Schaffer, Benjamin Peters.

Middletown, Middle ward—R. N. Hendricks, Michael Rambler, J. W. Rewalt.

Middletown, North ward—John W. Rife, Joseph H. Nissley, S. L. Yetter.

Londonderry—John S. Longenecker, Christian Gingrich, H. Techtmeyer.

West Londonderry—William Shireman, Adam Metzger, John Reill.

Conewago—George Redsecker, D. E. F. Nissley, S. S. Bachman.

Derry—John F. Strickler, Martin L. Hershey, Jacob Hocker.

South Hanover—Henry W. Kettering, John Cassel, A. Meatter.

East Hanover—D. A. Boyer, William E. Shell, Samuel Cassel.

West Hanover—Christian Cassel, G. W. Fox, Amos Hicks.

Lower Paxtang—E. M. Shaner, Benjamin Engle, E. B. Care, Jr.

Middle Paxtang—Eli Schartzer, Lewis Heck, G. R. Dennison.

Reed—Samuel Newbaker, George Warner, J. B. Carpenter.

Jefferson—Alexander McLaughlin, John Sheetz, Henry Buffington.

Jackson—George W. B. Enders, Isaac P. Miller, James Miller.

Halifax—Frank Bowman, John Sweigard, Uriah Rutter.

Halifax borough—A. S. Loomis, Newton Noblit, J. T. Thompson.

Millersburg—John B. Seal, Jeremiah S. Gilbert, J. L. Bomgardner.

Upper Paxtang—Henry B. Hoffman, Philip Moyer, Daniel Lenler.

Washington—Frederick Horner, Peter Stine, James Miller.

Mifflin—Jonathan Reigle, George Moyer, Nelson Wade.

Uniontown—George Moyer, John Hoffman, Emanuel W. Lyter.

Wiconisco—Lane S. Scholfield, Louis M. Neifer, Clay Keene.

Lykens—J. W. Hoffman, Daniel Buffington, William Sweitzer.

Gratz—Dr. I. S. Schminkey, D. E. Blyler, Jonathan Moyer.

Dauphin—Charles Rodearmel,A.T. Poffenberger,Andrew Gerberich.
Wayne township—E. W. Welker, Amos Sponsler, S. V. Enders.
Steelton, First—Frederick W. Wood, Edward J. Grunden, Moses B.
Young.
Steelton, Second—J. B. Meredith, L. S. Shelly, Jacob Sharr.
Steelton, Third—Charles F. Reehling, Adam Beinhower, D. B.
Hoffman.

CONTRIBUTORS TO CENTENNIAL FUND.

The following list does not include all who contributed to the general Centennial fund, many contributions being designated on the collectors' books as "cash." It has been deemed advisable not to give the amount of each subscription—for the greater number of individuals after the grand success of the Centennial would be mortified at the record of their amazing (?) generosity. The facts are, and it may as well be told here, that had it not been for the benevolence of less than twenty persons or firms, with the amount realized from the Antiquarian exhibition, the financial portion of the Centennial would have proved a disastrous failure.

HARRISBURG.

Abele, Rev. John G.,
Adams, Richard,
Aldinger, William,
Alricks, Levi B.,
Alricks, Hamilton,
Altmeyer, Peter A.,
Aldinger, Philip,
Anderson, W. H.,

Anderson, B. P.,
Arnold, Henry,
Atkinson, B. F.
Aughinbaugh, Henry E.,
Aughinbaugh, Charles A.,
Awl, J. Wesley,
Bateman, S.,
Bailetz, R.,

Bailetz, Jacob,
Barringer, A.,
Barringer, John A.,
Bacon, Daniel,
Bashore, F. D.,
Bailey, George,
Ball, Joseph,
Barnes, George W.,
Bailey & Co., Charles L.,
Barnitz, George C.,
Baumgardner, H.,
Bahel, James,
Barth, John,
Baum, E. F.,
Baltimore O. P. Clothing Store,
Baumiller, P.,
Barnhart, B. W.,
Bacon, George N.,
Banford, Robert,
Baker & Clark,
Becker, William H.,
Beatty, William, Sr.,
Beatty, Henry J.,
Beatty, P. S.,
Benitz, Constantine,
Bender, Frederick,
Bell, Thornton A.,
Bell, John,
Bell, George H.,
Bell, Misses,
Bent, George,
Beatty, G. Irwin,
Beaver, Charles,
Berrier, Joseph,
Berghaus, Mrs. Mary,
Bergner Brothers,
Bear, John,
Berry, Mrs.,
Bennett, George,
Burkholder, C. W.,

Biester, George,
Bishop, E. M.,
Bigler, Charles,
Bishop, W. O.,
Black, E. B.,
Black, Joseph M.,
Black, Andrew K.,
Blust, Joseph,
Black, W. A.,
Blumenstein, Conrad,
Bowermaster, Benjamin,
Bougher, Charles,
Boyer, George G.,
Bowman & Co.,
Boude, S. Bethel,
Boyd, James,
Boas, William S.,
Boas, Harry D.,
Boyd, Truman,
Boyd & Co.,
Boehmer, F. A.,
Boas, Charles A.,
Bowers, Moses K.,
Boyer, Harry F.,
Bollinger, John,
Bowen, Edwin,
Boyd, Mrs.,
Bomgardner, Alfred,
Boyer, Edward,
Bomgardner, George,
Bomberger, Jacob C.,
Boyd, A. B.,
Bowers, Michael,
Bomgardner, Mrs. Jane,
Brackenridge, Alfred,
Brua, John P.,
Brubaker, Calvin B.,
Brandt, A. F.,
Breckenridge, A. K.,
Brady, Mrs. William,

Brenizer, Mrs. E.,
Brenizer, Joseph,
Brandt, Levi,
Brubaker, David H.,
Brown, Mrs.,
Bradley, James,
Britten, C.,
Brightbill, Jacob A.,
Brightbill, B.,
Breitinger, W. H.,
Brady, James,
Brown & Reel,
Butler, W. H.,
Buehler, Jacob,
Buehler, H. B.,
Buckingham, A.,
Burkholder, J. N.,
Burtnett, Handy,
Byers, Frederick E.,
Cameron, Simon,
Calder, Mrs. Regina C.,
Calder, Theodore G.,
Calder, William J.,
Cameron, J. Donald,
Cass, Thomas,
Carroll, John,
Carson, James,
Cartwright, Jacob,
Cassel, Monroe,
Cadwallader, David R.,
Cadwallader, Horatio B.,
Calder, Frank,
Cassel, W. H.,
Cameron, William H.,
Campbell, Mrs.,
Chamberlin, James I.,
Clute, Horace A.,
Clarke, James,
Cline, John,
Clinton, Mrs.,

Clemson, L. C.,
Clark, J. Nelson,
Cleveland, Albert M.,
Clay, A. M.,
Cohen, Harris,
Colestock, Samuel,
Coover, Dr. Fred W.,
Cummings, J. E.,
Cowden, J. H.,
Coates, F. P.,
Coover, Dr. David H.,
Coover, Morrett,
Cooper, Albert,
Coffin, D. H.,
Compton, F. S.,
Coble, Mrs.,
Cobler, John,
Coover, Dr. Eli H.,
Corbett, W.,
Compton, W.,
Colbert, Mrs.,
Costello, J. C.,
Cowden, Benjamin F.,
Crawford, Samuel,
Crawshaw, William,
Crone, Charles,
Crowe, J. A.,
Craiglow, David,
Croft, John,
Cruikshank, William,
Crumley, George,
Cramp, Jacob,
Cross, W. H.,
Cripple, C. F.,
Curley, John,
Cummings, Jacob S.,
Cummings, A. E.,
Commings, Charles R.,
Currand, Mrs.,
Cunkle, John,

Curtis, Robert W.,
Cummings, H. H.,
Cummings, A. G.,
Cunningham, Mrs.,
Davies, Newton H.,
Dasher, E.,
Dasher, F. K.,
Dare, E. O.,
Dapp, Gotleib,
Dapp, Conrad,
Deil, Frank,
Derr, H. Walton,
Detweiler, William,
Deiker, Mrs.,
DeHaven, J. H.,
Deisroth, M. O.,
Deeter, J. N.,
Deihl, C. E.,
Derr, Mrs., Anthony,
Demming, Henry C.,
Detweiler, Samuel,
Denehey, William P.,
Demmy, Clayton,
Deihl, George A.
Deaner, Philip,
DeHaven, William H.,
Devout, Bartholomew,
Dentler, Jacob,
Dellone, Louis,
Dives, Pomeroy & Stewart,
Dietrich, P. E.,
Dipner & Bro.,
Dietrich, Howard D.,
Dorbet, Fred.,
Donleve, William,
Doninger, J. W.,
Doehne, George,
Donner, John,
Dow, F. M.,
Dohoney, Mrs. P.,

Dohoney, Mrs. Thomas,
Dorwent, William,
Drinkwater, Edward,
Drabenstadt, Amos,
Drumheller & Co.,
Dravenstadt, A. L.,
Drake, Mrs. William,
Duttenhoffer, C.,
Duffner, Theodore,
Dunn, Mrs.,
Drummonds, Henry,
Dunef, C. A.,
Duncan, D. L.,
Dunn, Alfred,
Dyer, H.,
Eby, Maurice C.,
Ebel, Fred W.,
Eby, W. H.,
Ebersole, H.,
Eberly, Samuel,
Ebersole, F. Jr.,
Egle, Dr. William H.,
Egle, Valentine,
Egle, Hiram,
Egenrieder, John,
Ehler, George W.,
Einstein, M. G.,
Einstein, Joseph V.,
Eisley, Edward,
Eitlebush, P. F.,
Elliot, Mrs.,
Elder, Mrs. R. O.,
Elder, David R.,
Ellenberger, Dr. John W.,
Emminger, Mrs. W. H.,
Emminger, James P.,
Engel, Ferdinand,
Ensminger, John T.,
Eppley, Daniel,
Eppler, Mrs. H. E.,

Erb, Martin,
Etter, B. Frank,
Etter, Calvin,
Evans, Thomas F.,
Evans, John,
Ewing, Joseph B.,
Eyster, Alfred E.,
Fager, Dr. Charles B.,
Fager, George C.,
Faust, Mrs. Mamie,
Fager, Dr. John H.,
Faus, Jacob,
Fager, Albert J.,
Feehrer, Mrs.,
Fehleisen, John,
Fesler, J. C.,
Fisher, Wesley,
Finney, Thomas J.,
Fisher, Charles,
Finn, James,
Fishinger, Mrs.,
Fitzgerald, Samuel,
Flanagan, William,
Fleming, David,
Fleming, Samuel W.,
Floyd, Isaac,
Fleck, Charles L.,
Flowers, E. M.,
Fogarty, Edward,
Fountain, Nelson,
Faerster, George, Jr.,
Faerster, George, Sr.,
Fountain, Oliver,
Forney & Stewart,
Foose, L. O.,
Forster, John E.,
Foltz, Mrs. A. B.,
Foley, Michael,
Floyd, James B.,
Fox, Richard V.,

Foltz, Andrew,
Forrer, Mrs.,
Forster, Mrs. M.,
Forney Bros. & Co.,
Fox, Wilson C.,
Foltz, J. B.,
Fry, Jerry,
Fry, J. B.,
Fromm, Joseph,
Franklin, Samuel,
Franck, George,
Fry, Amos F.,
Frisch, B.,
French, M. W.,
Frenie, Anthony,
Fry, W. H.,
Fraley, Il.,
Frank, Charles,
Frick, Augustus,
Fraim, Harry S.,
Freed, Isaac,
Frantz, Mrs.,
Froehlich, H.,
Funk, Dr. David S.,
Gastrock, William,
Gastrock, L.,
Garner, Mr.,
Gardner, W. L.,
Garmhausen, F. C.,
Gardner, Robert,
Garman, D. E.,
Garverich, George,
Garverich, W. M.,
Gates, William,
Gastrock, Lewis,
Gastrock, John,
Gastrock, W. M.,
Garverich, James,
George, J. C.,
Geiger, E. K.,

7

Gehr, George S.,
Geistweit, Mary and Sarah,
George, Charles T.,
Gerlock, F. G.,
Gilmore, John A.,
Gilbert, Lyman D.,
Gill, P. M.,
Giering, J. X.,
Gilman, Jeff,
Giede, C.,
Gilbert, C. P.,
Gilliland, Mr.,
Guiles, Isaac W.,
Ginger, W. H.,
Gough, Mrs.,
Golden Bros.,
Gohl, Fred.,
Gorgas, George A.,
Goodyear, M. S.,
Goodman, B. E.,
Gohl, Augustus,
Goetze, Theodore,
Gorgas. William R.,
Gould, Christian,
Graham, Hiram,
Greenawalt, Theodore D.,
Groff, Wesley K.,
Greenawalt, Jacob K.,
Grove, O. P.,
Greek, L.,
Groff, George M.,
Groff, Albert L.,
Graydon, H. Murray,
Gross, Daniel W. & Co.,
Gregory, Henry,
Gregory, William,
Grimes, John,
Gramm, Mrs. John A.,
Gray, J. W.,
Greenawalt, J. R.,

Gran, Pailus,
Groninger, Stewart,
Hand, Mrs.,
Hamlin, Rev. Benjamin B.,
Haas, Frederick,
Haines, Mrs.,
Hamilton, Dr. Hugh,
Harrisburg O. P. Clothing House.
Hamilton, Naudain,
Hamilton, A. Boyd,
Haulen Bros.,
Hammond, William B.,
Handshaw, Mrs.,
Hartranft, Howard H.,
Hart, Lane S.,
Hall, Louis W.,
Handshaw, James,
Hayes, James,
Hackett, George E.,
Harvey, Gwinn M.,
Haehnlen, Jacob F.,
Haldeman, Edwin M.,
Haldeman, Jacob S.,
Hamaker, Daniel H.,
Hammersley & Co.,
Hawkins, J. D.,
Hamer, John,
Hanshaw, Daniel,
Harris, J. R.,
Hake, A. F.,
Harm, L.,
Hahn, Mrs.,
Harlacker, J. C.,
Hess, Edward H.,
Hebner, John,
Hessenberger, Charles F.,
Hershey, H. M.,
Hench, S. A.,
Herman, John A.,
Heisey, Daniel H.,

Herman, John C.,
Herman, Edward S.,
Heckendorn, Mrs.,
Hess, Jacob,
Hemperley, James M.,
Hess, John,
Herr, Daniel C.,
Herr, Andrew J.,
Heist, Thomas H.,
Hess, Abraham M.,
Hess, Frank J.,
Herr, John B.,
Hess, Hiram W.,
Heffelfinger, E. A.,
Herbert, George D.,
Hemler, Hamilton D.,
Herr, Daniel S.,
Hicks, William C.,
Hildrup, John J.,
Hiltz, G F.,
Hickok, William O.,
Hinkel, George B.,
Hogentogler, Joseph,
Hocker, John A.,
Hoyley, John W.,
Hoopes, Jacob,
Hoyer & Milnor,
Houtz, Oscar S.,
Horner, J. W.,
Hoopes, Harry A.,
Hart, William B.,
Howell, Mathias,
Horting, Mrs. Matilda.
Holtzman, David,
Hoover & Gamble,
Hoffer, John,
Hoffman, A. A.,
Hoffer, John M.,
Honich, A. R.,
Hoffa, J. Wilson,

Hoerner, John W.,
Hoerner, Marcus D.,
Hoke, William,
Horner, William M.,
Howell, C.,
Holbert, Robert S.,
Hoffman, John,
Huss, A. M.,
Hummel, Samuel A.,
Hughes, William E.,
Hughes, James,
Hutchinson, Mr.,
Huntzberger, Mrs. M. A.,
Hursh, Martin,
Hutchinson, Mrs. Jennie,
Hutter, Frank L.,
Hubertis, Stephen,
Hummel, Mrs. Albert,
Hummel, Mrs. E. B.,
Hummel, Mrs. Sarah.
Hummel, John F.,
Hummel, Albert, Estate of,
Hutman, John,
Hubler, J. N.,
Hunter, Robert L.,
Ingram, Samuel D.,
Irwin, George H.,
Jauss, David L.,
Jauss, Luther D.,
Jackson, Mrs. Eliza K.,
Jackson, Andrew,
Jacobs, John M.,
Jauss, John G.,
Jauss, Mrs. Anna C.,
Jennings, William W.,
Jenkins, Henry S.,
Johnston, Samuel,
Johnston, Thomas H.,
Jones, Joshua W.,
Jones, Thomas M.,

Johnston & Co.,
Johnston, Andrew P. W.,
Johnson, Mrs. Jane A.,
Jones, William,
Jones, Harry C.,
Johnson, George,
Jones, Edward C.,
Jones, Erastus Jay,
Johnson, Lewis C.,
Jordan, Francis,
Kauffman, Stephen J.,
Kahnweiler, Joseph,
Karle, Augustus,
Kauffman, George W.,
Kapphan, Charles L.,
Kauffman, Levi,
Karns, Andrew,
Keil, John,
Keil, William,
Keil, Katie,
Kivler, George W.,
Keister, Robert,
Keet, Frank S.,
Kerper, John F.,
Kepner, Edward A.,
Kessack, George G.,
Keener, John,
Kepner, Mrs.,
Kepple, John,
Kelker, Henry A.,
Kelker & Sons,
Kelker, Rudolph F.,
Kerr, Mrs. Isabella S.,
Kelker, William A.,
Keeling, Rev. Robert J.,
Keenan, Mrs. Jane M.,
Keepers, Stephen,
Keiler, John F.,
Keller, John P.,
Kelker, Luther R.,

Keen, John,
Keith, Rev. William H.,
Keyser, Joseph,
Kelley, Carpenter H.,
Kelley, Henry M.,
Keffer, John J.,
Keen, John,
Kehl, Mrs. Caroline,
Kiney, Peter,
Kingport, A. E.,
Kilgore, W. W.,
Killinger, John,
Kinzer, Elias E.,
Kirby, William C.,
Kiman, J.,
Kindler, John,
Kilpatrick, T.,
Kime, H. B.,
Kinzer, J. D.,
Kinter, Mrs.,
Kline, William E.,
Klugh, George H.,
Klawansky, Abraham,
Knull & Co.,
Knoche, William,
Knisely, Samuel H.,
Knisely, Lincoln L.,
Knabie, William,
Knisely, William,
Knier, Harry L.,
Knoche, Frank,
Knox, Hiram,
Koppernagle, Rev. C. A.,
Koons, John,
Kohler, Stephen,
Koenig, Mrs.,
Koch, Jacob,
Krich, Conrad E.,
Krabin, J. O.,
Kruber, Charles,

Kraus, H.,
Krause, George W.,
Krichbaum, Mrs. George,
Krouse, John W.,
Kramer, Ira W.,
Kramer, Christian D.,
Kreider, Peter,
Kramer, John A.,
Knebler, Frederick,
Kunkel, Samuel,
Kuhn, Amos K.,
Kunkel, John C.,
Kunkel, Charles A.,
Kunkel, Samuel,
Lau, John,
Lawser, William,
Langletz, George W.,
Lauer, William,
Langletz, Mrs.,
Lauer, Jacob F.,
Lauer, Jacob F., Jr.,
Laverty, F.,
Laubenstein, E.,
Leedy, John W.
Lett, James,
Leedy, William,
Leib, Sobieski,
Lemer, LeRue.
Lebo, William,
Leeds, Richard,
Levan, William F.,
Liesman, Frederick W.,
Little, Augustus L.,
Liebtreu, Conrad H.,
Lingle, C. H.,
Lodge & Robinson,
Longnecker, Mrs. E.,
Lloyd, Patrick,
Lowry, J. M.,
Lochman, G. W.,

Low, John,
Lupold, John,
Lusk, A. Penrose,
Lutz, James N.,
Lucas, Robert A.,
Lutz, Horace,
Ludwick, John,
Lyme, John M,
Lynch, Christian W.,
Lynch, John S.,
Lyter, William H.,
Mason, Charles P.,
March, Daniel,
Macken, J. S.,
Macken, Mrs.,
Maxwell, W. H.,
Mailey, Mrs. Amos A.,
Mayer, Charles.
Marks, Herman,
Mayers, J.,
Markley, George H.,
Maguire, John J.,
Martin, S. Boyd.
Mason, Mr.,
Maurer, Daniel C.,
Martin, William D.,
Mayer, Thomas,
Maeyer, David,
Macklin, William E.,
Mondly, M.,
Mather, Edmund.
Mascher, C. F.,
Mauer, R.,
Martin, Charles,
Manum, Michael.
May, John K.,
Marzolf, Michael.
Machlin, James,
McCarty, Jerry,
McQuaddle, John,

McCrone, John A.,
McNeal, D. W.,
McCrone, A. F.,
McAlarney, Mathias W.,
McAlarney, Mrs. Ada,
McCarrell, Samuel J. M.,
McGowan, Dr. Hiram,
McBride, Rev. M. J.,
McManus, Mrs.,
McFadden, William C.,
McCarrell, William,
McCauley, Gilbert M.,
McCormick, Henry,
McCormick, James,
McCamant, Thomas,
McGlinn, M. C.,
McGlinn, C. A.,
McNear, William,
McCulloch, Thomas,
McIlhenny, Samuel W.,
McFadden, John,
McClure, Thomas, H.,
McDevitt, Mrs. John,
McCleaster, James,
McFadden, Andrew B.,
McCamant, Joel B.,
McIntyre, Mrs. Rose
McManus, Mrs. Edward,
McCarty, Callaughan,
McManus, Edward,
Metzger, Edward,
Metzgar, William B.,
Meyers, Abraham,
Meyers, Edwin K.,
Metzgar, Charles E.,
Meyers, Samuel W.,
Meals, E. S.,
Meese, J. W.,
Meals, Theodore S.,
Meredith, Eliza,

Melick, John P.,
Meiley, George W.,
Metzgar, L. F.,
Mehring, J. C.,
Messimer, B. F.,
Miller, Mrs. F.,
Muench, William,
Miller, David R.,
Miller, Jesse I.,
Miller, Albert,
Mittin, John,
Miller, Charles A.,
Miller, Mrs. M. P.,
Miller, George F.,
Miller, John,
Milleisen, L.,
Miller, Dr. Jacob A.,
Mitchell, Ehrman B.,
Middleton, William A.,
Mitchell, Horace B.,
Miller, Charles F., Jr.,
Miller, Charles F.,
Miller, Samuel C.,
Miller, J. Peter,
Miller, R. J.,
Miller, Benjamin K.,
Miller, John R.,
Miller, John,
Miller, Edwin S.,
Miller, Harry,
Miller, John,
Millhouse, Mrs. A.,
Morrow, Herbert,
Morrison, Alexander,
Montgomery, Joseph,
Moore, Brooke,
Morganthaler, Christian,
Montgomery, Mrs. L. A.,
Morley, Winfield S.,
Moyer, Isaac,

Montgomery, James B.,
Morley, Mrs. Fanny H.,
Moeslein, Edward,
Mumma, David,
Murphy, Samuel E.,
Musgrove, Alice,
Muench, Isaac S.,
Myers, William,
Myers, Mrs. Helen M.,
Nalen, James,
Neely, J. M.,
Neidig, James,
Neely, William F.,
Neidig, Jacob,
Neff, Jacob,
Nead, Benjamin M.,
Nise, W. H.,
Nickolas, Theodore J.,
Nipley, George,
Nutt, John C.,
O'Connor, Mrs. Dr.,
Ogelsby, J. J.,
Ogelsby, George A.,
Olmsted, Marlin E.,
Omit, Henry,
Orth, J. Fred.,
Orth, Henry C.,
Orsinger, Vincent,
Oves, Abraham,
Oyster, S. W.,
Pancake, George,
Pass, H. O.,
Parsons, George W.,
Pattison, Governor Robert E.,
Paganilli, Lewis,
Peters, William,
Peters & Son,
Pearson, Hon. John J.,
Peters, Mrs. Benjamin S.,
Pearson, Miss Carrie,

Pearson, Miss Ella,
Pearson, William,
Pennell, John A., -
Perry, Daniel W.,
Peters, John D.,
Phillips, Lewis O.,
Pfuhl, Rev. John G.,
Plack, William,
Potts, Howard D.,
Poole, Washington I.,
Potts, Milton G.,
Powell, W. L. & Co.,
Potts, Lewis,
Pritchard, Mrs.,
Pye, Joseph N.,
Pyper, William,
Quast, A.,
Quigley, J. X.,
Raysor, Michael F.,
Ray, Mrs. Susan B.,
Rahter, Dr. Charles A.,
Reel, Peter,
Reed & May,
Reed, George,
Reed, George E.,
Reinhard, J. Albert,
Reel, Adam,
Reese, Isaiah,
Reese, John,
Reeser, Richard,
Reed, Samuel B.,
Reily, Dr. George W.,
Reuwer, Henry,
Rhoads, Mrs.,
Rhoads, Daniel H.,
Rhine, Edward M.,
Rhoads, P.,
Rineer, John,
Rice, George H.,
Ritner, Thomas M.,

Ripper, Mrs. C.,
Ripper, John P.,
Rice, Rev. A. H.,
Ringland, Mrs. A.,
Riley, Harry M.,
Riegle, Hanson S.,
Rohrer, Martin,
Romich, Henry,
· Rauch, Edward C.,
Rodearmel, William,
Rockafellar, Thomas B.,
Ross, Joseph D.,
Roberts, Alexander,
Roop, Dr. J. Warren,
Rohrer & Morrow,
Rock, Mary,
Roumfort, Charles E.,
Roe, Francis M.,
Rohrer, John F.,
Russ, Patrick,
Russ, James,
Rudy, C. L.,
Rutherford, Mrs. E. R.,
Rutherford, William S.,
Russ, Narcissus,
Rumpf, Charles C.,
Reighard, Isaac,
Runk, DeWitt C.,
Ryan, William,
Santo, Martin M.,
Sayford, William,
Sample, Mrs. Ellen,
Sample, G.,
Santo, Jacob H.,
Sayford, Joseph,
Schaeffer, L. J.,
Schriver, Cornelius C.,
Schmidt, John,
Schermerhorn, John R.,
Scott, Mr.,

Schlayer, W. Harry,
Schlayer, Andrew,
Scheffer, B. Frank,
Schlayer, Jacob F.,
Schmidt, John,
Schlosser, John W.,
Schutzenbach, H.,
Schuddemage, Henry,
Schmidt, Joseph,
Sellers, John R.,
Sensenmayer, J.,
Segelbaum, Levi,
Segelbaum, Charles S.,
Senseman, Alfred J.,
Seiler, Jacob F.,
Seiler, William,
Seitz, Dr. John L.,
Seabold, Samuel,
Seiler, Dr. John P.,
Seabourn, Washington,
Seaman, Henry G,
Shue, Dr. John R.,
Shearer, J. L.,
Sheahan, Malachi,
Sherk, David L.,
Shellenberger, I.,
Shoemaker, Samuel W.,
Sharp, Jacob,
Shearer, Aquilla B.,
Shearer, John W.,
Shanahan, Rt. Rev. J. F.,
Sheaffer, Mrs.,
Shaffer, William S.,
Shoemaker, John P.,
Sheesley, William,
Sheesley, Daniel,
Sheesley, George,
Sheesley, Mrs. Daniel,
Shipley, George W.,
Shannon, J. Filmore,

Sheesley, Samuel,
Short, Charles,
Shindler, Louis B.,
Shellenberger, Augustus R.,
Shellenberger, Edwin D.,
Shoemaker & Holbert,
Shisler, Josephus,
Shiffler, John,
Shattuck, Charles,
Shopp, J. H.,
Shelly, J. F.,
Sharp, Mrs. E. G.,
Shunk, Mrs. William F.,
Shanklin, John,
Shoemaker, W. H.,
Silvius, John R.,
Simon, John B.,
Simonton, Hon. John W.,
Sible, John S.,
Simons, David, Sr.,
Sible, William H.,
Slentz, James A.,
Sloan Bros.,
Sloan, J. A.,
Smith, J.,
Smith, Henry,
Smith & Keffer,
Smith, W. H.,
Small, Charles H.,
Smith, George,
Smith, Mrs. T. Rockhill,
Smull, William P.,
Smith, Mrs. William D.,
Smith, Samuel R.,
Smith, David A.,
Smith, John W.,
Smith, Joseph,
Snodgrass, Robert,
Snavely, George,
Snyder, Eugene,
8

Snyder, Mrs.
Snyder, P. C.,
Sollers, William T.,
Sollers, Charles,
Sourbeer, Henry, Jr.,
Sourbeer, Henry S.,
Spahr, J.,
Spicer, John H.,
Speel, Alexander R.,
Sprenkel, Petter K.,
Spicer, W. I.,
Spahr, John H.,
Sponsler, Joseph A.,
Strouse Bros.,
Stern, Louis,
Stern, Emanuel,
Strouse, Joseph,
Stine, George W.,
Studebaker, Clement,
Stoose, John C.,
Stiner, Charles,
Stewart, Mrs.,
Sturgeon, Mrs. Susanna,
Stahl, John A.,
Stott, John E.,
Stackpole, Edward H. H.,
Stormfeltz, Henry E.,
Stroh, H. C.,
Stormfeltz, John W.,
Steever, A. M.,
Stoey, Washington I.,
Stewart, C.,
Stoey, John R.,
Steel, Mrs. Frank,
Stenner, Mrs. S. C.,
Stouffer, D. H.,
Stouffer, H. H.,
Starr, Hiram,
Steckley, Michael,
Stevens, Dr. John D.,

Stinson, Mrs. Samuel,
Stephens, William,
Stewart, John M.,
Stoner, Mrs.,
Stanton, Mrs.,
Strohm, S. W.,
Stutsman, John,
Stoner, A. H.,
Stine, J. W.,
Sullivan, P. M.,
Suydam, Eugene W.,
Sullenberger, Mrs.,
Swartz, Dr. J. Ross,
Swope, A. Carl,
Swab, Philip C.,
Swartz, George C. B.,
Swartz, Abraham,
Swivel, H.,
Taylor, Mars C.,
Tack, Albert B.,
Templar, James E.,
Tuepser, Adolph P.,
Techmeyer, H. W.,
Thorley, Thomas A.,
Thomas, Joseph H.,
Thompson, James B.,
Tilghman, David H.,
Tilghman, John,
Tippett, David L.,
Tippett, Robert Sons,
Toomey, Cornelius,
Toomey, John,
Tomlinson, Isaac R.,
Todd, Ira,
Trace, Mrs. Frederick,
Trewick, Walter L.,
Trostle, Israel S.,
Trippstein, George,
Tucker, Edward A.,
Uhler, Jeremiah,

Uhler, Henry,
Updegrove, Mrs.,
Uhler Brothers,
Umberger, B. F.,
Ulmer, William,
Umberger, H. L.,
Vallerchamp, John.
Vaughn, Robert,
Vanzandt, Harry M.,
VanCamp, William L.,
Vandling, John S.,
Vonstatten, John,
Wallower, Elias Z.,
Wagner, Edward L.,
Walmer, Noah A.,
Walker, Thomas,
Wallace, Thomas L.,
Wagner, Ferdinand F.,
Wagner, Frederick,
Walters, Jacob,
Walter, Henry,
Walters, William,
Warden, John,
Wharton, Mrs.,
Wagner, Samuel,
Walters, H. B.,
Warden, H. M.,
Warner, John,
Walters Brothers,
Weaver, Richard H.,
Weikle, R. G.,
Welzel, Frederick L.,
Weinman, Jacob,
West, Joseph R.,
Wehmeier, Emil,
Wechter, Hervey L.,
Wells, James B.,
Werner, Augustus F.,
Weisman, John,
Weaver, C.,

Weaver & Hubley,
Westbrook, Cherrick, Jr.,
Weills, Dr. W. M. L.,
Weimer, J. T.,
Weigner, Henry,
Weitmyer, J. H..
Wells, Joseph E.,
Weidling, H. C.,
Weaver, Frederick,
Weaver, Levi A.,
Whitman, John,
Whisler & Kline,
Whitman, Mrs. George,
Wilhelm. Jacob,
Wilson, David.
Wierman, Thomas T., Jr.,
Witman, Dr. Henry O.,
Wiestling, Samuel C.,
Wilhelm, Charles A.,
Winters, Thomas J.,
Wiestling, Joshua M.,
Wildman, Augustus,
Winters, John,
Wickert, Amos,
Wierman, Thomas T., Sr.,
Wilson, Albert,
Woolworth & Hasslet,
Woodward, L. B.,
Woods, Thomas A.,

Wohlfarth, Leopold,
Wolford, George W.,
Wollerton, Harry,
Wollerton. Charles.
Wolz, Herman J..
Wolz, M.,
Wright, William Wesley,
Wright, James,
Wyeth, Francis,
Wykoff, William,
Weidler. Mrs. Anna E.,
Yeagley. Edwin M.,
Yingst. Frederick W.,
Young, Mrs.,
Young, Joseph,
Young, L.,
Young, Rev. Jesse Bowman.
York, Henry,
Yount, Charles E..
Yost, Zachariah,
Zeil, Herman R.,
Ziegler, Richard B.,
Zeigenthaler, Mrs..
Ziegler, John H.,
Zimmerman, Luther R.,
Zimmerman, Mrs.,
Zollinger & Kline,
Zollinger, Samuel W.,
Zollinger, Warren A.

LYKENS TOWNSHIP.

Buffington, Daniel,
Beisel, Frank,
Bowman, C. T.,
Ferrier, F. P.,
Heminger, S.,

Hoffman, J. W.,
Hess, Charles,
Kessler, Reuben,
Kebach, Henry,
Kissinger, Jacob,

WICONISCO TOWNSHIP.

Englebert, A. F.,
Heilm, Milt,

Keen. H. Clay,
Neiffer, Lewis M.,

Schofield, E. Lane.

HUMMELSTOWN.

Baker, Dr. W. C.,
Balsbaugh, Jere.,
Balsbaugh, H. L.,
Bear, S. M.,
Bear, A. J.,
Blessing, F. D.,
Burkholder, M. K.,
Cassel, D. B.,
Clark, Dr. Charles,
Dasher, J. P.,
Earnest, Napoleon,
Fox, Dr. Thomas G.,
Fox, George,
Gerberich, H. T.,
Greenawalt, Samuel H.,
Grove, G. H.,
Greaff, M. F.,
Hoffer, E. M.,
Hoverter & Co.,
Hoffman, Mrs. Joseph F.,
Holler, Charles,
Hummel & Son, R. T.,
Hummel, Adaline,

Hummel, David,
Hummel, F. L.,
Hummel, Christian,
Hummel, H. J.,
Hummel, Luther,
Landis, Hiram,
McCurdy, E. E.,
Nissley, John J.,
Remsberger, J. M.,
Shope, Dr. Jacob,
Shreiner, W. H.,
Shope, E. M.,
Shaffner, F.,
Shope, Peter,
Siple, W. H.,
Smith, F.,
Spidle, F.,
Spidle, John G.,
Strickler, J. F.,
Strickler, A.,
Ulrich, William H.,
Walton, Allen,
Walmer & Fox.

MILLERSBURG.

Albin, James,
Bomgardner, J. L.,
Bowman, H. E.,
Brubaker, W. L.,
Dreibelbis, J. W.,
Freck, Roland,
Gilbert J. S.,
Gilbert, H. L.,
Heckert, J. H.,
Hillier, William,
High, S. B.,
Holtzman, D. R.,
Hoffman, I. W.,
Jury, B. W.,

Kahler, J. H.,
Kerchner, J. B.,
Kline, George W.,
Knouff, Frank L.,
Lincoln, J. H.,
Martz, J. C.,
Matteer, John,
McNeal, R.,
Miller, Levi,
Moyer, R. E.,
Penrose, John W.,
Penrose, C. H.,
Seal, Hon. John B.,
Steever, E. W.,

JEFFERSON TOWNSHIP.

Bowerman, G. W.,
Buffington, Henry,
Etzweiler, D. M.,
Etzweiler, Michael,
McLaughlin, Alexander,
Runnel, Daniel,

Shope, R. G.,
Sheetz, John,
Smith, Michael,
Snyder, Clinton,
Swigert, Emanuel,
Zimmerman, A. D.,

SWATARA TOWNSHIP—SECOND PRECINCT.

Basley, William,
Banlitz, Jonas,
Bare, Joseph,
Bartles, Joseph,
Brent, Moses,
Crumble, John,
Cumbler, G. W.,
Fetrow, S. C.,
Fishburn, John,
Foorman, Edward,
France, Smith,
Grasman, Henry,
Herr, Newton,
Horn, Adawort,
Martin, John,
McCreary, Joseph,
Mitta, Martin,
Naugle, Thomas,

Poorman, John,
Rigs, John W.,
Rink, Ferdinand,
Rink, Michael,
Rupp, David,
Seiders, F. B.,
Seward, John,
Seace, John H.,
Seiders, Emanuel,
Shafer, John,
Shipley, George,
Shafner, F. C.,
Simpson, Aaron,
Smith, Charles,
Swoveland, Henry,
Whitman, James,
Wolf, Duncan,
Wright, Irvin,

HALIFAX BOROUGH.

Cumbler, I. H.,
Fortenbaugh, Abram,
Freeburn, J. M.,
Landis, J. B.,
Lodge, William,
Loomis, Alfred S.,

Lyter, Isaac,
Rouch, Jesse,
Ryan, Charles W.,
Shammo, B. A.,
Zimmerman, C. C.,
Kline, William.

JACKSON TOWNSHIP.

Bixler, Cornelius,
Bowman, John F.,
Enders, George D.,

Erb, Peter,
Miller, James,
Naus, Dr. R. P.,

Snyder, Josiah.

LYKENS BOROUGH.

Bergstresser, E. L.,
Blum & Delaney,
Brubaker, G. B.,
Brallier & Co.,
Bueck, H.,
Deibler, E. W.,
Durbin, J. C.,
Eby, B. F.,
Fenn, W. H.,
Feindt, H.,
Forster, J. Frank,
Garman, J.,
Gemberling, D. R.,
Griesbam, William,
Hensel, W.,
Huhn & Miller,
Joseps, H. H.,
Koeher, W. S.,
Kuntzelman, A.,
Lebo, Edward,

Leum, Samuel,
LeFinn, Samuel,
Ludes, John,
Matter, J. L.,
Matter & Fear,
Marks, L.,
Marten, D.,
Myers, Dr. H. K.,
Sanner, E. A.,
Smith, W. H.,
Snyder, H. W.,
Stanley, A. G.,
Thompson, Alexander F.,
Trout, Jacob,
Vogle, Mrs.
Warner, John,
Weller, George.
Winters, W. J.,
Wolcott, Charles,
W——, J. B.,
Young, W. S.

WASHINGTON TOWNSHIP.

Lyter, Peter B.,
Miller, James,

Smith, Hiram,
Weaver, Frederick,
Ziegler, Lewis H.

WAYNE TOWNSHIP.

Etrider, Samuel,
Etzwiler, John,
Fowler, Frederick,

Hoffman, John,
Sponsler, Amos,
Swigard, C.,
Warner, John.

SUSQUEHANNA TOWNSHIP—NORTH PRECINCT.

Ott, Leander, N.,
Ott, Fred M.

BERRYSBURG BOROUGH.

Lenker, Valentine.

MIDDLE PAXTANG TOWNSHIP.

Heck, Dr. Lewis H.

WILLIAMS TOWNSHIP.

Armbruster, F.,
Carl, J. R.,
Challinger, D.,
Coller, Jacob,
Curtis, C.,
Day, R. W.,
Falk, R. G.,
Fitch, T. B.,
Frank, William,
Griffiths, John,
Haskins, J. P.,
Hess, Solomon,
Lebo, Amos.

Matter, G. F.,
Miller, E. H.,
Michan, John
Park, J. W.,
Powell, George,
Rank, H.
Reisig, Valentine,
Rickert, C. M.,
Stroup, J. N.,
Thomas, Robert,
Thompson, Robert.
Welsh, J. B.,
Willson, E. H.,

THE GENERAL FUND.

Statement of the receipts and expenditures of T. D. Greenawalt, Treasurer of the Dauphin County Centennial.

Debtor—T. D. Greenawalt, Treasurer Dauphin County Centennial September, 1885.

Cash received, individual contributions		$402 75
Cash received, committee contributions		3,331 75
Cash appropriated by Councils	$100 00	
Cash 324 medals sold	65 20	
Cash S. W. Fleming, account, medals	260 30	
		425 50
Total receipts		$4,160 00

Credit, September, 1885, orders numbered as follows:

1.	Frank R. Leib, chairman Military Day	$100 00
2.	Peter L. Krider, disc of medal	75 00
3.	A. B. Hamilton, postage, etc	20 00
4.	A. B. Hamilton, postage stamps	30 00
5.	Wilson Elder, services to Finance Committee	45 00
6.	M. W. McAlarney, engraving and printing	70 10
7.	S. W. Fleming, stationery	17 45
8.	C. O. Zimmerman, rent	20 00
6.	C. M. Bowman, Lebanon, advertising	3 00
10.	Peter L. Krider, 930 medals	93 00
11.	A. B. Hamilton, expressage	16 75
12.	Frank R. Leib, chairman Military Day	500 00
13.	S. A. Hummel, treasurer Industrial Day	500 00
14.	Patriot Publishing Company, printing	50 00
15.	Worth & Reinœhl, Lebanon, advertising	2 00
16.	W. R. Hendricks. Hummelstown, adv., 50c. . . . . [not presented]	
17.	C. M. Bowman, Lebanon, advertising	5 00
18.	D. Mumma, Committee on Inaugural Ceremonies	250 00
19.	F. R. Leib, Committee on Military Day	400 00

20. S. A. Hummel, treasurer Industrial Day 300 00
21. J. Brisbin Boyd, Committee on Salutes 62 00
22. Peter L. Krider, for medals 167 30
23. William K. Alricks, treasurer Firemen's Union . . .   500 00
24. George A. Gross, rent of office 25 00
25. W. W. Jennings, Finance Committee 100 00
26. J. M. Neely, hauling 42 75
27. General Secretary, express and telegrams 15 17
28. S. W. Fleming, stationery. 2 73
29. George Trullinger & Co., lumber 168 90
30. D. D. Boas' Estate, lumber 4 50
31. Dr. Thomas G. Fox, express 1 00
32. Wilson Elder, clerical services. 45 00
33. J. R. Orwig, clerical services 25 00
54. William Roberts, services at office 10 00
35. J. F. Rohrer, balance rent on Shakespeare 162 00
36. John I. Beggs, for electric light 160 50
37. Peter L. Krider, silver medals 100 00
38. James M. Lamberton, treasurer Dauphin County Historical Society, balance. 5 40

$4,160 00

Attest: GEORGE J. SHOEMAKER, Centennial Auditor.
March 11, 1886.

MILITARY SALUTES.

SEPTEMBER 14, 15, 16 AND 17, 1885.

COMMITTEE.

J. BRISBIN BOYD, *Chairman.*

SIMON DUEY,	WILLIAM PEARSON,
CHARLES A. WILHELM,	GEORGE H. HOUSER,
JOHN E. PATTERSON,	JOSEPH V. EINSTEIN.

Resolved, That a committee of seven be appointed, charged with the superintendence of salutes of thirteen guns each at the hour of six o'clock A. M., to wit: On Monday September 14, at Herr and Fifteenth streets; on Tuesday September 15, at Crescent and Kittatinny streets; on Wednesday September 16, at Herr and Fifteenth streets, and on Thursday September 17, at Crescent and Kittatinny streets.—*Proceedings of General Committee August 14, 1885.*

RELIGIOUS CELEBRATION.

SUNDAY, SEPTEMBER 13, 1885.

COMMITTEE.

JAMES McCORMICK, *Chairman.*

GILBERT M. McCAULEY,	E. W. S. PARTHEMORE, *Secretary.*
HENRY A. KELKER,	DANIEL EPPLEY,
JOHN J. CLYDE,	JOHN C. FORNEY,
LEVI B. ALRICKS,	JAMES BRADY.

CIRCULAR TO THE OFFICIATING CLERGY OF THE COUNTY OF DAUPHIN.

HARRISBURG, JULY 4, 1885.

DEAR SIR : We have been appointed a committee to confer with and invite the co-operation of the Clergy of all the Congregations or Churches in the County of Dauphin, in the celebration of the One Hundredth Anniversary of the erection of the County and the founding of the City of Harrisburg, and we request you to deliver a commemorative Sermon, or Discourse, on SUNDAY, THE 13TH OF SEPTEMBER, 1885, and forward a copy thereof to our Secrtary, to be deposited for preservation with the Dauphin County Historical Society.

Yours Respectfully,

JAMES McCORMICK, *Chairman.*

GILBERT M. McCAULEY,	DANIEL EPPLEY,
HENRY A. KELKER,	JOHN C. FORNEY,
JOHN J. CLYDE,	JAMES BRADY,
LEVI B. ALRICKS,	

E. W. S. PARTHEMORE, *Secretary*,

COMMEMORATIVE DISCOURSES.

No brighter autumn Sabbath ever dawned than that of the 13th of September, 1885. It was the opening of the Centennial celebration, and in the history of the town and county never was the attendance on religious service so universally large. It augured well for the week-day ceremonies to follow. Every one felt that under the protection of Divine Providence we had greatly prospered as a people. The pastors of the city preached commemorative sermons—while interesting services suitable to the occasion were also held in the various Sunday schools.

The pulpit of St. Stephen's P. Episcopal church was filled by the only surviving grandson of John Harris, Rev. William A. Harris, rector emeritus of Washington, D. C. Mr. Harris' sermon was an excellent one, the text being "The path of the just is as the shining light, that shineth more and more unto the perfect day." Proverbs iv:18. The reverend gentleman, although advanced in years, spoke with a full, rich, clear voice, and to the large multitude of people gathered to hear him his sermon was instructive, interesting and pleasing.

The services of the First Free Baptist church, corner State and Fourth streets, were conducted by Rev. James Calder, D. D., the pastor. Dr. Calder is probably about the only one of the city ministers who is a native of the county. He spoke of the characteristics, manners and motives as well as experiences of the early settlers, and was entertaining and instructive throughout his entire sermon.

The services at Westminster Presbyterian church were unusually interesting. Rev. William A. West's sermons were excellent and the large congregations were deeply interested. He spoke of the early efforts of the churches and their steady growth. He referred to the manufactories of our city, to our county almshouse, our hospital, our Home for the Friendless and Industrial Home and to the Y. M. C. A. as indications of progress. In the evening his discourse was from Isaiah iv : 18, " Remember ye not the former things neither consider the things of old."

Rev. B. C. Conner, of the Ridge Avenue Methodist church, preached an eloquent sermon in the morning to a large concourse of people. He spoke at length concerning the advancement of the freedmen in this country, and drew pleasing comparisons between their condition of to-day and that of one hundred years ago.

Rev. George W. Snyder, at the Second Reformed church, preached an historical sermon in the morning, giving a general history of the organization of the churches of the various denominations in the city and county, and a special history of the Second Reformed church, of which he is pastor. He stated that the Reformed Church was second in date of organization in the county, but first in this city. His text was from Hebrews x : 32, " But call to remembrance the former days."

The Centennial services at the Chestnut Street Salem Reformed church were conducted by the pastor,

Rev. W. H. H. Snyder, who made a short, pithy and interesting address. He was followed by Mr. Rudolph F. Kelker, who spoke at some length on the early history of the church. J. M. Wiestling and G. Z. Kunkel spoke of personal remembrances of the past history of the congregation.

There was a very large attendance at the Nagle Street Church of God to hear Rev. Jesse Bergstresser discourse from II. Kings, ii : 19, "The situation of this city is pleasant." The city referred to in the text meaning Jericho, which is located on the Jordan near the Dead Sea. In conclusion the speaker said : "The situation of Harrisburg is pleasant. When we survey the lofty scenery of nature and gaze upon her sunlit prospects in which every object is adorned with beauty, and hear the sweetest melodies wafted on the breeze, we exclaim: 'Truly our heritage is a good one.'"

Probably the most elaborate celebration of the day was at the Memorial Lutheran church, on Allison's Hill. The programme consisted of music and responsive reading of Scripture. Rev. J. R. Dimm, D. D., in the absence of the pastor, Rev. Mr. Dasher, preached an able sermon. In the afternoon there was more responsive reading and several addresses.

Rev. Leroy F. Baker, rector of St. Paul's Episcopal church preached two sermons touching on the Centennial. He referred to the many incidents in the early history of this county, the adversities that the first settlers encountered, their struggles with the ever-treacherous red man, the gradual, but permanent advances made, and compared the present with the past. Such history, he said, was full of its useful lessons and we must give especial thanks to a good God for the privileges now enjoyed. Rev. Baker's sermons were carefully prepared and proved very interesting to the large congregations.

Rev. D. W. Proffit, of the Memorial U. B. church, Boas street, preached a Centennial sermon this day in which were illustrated many beautiful comparisons between living in the age of civilization and that of heathendom: "It is the Centennial or one hundredth anniversary of this County, and we, as citizens, may without reproach congratulate our children upon the dawn of this Centennial year.

The Rev. M. J. McBride, at the Pro-Cathedral, spoke of the anniversary in fitting terms, contrasting the bountiful blessings we enjoy with the dangers and struggles, and self-denial of our ancestors.

Rev. J. H. Shively, of Carlisle, in the absence of Rev. Mr. Young, filled the pulpit of Grace Methodist church both morning and evening to larger audiences than have been seen in that edifice for some time. He alluded in pleasing terms to the Centenary of the county, and how thankful we ought to be to God for his blessings to us as a community.

The Centennial sermon in the Trinity Evangelical church, Dauphin, by Rev. D. W. Bicksler, was listened to by a large audience. His text was from I Samuel vii: 12.

Rev. M. P. Hocker, of the Lutheran church, Steelton, preached from the text found in Zachariah i: 5 —"Your fathers, where are they?"

Rev. Z. A. Weidler, pastor of the U. B. church, at

Highspire, preached his Centennial sermon from Hebrews xii: 1, " Wherefore seeing we also are compassed about with so great a cloud of witnesses." The services were largely attended.

At the Steelton U. B. Church, the subject taken by Rev. J. B. Hutchinson, the pastor, "A walk about Zion," from Psalms, xviii: 12, 13, "Walk about Zion, and go around about her, tell the towers thereof, mark ye well her bulwarks, consider her palaces, that ye may tell it to the generations following." The speaker said of the 140 churches in Dauphin county, twenty-six were United Brethren.

At Trinity Protestant Episcopal church, Steelton, Rev. Stoddard delivered a telling sermon, on a text taken from Matthew, 26th chapter and 8th verse. His closing words were as follows: In the events of this week, in the display made, and in the time and means employed, it would be strange if some did not say "to what purpose is this waste." But it will not seem a waste to those who realize what the object is. Self-sacrifice always gains respect. The sturdy pioneers who reared cabins and stockades; who had to fight wild beasts and contend against savages in human form deserve to be remembered. In traveling through a country however beautiful the scenery, it leaves far more impression upon the mind if connected with some historical event. The event about to be commemorated throws an additional charm about that old mulberry tree and the single grave beside it. There is nothing out of place in crowning that old tree with ivy or in filling the enclosure, in which it stands, and in decking the grave of him,

who was once bound to it, with flowers. It tells the
story of self-sacrifice at an early day, and yet, it tells
more than this. It serves to refute the saying that
"the only good Indian is a dead one." When a
roving fiend, maddened by rum, bound the first settler to this tree, intending to burn him to death, he
was saved by the Shawanese at the risk of their own
lives, who held him in high esteem. What wonder
then, when about to die, he made a request to be
buried under the shade of that mulberry tree! No
monument, however costly, can outlive the scene
where a noble deed is done. So the pioneer believed;
so those who came after him have shown by the
costly manner in which the tree is protected. And
so we will find if we are willing to work for some
good cause. The eyes of the world may not be upon
us. But what did the Saviour say of Mary's deed?
"I tell you throughout the whole world this shall be
told for a memorial of her." If your actions are
similar the reward will be the same.

It is probable that from every pulpit throughout
the county of Dauphin, were heard similar acknowl-
edgements to the Divine Ruler for all spiritual and
temporal blessings which we have enjoyed as citizens
of a prosperous city and thrifty county. In this
connection we have deemed it proper to preserve
the list of the clergy within the limits of the county
who so cordially entered with the spirit of the hour
and the occasion. Their names follow, with their
denomination and post-office address:

Baptist.
Rev. James Calder, D. D., Harrisburg.

Presbyterian.

Rev. William A. West, Harrisburg.

Rev. George B. Stewart, Harrisburg.

Rev. George S. Chambers, Harrisburg.

Rev. Francis M. Baker, Dauphin.

[The churches at Middletown, Steelton, Paxtang, Derry and Seventh street, Harrisburg, were without regular pastors.]

Lutheran.

Rev. A. H. Studebaker, Harrisburg.

Rev. H. S. Cook, Harrisburg.

Rev. Solomon Dasher, Harrisburg.

Rev. J. G. Pfuhl, Harrisburg.

Rev. John G. Abele, Harrisburg.

Rev. C. K. Drumheller, Pillow.

Rev. J. Fishburn, Millersburg.

Rev. M. L. Heisler, Lykens.

Rev. M. V. Shadow, Fisherville.

Rev. H. A. Letterman, Dauphin.

Rev. M. P. Hocker, Steelton.

Rev. H. C. Holloway, Middletown.

Rev. J. B. Crist, Hummelstown.

Reformed.

Rev. W. H. H. Snyder, Harrisburg.

Rev. George W. Snyder, Harrisburg.

Rev. John Kuelling, D. D., Harrisburg.

Rev. Albert S. Stauffer, Hummelstown.

Rev. Jacob B. Kerschner, Millersburg.

Rev. William G. Engle, Pillow.

Rev. Samuel Kuhn, Elizabethville.

Protestant Episcopal.

Rev. Robert J. Keeling, D. D., Harrisburg.

Rev. LeRoy F. Baker, Harrisburg.

Rev. Henry C. Pastorius, Lykens.

Rev. James Stoddard, Steelton.

Roman Catholic.

Rt. Rev. J. F. Shanahan, D. D., Bishop, Harrisburg.

Rev. C. A. Koppernagel, Harrisburg.

Rev. M. J. McBride, Harrisburg.

Rev. M. A. O'Neil, Lykens.

Rev. J. F. Foine, Middletown.

Methodist Episcopal.

Rev. Jesse B. Young, Harrisburg.
Rev. B. C. Conner, Harrisburg.
Rev. William H. Keith, Harrisburg.
Rev. J. Patton Moore, Harrisburg.
Rev. Horace Jacobs, Harrisburg.
Rev. Morris Graves, Middletown.
Rev. George Alcorn, Hummelstown.
Rev. G. A. Wolfe, Steelton.
Rev. William Powick, Dauphin.
Rev. William Redheffer, Halifax.
Rev. E. C. Yerkes, Millersburg.
Rev. William Furgeson, Wiconisco.
Rev. John O'Neill, Williamstown.

Church of God.

Rev. Carlton Price, Harrisburg.
Rev. J. Bergstresser, Harrisburg.
Rev. M. M. Foose, Harrisburg.
Rev. J. Jones (colored), Harrisburg.
Rev. S. C. Stonesifer, Hummelstown.
Rev. J. B. Lockwood, Middletown.
Rev. C. Kahler, Rockville.
Rev. Thomas Still, Steelton.
Rev. J. M. Wagner, Halifax.
Rev. F. G. Widenhammer, Highspire.
Rev. H. E. Reever, Linglestown.

Evangelical.

Rev. Samuel S. Chubb, Harrisburg.
Rev. D. W. Bicksler, Dauphin.
Rev. G. B. Fisher, Berrysburg.
Rev. D. A. Medlar, Millersburg.
Rev. B. J. Smoyer, Millersburg.
Rev. J. S. Overholzer, Lykens.
Rev. G. D. Sweigart, Williamstown.
Rev. C. J. Warmkessel, Pillow.

Mennonite.

Rev. John Erb, Harrisburg.
Rev. Henry Shope, Middletown.
Rev. John Stouffer, Bachmansville.
Rev. Menno Hershey, Hockersville.

United Brethren.

Rev. D. W. Proffitt, Harrisburg.
Rev. A. H. Rice, Harrisburg.
Rev. C. W. Hartzler, Harrisburg.
Rev. J. D. Killian, Hummelstown.
Rev. G. W. Lightner, Halifax.
Rev. J. B. Hutchinson, Steelton.
Rev. Z. A. Weidler, Highspire.
Rev. W. H. Wagner, Middletown.
Rev. P. L. Haines, Derry.
Rev. Ephraim Light, Swatara.
Rev. J. Runk, Grantville.
Rev. J. Von Neida, Lykens.

Dunkard—River Brethren.

Rev. Matthias Brinser, Middletown.
Rev. Solomon Brinser, Middletown.
Rev. Samuel Kieffer, Middletown.
Rev. Joseph Nissley, Hummelstown.
Rev. Daniel Kieffer, Union Deposit.

Dunkard—Old Brethren.

Rev. Adam Shope, Union Deposit.
Rev. David Smith, Union Deposit.
Rev. David Etter, Union Deposit.
Rev. John Witmer, Union Deposit.
Rev. William Hartsler, Elizabethtown.
Rev. Samuel Behm, Hummelstown.
Rev. D. Stroub, Elizabethville.
Rev. John Kuhn, Hockersville.

African M. E. and other Colored Churches.

Rev. Wallace Jackson, Harrisburg.
Rev. B. S. Jones, Harrisburg.
Rev. Horace R. Phoenix, Harrisburg.
Rev. Theodore Gould, Harrisburg.
Rev. Charles W. W. Frazier, Harrisburg.

THE FIRST DAY.

MONDAY, SEPTEMBER 14, 1885.

COMMITTEE.

DAVID MUMMA, *Chairman*

EHRMAN B. MITHELL,	ALFRED E. EYSTER,
HENRY L. HARRIS,	JOHN P. KELLER,
GEORGE KUNKEL,	W. FRANKLIN RUTHERFORD,
H. MURRAY GRAYDON,	HUGH HAMILTON.

PROGRAMME.

At 9 A. M.—Assemblage of school children at Harris Park.

AT THE COURT HOUSE, 11 A. M.

Music.

Prayer . . . . Rev. William A. Harris, D. D.
Introductory Address . . . . Hon. David Mumma.

Music.

Addresses :

Robert E. Pattison, Governor; Hon. John W. Simonton, President Judge; S. Cameron Wilson, Esq., Mayor.

Music.

Five Minute Addresses by Old Citizens.

Music.

AT THE COURT HOUSE, 7:30 P. M.

Hon. Simon Cameron, *Chairman.*

Music . . . . Chorus.
Historical Address . . . . Hon. John B. McPherson.
Music . . . . Chorus.
Centennial Poem . . . . Dr. Charles C. Bombaugh.
Music . . . . Chorus.

Mr. Leonard H. Kinnard, *Musical Conductor.*

THE CHILDREN'S DAY.

The wild Indian who over a century ago stood on the mountains near where Rockville now stands, and looking down the river saw the smoke arise from the abode of John Harris, and placed little significance on the fact that the white man was with him, would have opened his eyes wide, scratched his frowsy poll and snorted with astonishment could he have appeared in the flesh on this day and witnessed Harrisburg awakening to the celebration of the Centennial of its existence. His astonishment would have increased some hours later when the cannons boomed and the bells rang out a merry welcome to the second century, and he might have turned away in disgust and buried himself for another hundred years, cursing himself meanwhile that he had not scalped the first settlers in a bunch, and so guaranteed the country to his red descendants. But his red descendants have passed away with him, and in their stead comes the white man with a whoop and hurrah, and ding dong, and boom and whizz, to usher in and cheer the anniversary of the first hundred years of the existence of Dauphin county and ye town of Harris' Ferry.

All Harrisburg went to bed Sunday night after offering up a fervent prayer for fair weather, and at the first boom of the gun in the morning all Harrisburg "lit out" of its bunk and rushing to the window, looked out, and shouted "Laus Deo, it's a-going to be a fine day!" And it was.

Early in the morning the visitors from the surrounding country began to pour into the city, and every wagon in the county brought its load of cousins, every train on the numerous railroads centering here were laden with people who wanted to be in at the start, and quite likely were here when the last red light went out on Thursday night. The railroads, while not taxed to their utmost, it being the first day, yet had enough to do to take care of the passengers all bound to Harrisburg to see the "Centen."

The hotels had all they could do to take care of the crowds, and the numerous boarding houses, sprung up in a night to catch the Centennial visitor, were kept busy storing him away and feeding him.

The streets were very lively. It was early when the bustle began, but there was a hearty greeting to "Old Hundred" by the thousands who were up and ready to say "How de do?" It must not be supposed that only Harrisburgers were up and about. The country cousins and the spruce residents of surrounding towns were here bright and early, all bent on having a good time, and we know they had it.

The wonder of all were the pretty arches and decorations. But like Harrisburg, it never awakened to the fact that it *ought to decorate* until the last hour, and then everybody made a rush for decorations. Flags, bunting, gay colored calico, flag-stripe, lanterns, every species of decorations were eagerly sought for, and in a short time purchasers were cry-ing for more, and dealers were worrying over the fact, that although warned in time, they had not followed the advice of the newspapers and prepared for a big rush. It seemed as if they realized for the first time that Harrisburg was really going to have a Centennial celebration to amount to something. The mail and telegraph were brought into play and large demands were made on New York and Philadelphia wholesale dealers, and by Monday morning huge bales of decorations were piled up in the express offices and hurried to the stores by merchants.

In the upper end of the city the decorations were very elaborate. Arches spanned every street, not only the work of organizations, but erected by individuals, who grasped the idea of celebrating in the proper spirit and carried it out. In front of every engine house the firemen had erected pretty arches, some of them being very elaborate. The citizens of the Fifth, Sixth, Seventh and Eighth wards spared no bunting to make things look bright. and they literally painted their localities "red." Private houses, in some instances, were literally covered with flags.

In the lower part of the city the residents caught the fever and made one vast decoration of their houses. The engine house arches were perfectly beautiful, and the private decorations eclipsed anything that had ever been seen in Harrisburg.

All Monday the work of decorating was going on, and by Tuesday morning the supply of bunting was exhausted, while the town was covered with a gaily striped uniform.

The period toward which expectancy had for

weeks turned her eager gaze in pleasureable antici-
pation—the day for which the people of Dauphin
county and their Capital City had long been looking
—the opening day of Centennial week—was ushered
in amid the booming of cannon, and as the echo of
this, the initial sound of rejoicing, swept back across
the city from the cliffs of the Cumberland shore of
the river, the people, roused from their dreams of the
coming festivities, arose to a realization of their an-
ticipations: the Centennial had begun. Amid the
booming of the guns, pulsating on the early morning
air like the heart-strokes of nature, the bustle of preparation for the great event was renewed, and soon
the busy hum in the streets told of the energies and
activities of a community which that day would
begin the first year of a new century of life. The
sun burst forth in glory, giving auspicious promise
of nature's benediction on the event, and thus announced—the roar of the rejoicing gun, followed by
the smiling "god of day"—the Centennial period
was ushured in.

Soon the bells of the city took up the glad refrain,
and from the many towers and steeples the brazen-
throated heralds clanged out their rejoicings. Prompt
to the hour of nine they began their joyous clamor,
and for full fifteen minutes the air was burdened
with such a medley of sounds as caused the very
earth to quake and the tympanum to ring with the
second emphatic reminder that the joyous time had
come. Ere the last sound of the song of the bells
had died away the city, full clad, well fed, with joy
in its great heart, had entered on the enjoyment of

the pleasures of Centennial week, a week which will ever be remembered by the present generation as "red-letter days" in the history of the city and county.

IN HARRIS PARK.

The school children took possession of Harrisburg on Monday. It was their day, and when they can't have a great, large time it is very cold. It was just the reverse when they began to gather at their school houses in the morning—it was hot. By 8:15, in response to the request of the committee, the children assembled at their respective rooms and were formed in line for marching to Harris Park, where the Centennial exercises were to begin. It was the subject of considerable unfavorable comment that a great many teachers absented themselves and refused to take part in the proceedings. This did not set back the small boy and girl. They were there to parade, and they did. They came from the highways and by-ways, from streets and avenues. They were of all sorts, sizes and conditions and colors. There were children of all nationalities—from the fresh-looking, sturdy thoroughbred American through the gamut of English, French, Swede, Irish, Italian, German and every other country. The boy whose father can count his money by the thousands marched linked arms with the lad whose father works for ninety cents a day as a laborer. And they both wore the American flag on their bosoms. The little colored boy bore aloft his flag and marched with the same saucy, independent step as his whiter school-fellow. And he cheered just as loud.

Each school marched to the Chestnut street school

house and received a banner. As they passed through the streets they began to cheer, and they kept it up right straight along. The boy who carried the banner was the King Bee and envied by every other boy. Every girl who got a banner to carry voted it perfectly lovely, and her girl companions said she looked just too sweet for anything. The costumes of some of the children were very appropriate. They all wore flags—flags pinned on their hats, on their bosoms, waving in their hands; some boys wore entire uniforms of flag calico, some of them wore flags pinned all over them. The girls were all dressed in white, except some patriotic little ones who had entire dresses of flag stuff, and all wore sashes over their shoulder. One little tot marched as a Goddess of Liberty with a gilt crown, clad in red, white and blue, with her long hair streaming down her back. One little boy in old Continental costume, was very proud and seemed to be a pet of the other boys. At the Chestnut street school, also, twenty-five children in ancient costumes, very quaint, clambered into a large wagon and took their seats on benches arranged on the vehicle. They represented an old-time school, and the schoolmaster, Mr. John Alter, dressed in ancient costume, with a bunch of switches on the desk in front of him, looked very much as if it would be no trouble for him to flog some of his refractory pupils, who insisted upon getting up and cheering. As fast as the schools were supplied with banners they marched to Harris Park where they gathered around the enclosure in which lie the remains of John Harris.

If old John Harris could have gotten up and took a look at the strange scene about him that morning, he would have been astonished at the sight. Thousands of children were grouped about the grave, and a livelier crowd was never seen. While the girls were quiet and well-behaved for the most part, and contented themselves with waving their handkerchiefs, the boys held high carnival. They were true boys, and it was strange if they did not have a few fights. A newspaper reporter separated two boys who were at it hammer and tongs to the great delight of their school-fellows. Two boys banged each other over the head with flag sticks, and were parted: but it was all in fun! and so then and there over the grounds the lads had little battles, which lasted a few minutes, and then the participants were good friends again.

At 9:10 o'clock the sound of a band was heard and this was the signal for renewed cheering on the part of the scholars. Pretty soon Drum Major Tagg appeared in sight and back of him was an array of brass and blue uniforms brought up at the rear by a bass drum. It was the State Capital Band, which was met by Major David Mumma and escorted to the fence around the park, where it took up a position overlooking the whole scene. At this interesting period, while the boys and girls were grouped, the photographer got his work in and caught a picture of the scene.

At 9:15 Major David Mumma, Dr. Egle, Judge Hiester, Dr. Bombaugh, of Baltimore, A. E. Eyster, Dr. J. P. Keller, H. Murray Graydon, A. Boyd Ham-

ilton, W. Frank Rutherford, J. S. Barnes, Howard D.
Potts, William H. Smith and other prominent gentlemen interested in the proceedings took their positions at the foot of the elevation below the band
From the verandah of the old Harris mansion, now
his own residence, General Simon Cameron and a
large party of friends watched the proceedings with
great interest.

Every child was furnished with a programme on
which was printed the song to be sung. Promptly
at 9:20 Professor Chambers waved his gold cornet
and the notes of the tune "Liberty" floated on the
air. Then Prof. L. H. Kinnard waved his baton
once, twice, thrice; and everybody sang as follows:

> "God bless our native land!
> Firm may she ever stand,
>   Through storms and night:
> When the wild tempests rave,
> Ruler of wind and wave,
> Do thou our country save,
>   By Thy great might."

> "For her our prayer shall rise
> To God above the skies:
>   On Him we wait.
> Thou who art ever nigh,
> Guarding with watchful eye,
> To Thee aloud we cry,
>   God save the State."

At the conclusion of the singing, which occupied
but a short time there was a loud cheer and considerable applause. Immediately steps were taken to
form the procession to march to Second and State
streets. It was no easy matter. The children were
massed, and the task of disentangling them was

stupendous. Finally Chief Marshal Thomas and his efficient aids, with the assistance of what few teachers were present, succeeded in straightening out matters, and the procession marched out Washington avenue and up Second street in the following order:

Platoon of Policemen.

State Capital Band.

Chief Marshal Finley I. Thomas, and J. Edwin Devoe and Wilson Snyder, Assistant Marshals.

Hamilton street school. There were over 602 children in this representation, a large proportion being girls.

Harris Park school, 550 boys and girls, in charge of Prof. S. P. Stambaugh, as marshal and Mr. John L. Bates, assistant marshal.

Emaus Orphan Home, of Middletown, in charge of Mr. William A. Crull, the principal, and Mr. George A. Lauman, the tutor. The children were dressed, boys in gray and girls in drab. They bore a transparency inscribed: "Emaus Orphan Home, Middletown, Pa., Founded by George Frey, 1830.

Pennsylvania avenue school, in charge of Miss Lyle George, 280 scholars.

Lochiel school, in charge of Prof. W. E. Kirk, supervisory principal, and assistants, 225 pupils.

Mt. Pleasant school, 350 children, in charge of Mr. J. C. Miller supervisory principal.

Fager school, 132 scholars.

Allison Hill school, in charge of supervisory principal, 164 children.

Maclay street school, 60 pupils in charge of teacher.

Verbeke street school, estimated 525 children in charge of supervisory principal and teacher.

Lincoln school (colored), North street, W. H. Layton, principal, 60 scholars.

Calder street school (colored), marshaled by Mr. Scott, 50 scholars.

Paxtang school, Miss Kate Miller, principal, 70 scholars.

Boas street school, 292 pupils in charge of the teachers.

Chestnut street school, 120 pupils in charge of supervisory principa and pupils.

DeWitt school, in charge of Messrs. Tomlinson and Lloyd, 103 children.

Stevens school, Miss Stambaugh, supervisory principal, 90 children.

Garfield school, in charge of Miss Jauss, 150 pupils.

Reily street school, in charge of supervisory principal, L. H. Gause and three assistants, 350 pupils.

Ayres school, 98 pupils in charge of Miss Minnie Shisler, principal.

The Steelton schools were represented by about 57 pupils in charge of Mr. L. L. Palmer.

RECAPITULATION OF PROCESSION.

Committeemen and others,	45
Teachers and assistants,	97
Hamilton street,	602
Harris Park,	556
Emaus Orphan school, Middletown,	39
Pennsylvania avenue,	280
Lochiel building,	225
Mt. Pleasant building,	350
Fager building,	132
Allison's Hill,	164
Maclay street,	60
Verbeke street,	525
Lincoln, building, colored,	60
Calder street, colored,	50
Paxtang school,	70
Boas street,	292
Chestnut street,	120
DeWitt building,	103
Stevens' school,	90
Garfield school,	150
Reily street school,	350
Ayres school,	98
Steelton,	57
School of the olden time,	25
	———
Total,	4542

Of course it was very difficult to count the children, as there was no regard, except in a few instances, paid to alignment and order. The girls, as a rule, marched better than the boys, although the Harris Park boys made a pretty appearance sixteen abreast marching up Second street. There were as above given in round numbers, 4,500 in line, and this may be regarded as pretty accurate; although by the time the column reached State street the number had increased to over 5,000. Where they all came from was a mystery, but they certainly presented a very pretty sight, and they assuredly were vociferous. They cheered at everybody and everything. The waving of a flag on the sidewalk would set the whole line in a cheer. A man with a large stone wagon was cheered until he got down and held the horses for fear they would run away. Two boys on bycicles came along and were cheered and chaffed and guyed until they were compelled to get off their bikes and hunt cover. The number and enthusiasm were great. As a general rule those teachers present marched with their scholars, and were highly commended by everybody for doing so. They seemed to take a pride in displaying the young citizens they were bringing up, and they enjoyed the cheering and the laughter of the merry little ones as if it was the first time they had ever heard it. All honor to them. Long before the procession had passed Market square, it was halted by the information that State street was full and the vicinity of the monument passed. It was determined to make a double line, and by a division at Pine street those in the rear were marched up side by side with those who had occupied more favorable positions in the line. Second and State streets was a sight to look upon, and the oldest inhabitants never saw its like, and never will if he lives his life over again.

AT THE SOLDIERS MONUMENT.

When the head of the greatest juvenile procession ever seen in Harrisburg reached the monument at State and Second streets, the children gathered about the base and led by the band, sang two verses of " My Country 'Tis of Thee," as follows :

> My country 'tis of thee,
> Sweet land of liberty,
>   Of thee I sing ;
> Land where our fathers died
> Land of the pilgrim's pride ;
> From every mountain side,
>   Let freedom ring.

> Our father's God! to Thee,
> Author of liberty,
>   To Thee we sing.
> Long may our land be bright
> With freedom's holy light,
> Protect us by Thy might,
>   Great God, our King.

Then the chief marshall got ready for the counter-march on West State street, when each child was to receive the souvenir. The crowd was so dense that the idea of a countermarch was almost abandoned, but the committee determined to carry out the programme and the band was ordered to play. It did so with a will and the countermarch began. The sea of humanity was literally forced back by the moving line, and as the children again passed the monument they were each presented with the souvenir. This was a neatly printed and engraved folding card, on the front of which was the inscription: "1785— Dauphin County Centennial—1885." Inaugural Ceremonies, Monday, September 14th. Children's Sou-

venir." The coat of arms of the State was the center
piece. Inside was the picture of the attempt to burn
John Harris at the stake. The last page contained
portraits of the old and new court houses. One of
these is preserved in this memorial volume. When
each child had received the souvenir, amid much
shouting and jostling and waving of flags and banners, the line was dismissed.

At 10:45 the great children's parade was a thing
of the past, and the children were dismissed
and permitted to have their own sweet will in the
matter of going where they pleased. They were
proud of the fact that they had opened the Centennial so auspiciously, and so was everybody who saw
them.

Chief Marshal Thomas returned thanks in the following card: I desire to return my sincere thanks
to teachers and scholars who took part in the parade
this morning. The promptness in reporting, the
completeness in organizing, the orderly procession,
were all commendable in the highest degree. The
parents have my heartfelt thanks for their co-operation, which was evinced by the beautiful appearance
of hundreds of the children. The assistant marshals
have my thanks for their valuable aid in forming
the thousands of boys and girls into line.

FINLEY I. THOMAS, *Chief Marshal.*

EXERCISES AT THE COURT HOUSE.

At 11 o'clock in the forenoon, the Court House was
well filled. It was there where the centennial ad-

dresses were to be delivered. Without, in all directions, the mass of people were making extensive preparations for the three days parades which were to follow. The audience although not so very great, was more thoroughly representative than any ever assembled there. Many of the oldest citizens were present. The Nestor of the assemblage was Samuel Shoch, now of Columbia, a native of Harrisburg, who is between 90 and 91 years old. Next in order of age came Mr. George Garverich, aged 88, who when 21 years of age witnessed the laying of the cornerstone of the capitol building and aided in the hauling of the heavy timbers for that edifice. Next came Judge Pearson, who is 86; Wm. R. Gorgas, who is 80; Hamilton Alricks, Esq., 79; A. O. Hiester, Esq., 78; Hon. David Fleming, Col. Francis Jordan, Joshua M. Wiestling, Esq., Hon. A. J. Herr, H. Murray Graydon, Esq., Messrs. Daniel Eppley, Wm. K. Verbeke, E. E. Kinzer, J. Montgomery Forster, Dr. J. P. Keller, A. Boyd Hamilton, A. E. Eyster, Dr. W. H. Egle, Hon. J. B. McPherson and Reverends Wm. A. West, Geo. W. Snyder, B. C. Conner, T. T. Everett and many others. The ladies of the city and county were largely represented, prominent among them being some of the descendants or connections of the founder of the city. These and many other prominent ladies and gentlemen of the city and county, the officers of the meeting and members of the several committees, with the orators of the day, comfortably filled the court room for the inaugural ceremonies of Centennial week.

The minute hand of the clock indicated 7 minutes past 11 when Prof. Chambers gave his baton a flourish which started his band on the American Overture, consisting of a medley of American patriotic airs and including the soul-stirring song of "America."

After the applause which followed the music had died away, Hon. David Mumma, Chairman of the committee arose and said:

LADIES AND GENTLEMEN: —We meet to-day in this place for the purpose of inaugurating a series of services in the celebration of the one hundredth anniversary of the erection of the County of Dauphin, and the founding of the City of Harrisburg. We have with us the grandson of the founder, the Rev. William A. Harris, D. D., of the city of Washington, who will now address the Throne of Grace.

INVOCATION BY REV. WILLIAM A. HARRIS, D. D.

Almighty God. Father of all mercies, we, thine unworthy servants, do give Thee most humble and hearty thanks for all Thy blessings, past and present, temporal and spiritual. We thank Thee for health and home, food and raiment, and all the other manifold favors and comforts which Thy gracious bounty has lavished upon us, our friends and fellow-creatures. As in the former times, Thou leddest our fathers forth, into a wealthy place, and didst set their feet in a large room: give Thy grace, we humbly beseech thee. to us their children, that we may always approve ourselves a people mindful of Thy favors, and glad to do Thy will. Bless our land with honorable industry, sound learning, and pure manners. Defend our liberties, preserve our unity, save us from violence, discord and confusion, from pride and arrogancy, and from every evil way. Fashion into one happy people the multitude brought hither out of many kindred and tongues, endue with the spirit of wisdom, those who in Thy name are entrusted with the authority of government, that there may be peace at home, and that He may keep our place among the nations of the earth,—in the time of prosperity, temperance, and self confidence, with thankfulness; and in the day of trouble, suffer not our trust in Thee to fail.

We commend to Thy continual care the home in which Thy people dwell. Put far from them every root of bitterness, the desire of vain glory, and the pride of life. Fill them with faith, virtue, knowledge, temperance, patience, godliness. Knit together in constant affection those who, in holy wedlock, are made one flesh : turn the hearts of the fathers to the children, and the hearts of the children to the fathers, and so kindle charity among us all, that we may be, each one kindly affectioned with brotherly love.

Almighty and Merciful God, who healeth those who are broken in heart, and turneth the sadness of the sorrowful to joy, let Thy fatherly goodness be upon all that Thou hast made. Especially, we beseech Thee to remember in pity such as are this day destitute, homeless, or forgotten of their fellow-men. Bless the congregation of Thy poor, uplift those who are cast down, mightily defend innocent suf-

ferers, and sanctify to them the endurance of their
wrongs : cheer with hope all discouraged and un-
happy people, and by Thy heavenly grace preserve
from falling those whose penury tempteth them to
sin. Bless all who participate in this celebration.
Protect them from accident and from danger. Ani-
mate them with one holy purpose, to seek Thy favor
and to do Thy will. Give us all wisdom to find the
straight gate, and guide us in the narrow way that
leadeth unto life. Sanctify us in body and in soul,
and lead us in thy path of holiness, and prayer, and
praise, to that glorious Kingdom, where Angels
praise thy name for evermore, and, where Thou
livest and reignest with Thy dearly beloved Son,
and the Holy Ghost, one true and everlasting God,
world without end.

We ask every blessing in the name of Jesus Christ
our Lord, who has taught us, when we pray to say,
Our Father, &c.

The audience joined, en masse, in repeating the
"Lord's Prayer."

ADDRESS BY HON. DAVID MUMMA.

LADIES AND GENTLEMEN :—Standing upon the
threshhold of the second century in the history of
Dauphin County, and taking a retrospective view in
the light of history, of the events which have
transpired during the century, the close of which
we are now about to celebrate—glancing at some
of the privations and dangers encountered by
those who first settled upon the territory now
composing our County, and who with their

descendants brought it up to its present prosperous condition, we at once realize, that the services we are about to inaugurate, are eminently proper.

These early settlers, many of whom lived to take part in the organization of the County, frequently found it necessary, in order to protect themselves and families from the attacks of Indians, to carry their trusted rifles with them to their fields of labor, and carry their rifle in one hand, while they wielded the implements of husbandry with the other.

Being possessed of strong faith in God, and of deep religious convictions, they early built houses of worship, in which they frequently found it necessary for their protection, to worship with their rifles in their pews.

Notwithstanding these precautions, the savages frequently burnt their houses, and carried off their women and children into a condition worse than death. They were an industrious, frugal, honest and patriotic race, and they in their day and generation, so impressed their descendants with their noble example, that in pursuance of the example impressed upon them they have kept pace with the improvements of the age, so that to-day we may claim for our County a prosperity equal to any in the Commonwealth. Agriculture has been advanced so that to-day the farms of our County are the equal of any in this country, and some of them the equal of, if not the superior of any in the world.

Our mineral resources have been developed, and manufactories established, so that in the production of iron and the manufacturing of it in its various

branches, we can boast of establishments equal to
any in the country.

Education has been advanced so that now a good
and comfortable school house can be met with at
every cross roads, and every child, however poor and
humble may get a good education free of cost.
Religion has been promoted, and you may now see a
church spire from every hill top in the county.
Well may we honor those who have contributed to
these results. During the last century, liberty has
received a new baptism, to which glorious result our
County has contributed her full share. Her sons
fought on every battle field, and many of them now
sleep in unknown graves, far from home and friends.

We now start in the second century in the history
of our County, with many advantages over our ancestors, who have long since passed away. But only
in the practice of honest industry, and integrity, and
in the worship of God in simplicity and faith, with
a singleness to the promotion of his kingdom on
earth, as practiced by them, can we stand still in
their foot steps.

In every thing else pertaining to the welfare of
mankind, we must move forward and onward.
The farmer must cultivate his farm, (I will not say
with more industry,) but with more skill, aided by
the knowledge, and science of his day.

The mechanic must use more skill in his trade,
aided by the improved tools at hand, and persons
engaged in all other pursuits must keep pace with
the improvements of their age, if our county is to
continue to maintain her present position of equality

with the other parts of our great Commonwealth.

Within the last century science has accomplished such mighty results, that it is far beyond the scope of human immagination to divine what the next century may bring forth.

Electricity which was a terror to our ancestors has been brought under the control of man, so that we can now sit under the lightning's continous flash, and read with as much safety as our ancestors could under the light of the pine knot, lard lamp or tallow candle.

No one will now venture to doubt, that before the close of the next century, man with the aid of science, will be able to arrest the tornado in its path of destruction, and command its mighty power for the comfort and pleasure of mankind.

"Abide With Us," a hymn, by Haydn, was impressively rendered by the band.

The chairman, Major Mumma, then said: "This being the Capital of the Commonwealth, to which the Founder gave of his land for public use forever, it is proper that the executive take part in our Centennial celebration. I have the honor, therefore, to present to you His Excellency Robert E. Pattison."

ADDRESS BY GOVERNOR ROBERT E. PATTISON.

It is to be regretted that the address of the governor was not stenographically reported. It certainly was one of the most interesting delivered on the occasion. The following resume, however, will convey some idea of what he said:

LADIES AND GENTLEMEN:—This is Dauphin

county's week—the close of the first century of her organization. Her citizens may proudly exchange congratulations. To her the State sends greetings. I fancy that upon just such day, beneath an unclouded sun, with the ringing of bells and the songs of children, a free people ushered in the first celebration of Independence. One hundred years ago John Dickinson was President of the Supreme Council of the State; Benjamin Franklin was returning in triumph from the court of France, soon to succeed Dickinson as Governor; Simon Snyder was moving into Northumberland county to engage in the business of store-keeping; Madison and Hamilton were busy in the efforts to secure a convention to consider articles of confederation; Washington was watching the progress of the movement with much solicitude from Mount Vernon; William Pitt was bringing forward as minister his reform measures in Parliament, and a corrupt government in France seeking to gratify its vicious appetites, was surely leading to the Revolution that followed; Reformation was advancing in Germany; Catharine of Russia left a people better by reason of her reign, and China's walls were giving away to foreign commerce; seventeen years after, to admit the first American consul. Amidst this organization and disorganization prevalent throughout the world—all tending to popular and better government—Dauphin County was organized. Then with a population of 4,000 now 76,000; then the State with 360,000 now nearly 5,000,000; then the nation with but 3,000,000 now a people of more than fifty millions. It is reserved to the historian to tell of the struggles of Bezalion, and Harris, and the Paxtang band. I cannot refrain, however, from referring to the grand old figure of the man upon the Susquehanna, standing as a companion to that other example upon the Delaware, William Penn, who saw the future Philadelphia, the great sea-coast town of a great State—whilst Harris saw here the natural crossing point of the Susquehanna river—literally the ferry of the western traffic of the country, and he planned accordingly. Nor have the centuries disappointed either prophet. Philadelphia realizes Penn's dreams and hopes, and Harris' Ferry of old time is the same in spirit, the passage point of traffic, but by a different agency. The ferry is a bridge now. The wagon paths are mighty railroads, but still this city is the point they pass—the ferriage for the traffic of the State. What of the next century? Our fathers builded not for themselves. As they builded for us, so we must build for those who will follow us. The globe has been belted by civilization. We stand here the proudest, freest people on the face of the earth, and in one hundred years we have indeed been blessed. God evidently intends to raise up a better people here than ever. Just as this people puts itself in accord with divine law, will this people prosper; just as the law is violated will this people go down. Society is made up of individuals. Society makes communities, communities make counties, counties make States, and States make the nation, and what injures any portion of the organization injures the whole.

Governor Pattison's address was replete with inter

esting statements and statistics, and was closely
listened to. At its conclusion the Governor was
warmly applauded.

Music by the band—"Auld Lang Syne."

The chairman on introducing Hon. John W.
Simonton, said, that next to the State comes the
county, the one whose formation a century ago we
are celebrating. It is fitting that the highest judicial
officer should speak for it.

ADDRESS BY HON. JOHN W. SIMONTON.

As in the case of Governor Pattison, the admirable
off-hand address of Hon. John W. Simonton was
not fully reported. It bristled with good points,
and in effect was as follows :

CITIZENS OF DAUPHIN COUNTY :—We have assembled here to celebrate the one hundreth anniversary
of Dauphin county, and this meeting shows that
we have not in this progressive age turned our
backs upon the events of the past and the deeds of our
forefathers, and this we may consider a favorable
augury for this community. There are lessons
which individuals and communities cannot learn
except by experience. No individual can understand
himself until he considers the maxims and impulses
which controlled him in the past. I think it is that
which impels us to look into the actions and deeds of
our ancestors. It is the early history that gives us the
key to the present and future. I might say that this
is the principle that leads us to this celebration.
And we may make it more than a passing show if
we are induced by it to study the lives and history

of our ancestors. The past is continually exerting its influence upon the future. When in recent years those who controlled Germany, impelled by a desire for national unity wished to inspire the soldiers and people with the same desire, they recounted the heroic deeds of the men of the past; so in the history of our own country, we may awaken inspiration in the people of to-day, by recalling the deeds of heroism of our ancestors.

Most of our early settlers came from Scotland, via Ireland, and from Germany. They were a people impelled by motives of right; their greatest love being that of liberty, and we are here to-day to show the fruits of their privations. They had none of the domestic comforts such as we have to-day; the utensils such as were used by the housewife of 100 years ago are no more used. We stand to-day a people more advanced in science, but in intellect and judgment they were our equals. And in conclusion, let us try to remember, as Governor Pattison has already said, that it is only so far as we obey God's commands that we can hope to continue prosperous as a Nation.

In introducing the next speaker, the chairman took occasion to say—that as this was the Centennial of the Founding of the Town as well as the Formation of the County, he took pleasure in presenting Hon. S Cameron Wilson, mayor of the city of Harrisburg.

ADDRESS OF MAYOR SIMON CAMERON WILSON.

FELLOW CITIZENS—I feel proud to-day of the honor which has been conferred upon me, as chief Magistrate of this city, to assist in the grand ceremonies incident

to the centennial year of the city of Harrisburg and
the county of Dauphin. Our minds will naturally
turn back to-day and note the changes—the wonderful transformations—which have been wrought by
the energies of men long since passed away, who
lived and toiled and wrought, not for themselves
alone, but for unborn generations; and their works
which have lived after them are destined to flourish
long after we too have passed the mysterious border
and entered upon other scenes and another life. To
the hardy pioneers, whose faith in their ability to
wrest from the wilderness this beautiful home we
now enjoy was only excelled by a devout love of
their God, we owe a debt which no posthumous honors
can repay. From these men and women we have
been instilled with that spirit of obedience to law and
order which has given us a proud name beyond our
borders. To these men and women we are indebted
for those features of economy, industry and integrity
that have so far crowned our enterprises with success
and made us a prosperous people. This is our inheritance, and to the pioneers of the wilderness we owe
the debt for what we now are. Peering through the
vista of a century past, we must be impressed with
the vast changes which have taken place since first
the rugged backwoodsman erected his rude home
here—a then outpost of civilization. The story is an
old one—has "oft been told in prose and verse," and
is to us to-day as a book—well studied and understood—therefore needless of repetition.

It is to the future, however, that we should direct
our energies and our genius—and should the same

11

proportionate success be ours through the coming
century as it has been through the past one, truly
our greatness will be beyond the conception of living
men. But to thus succeed, we must lay aside the
village ideas—must let the fogyisms of the days that
are gone be matters of past history only, and filed
away among our musty archives, to be displayed at
some future centennial among the relics of the antiquarian, and then by seeking in all honorable ways
to outrival our rivals—getting out of the ruts in
which we have too long traveled, strive to reach that
pinnacle of municipal government which, while cos-
mopolitan in its features, is, in the hands of honest
and good citizens, the best government we can attain.

I congratulate my fellow-citizens to-day upon the
auspicious commencement of the grand celebration
of their Centennial, and their efforts to make it a
complete success—an object they have fully attained.
To them, and for them, be all commendation and
honor. There are but few occasions arise where
men have an honest opportunity to glorify their own
success while honoring others, and as this *is* one of
those occasions, I know of no people who have a
better right or a better cause so to do than our good
people of Harrisburg.

After a short selection by the band, Hon. A. O.
Hiester was introduced as the first old citizen to
address the meeting.

ADDRESS OF JUDGE HIESTER.

MR. CHAIRMAN, LADIES AND GENTLEMEN:—The
letter of the secretary of your committee inviting me
to deliver a short address at the inaugural ceremo-

nies of the Dauphin county centennial, carries with it the thought, that in all past ages festivals have been observed to commemorate events of importance in the lives of individuals and communities. The most important to us as citizens of the United States, is the celebration of the Declaration of Independence, and the birthday of Washington.

In speaking of the first event, John Adams said to the convention of patriots in session at Philadelphia, we shall make this a glorious and immortal day—when we are in our graves our children will honor it, they will celebrate it with thanksgiving, with festivity, with bonfires, with illuminations—this prophecy has been fulfilled.

In the celebration of Independence and Washington's birthday, all, of different political opinions and different principles can and do associate together; so may it ever be, and heaven grant that on every recurrence of the event, the recital of the sufferings of our forefathers, through eight long years of war, may conduce to the patriotism and fidelity to the Union of the body of our citizens.

By the festival which calls us together to-day, we are reminded of the sufferings of the early settlers of our county, in their contests with the Indians, of the massacres of women and children, and the burning of homes and of crops; and by contrast, of the peace, the order, and prosperity that surround us at this time.

In 1749, the territory composing the county, then included in Lancaster was purchased from the Indians.

An interesting chapter of history may be gleaned from the able petitions and remonstrances for, and against the formation of the County of Dauphin, out of a part of Lancaster, and of the contest between Middletown and Harrisburg from 1782 to 1785 for the seat of justice.

In 1756 this section was surrounded with stockade forts and block houses, at Halifax, McKees' Half Falls, Fort Hunter, Manada Gap, Harris' Ferry and Robinson's Mill, places of refuge from the intrusion of the Indians, for women and children.

Though no mention is made in the history of the county of a store house for ammunition and provisions for these forts, yet so late as 1836, when I moved to my farm, there was a large store house standing on the bank of the river a hundred yards below my present dwelling in which was stored a number of very strong iron-bound boxes, some empty, others, containing cast iron bullets, bayonets and other implements of war. These were destroyed on the burning of my barn in 1848.

Now for a few reminiscences during the last sixty years. In nothing in my experience as a farmer, has there been greater progress and improvement than in farm implements, and farm work, unless it be in the good conduct of the people, as I shall hereafter show.

In early years I made a regular pilgrimage to Powell's and Lyken's Valleys during the month of May to engage eight or ten skilled workmen with scythe and cradle to help with haying and harvest.

In those days the ministers of the gospel for the

sake of health and social enjoyment, came to the country and made a hand in the field; now they go to the sea shore.

For several years the Rev. Mr. Stem, of the Protestant Episcopal church, made me a visit during hay-making, and delighted to pitch hay on the wagon against my teamster. At noon and supper time he would come to the house as wet as if he had been dragged through the river. Then by taking a bath would, by morning, be as bright as a lark.

The Rev. John McCauly for several years, led my men with scythe and cradle, and I never had a better leader. McCauley was a grand singer, and in the evening would lead the party in singing hymns of praise.

Now we send one man with a pair of horses and mower to the field, and he will do the work of ten men in a day. The next day a man with a tedder and one horse, and he will do the work of ten men in turning the grass. Again we send a man and one horse with a rake and he will do the work of ten men in gathering into winrows, and when the hay is ready for the barn, with the hay fork and horse power we unload a ton and a half of hay in twenty minutes.

So with threshing, instead of spending half the winter in tramping out the grain with horses, we engage a steamer and in a few days, by threshing 400 bushels of wheat or 600 of oats a day, the work is done.

So with farm implements. In none has there been greater improvement than the grain drill. I had perhaps the first, at least the first I know of that was brought to the county. It was a simple concern. A wooden cylinder with perforated holes, small hopper on the top, and six teeth, and pair of handles projecting behind, by which the driver carried it around at the end of the field, while a boy turned his horses. Now they are improved to indicate the exact number of acres sowed, the quantity of grain dropped, adjusted to sow it at equal depth on hard or soft ground, to drop the fertilizer, and roll the ground on each drill equally, all at one operation.

With regard to the improvements around town, the young people of the present day will hardly be able to realize, that back of the Capitol, along Pennsylvania avenue, and from there to Paxtang creek, now covered with thriving manufactories and handsome residences, that in my short recollection, it was a swamp grown up with tussocks, and that when a boy I often after an early supper, would take my dog and gun before dark till my game bag with woodcock, snipe and quail which then abounded, with a few wing shots to thin them.

There is a reminiscence that presents itself to me that is appropriate to the occasion, as it is calculated to show the great change that has taken place in public sentiment and the improvement in manners of the people of Harrisburg, in hearing with respect the opinion of those who may differ with them on great national and moral questions. In fact I believe it is an argument in favor of the moot question, that people are growing better.

We should hardly be able to realize that so late as

1834, when a small body of ladies and gentlemen, the very elite of the citizens for culture and wealth, met in a little building on Mulberry street, used as a place of worship, to listen to a lecture by the world renowned Burleigh, as to how best to use their influence and their means to alleviate the condition of the slave, and to rid the country from the foul blot that was making our land a by-word and reproach to the nations of the world, that they should have been disturbed by having stones thrown through the windows, and when the meeting was closed, that the lecturer should have been followed by a howling mob.

I remember that James W. Weir, of blessed memory, sent me a note at Fairview rolling mills, where I then resided, asking me to come over, and to come prepared, as they apprehended violence. As we left the door, Dr. Rutherford took Mr. Burleigh on his arm to escort him to his hospitable mansion on Front street. James Weir and I followed, Doctor William Elder and John A. Weir came next. The rabble followed by our side and in the rear, shouting and yelling. Had we been assaulted at least six barrels of a revolver would have been emptied by one who knew how to handle it, and that not in the air.

There is another reminiscence that goes to show the change in the habits of the people. I remember that on a beautiful evening in 1833 while sitting in Doctor Dean's office on Second near Walnut street, with his students, Doctors Rutherford and Elder, Major Hannah, bridge inspector for Washington county, a man of great physical proportions, fully six feet tall came into the office and introduced himself as an athlete, saying he understood since he arrived in town, that Doctor Rutherford was a great wrestler, and that he had called to ask him to have a fall with him. A bottle of wine was soon staked upon the result, and we repaired to the green in front of the capitol. Arrived upon the spot, the bridge inspector disrobed and put on a pair of buckskin breeches which he said he always carried with him, and then they took a back hold. The moon was full, and not a leaf intervened to break the reflection upon the group. I think I can see them now as they swayed to and fro with the shadow apparently twenty feet long following them at every turn of their bodies, and trip of their feet, until they fell heavily upon the sod. You will ask who won? Our townsman, Doctor Rutherford, and we had a grand jubilation, calling in some of our friends to make merry with us over the event.

And now the thought suggests itself to me, and it is appropriate to the occasion, where are the friends of those days, the friends from '24 to '36, where Doctor Dean, Doctor Rutherford, Doctor Elder, Doctor Roberts, Doctor Berghaus, Doctor Benjamin J. Wiestling, where William Buehler, James Lesley, James W. Weir, John A. Weir, Robert J. Ross, Herman Alricks, Charles H. Rawn, James Burnside, John H. Briggs, John C. Berryhill, all of town? Where are my old country friends and neighbors, John P. Rutherford, John H. Fox, Isaac Updegrove, George Kinter, John C. McAllister and Jacob Grove, all men re-

spected in their day? They have been all called to
give an account of their stewardship, and many of
them I helped to carry to their last resting place.

How many remain? Our worthy chairman, who
at that early day was a little boy, being prepared by
the watchful care of a good mother (to whose memory
he so lately rendered a beautiful tribute of praise at
Shoop's church), for the duties and trials of life, Hamilton Alricks, A. Boyd Hamilton, Francis Wyeth,
Louis Heck, Daniel W. Gross, Rudolph F. Kelker
and Frederick K. Boas, names that I can count on
the fingers of my one hand—men respected and
honored where they were known, lingering nearly all
alone on the shores of time, and waiting with your
speaker to join the company of loved ones, who are
watching to greet them on the other side.

Another musical selection rehearsed by the band
closed the morning exercises.

IN THE EVENING.

As at the opening ceremonies of the morning, so
in the evening the Court House was well filled with an
intelligent audience, who, doubtless anticipating the
intellectual treat in store, gathered to hear what orator and poet had to say about the city and county
we all so dearly love. As in the forenoon, also many
ladies graced the occasion with their smiling, beau-
teous and benign presence. Prominent among
those seated within the bar were Judge Pearson,
Judge Simonton, Rev. Wm. A. Harris, Alexander

Sloan, David Fleming, Francis Jordan, Col. Henry McCormick, Rudolph F. Kelker, George Z. Kunkel, Rev. A. H. Studebaker, and many others whose names are well known throughout the city and county. Shortly before the meeting was opened General Simon Cameron entered and walked up the aisle. When his tall and upright form, topped with his massive head, crowned with silver, met the eyes of the waiting audience, he was greeted with an outburst of hearty applause. He was followed soon after by Governor Pattison, who was invited to a seat at the right hand of the venerable president of the meeting. Soon another stalwart form, its ample head with silver glory crowned, claimed the attention of the audience, and Governor Ramsey, of Minnesota, a son of Dauphin, of whom all Pennsylvania is justly proud, took his seat beside his friend General Cameron.

The exercises were opened by a chorus, "American Hymn, by Keller," sung by a choir of nine ladies and seven gentlemen, under the direction of Mr. L. H. Kinnard. Prof. Knoche played the organ. After the music, General Cameron said he had been chosen to preside at the meeting. He named the features of the programme, and after saying that he had no remarks to make at the time, but might have something to say later, he introduced the orator of the evening, Hon. John Bayard McPherson.

HISTORICAL ADDRESS BY JUDGE M'PHERSON.

LADIES AND GENTLEMEN:—Individual life is for the most part a process of connected and continuous

growth. Its movement is so slow that from day to
day, perhaps from year to year, it registers no conscious change. In the vast majority of lives there
are no periods of sudden development, no rapid and
surprising changes, no inward flashes of revealing
light. Doubtless, such experiences are not unknown, and in truth they seem to come at times to
most of us, at intervals so rare and with effect so
vivid, that the memory holds them fast indeed, and
all our after life is often seen to wear their color and
to follow in the path they point. But while the effect is real and may be lasting, its true cause and
character may well fail of proper notice. Laying
aside the special cases to which I have referred, I
think it may be safely said that, if we closely look at
what has gone before such epoch-making moments
in our lives, we shall surely find they are the last
step only in our progress toward a goal we did not
clearly see; the successful end of some long struggle
for a good the greatness of whose value only then
grew plain; the bursting into flower of a plant whose
growth we had not watched; the splendid surprise
that waits our vision round the winding of some
toilsome road. Nature does not work her marvels
suddenly, and there is no sudden growth in mind
and soul—what often seems so is only seeming. Before the blessed burst of sunlight comes to eyes long
closed in darkness, there is first the dim sight of
men as trees walking, a sight forgotten in the full
joy of vision; and before the light of knowledge or of
loftier wisdom brings its gladness to the darkened
mind, there are many cheering gleams of brightness,

which fade from memory when the night is fully past. And so it is with higher things. Sometimes the meaning and the purpose of our life flash upon the startled spirit with a clearness that needs no further witness to its truth, and we think that sudden brightness to be wholly new. In truth, it is not wholly new; such insight does not come to those whose souls are blind, who have not seen, although it be but dimly, the heralds of the rising sun, and have not turned their ardent faces toward the glowing east.

We belong to our past according to a law that knows no change, a law we overlook too often and thus miss great lessons we are set to learn, the need of constant effort, of caring lest our sympathies grow cold, of long perhaps of weary striving for the joy, which dawns at last, of conscious growth. Thus, too, it often comes we pass our days in longing vainly for some outward power to lift us where we ought to climb, to flood us with a light we could not bear, and mould us in our own, despite upon some goodly, or perhaps, some glorious pattern. Such dreams are beautiful indeed : they lend to earnest struggle a real support and inspiration, but their help is not for him who only dreams and does not also toil. To him they bring no inspiration, but only soothe to careless ease; no call to present battle, but the far-off sound of arms, which scarce disturbs his slumber; no sure promise of reward, but the phantom of that victory which only comes to those who fight.

Do you ask me why, at such a time as this, I turn

your minds to thoughts like these? I answer, because the nation's life is yours, and yours alone. In
common speech, we call ourselves a nation, a state, a
community, and speak of corporate life, of national
character, as if in some way a group of men was different from the single men which make it up, concealing thus the truth that as the people are, so is
the state; that institutions but express the wants and
belief of individuals, and that the upward progress
of a nation is not possible while its men and women
sit with folded hands. Bound in one community by
many ties of race and blood and neighborhood, we
have reached in company, and suddenly as it seems,
a summit of our forward way. Behind us lies the
past, and seemingly at far greater distance than before this century closed. The tie that binds us to
that early day seems much less close. We
almost seem to have sprung to prosperity at a single
bound, to have almost unawares attained to largeness in our public life, and in this result our fathers'
part looks dim and vague. It is well, therefore, to
scan closely the road by which in truth we came,
and see that here, too, we are of the past and are indeed its fruit and outcome. It is well to trace again
the windings of the path that led us here, to take
ourselves to task because our memory has grown
slack, to fairly face and duly recognize our debt to
those long dead who made our living possible, and
set the framework for this pleasant habitation.
Thus we may best be able to feel again the bonds
that make us one with all the forces of that bygone
day, to clearly see the unbroken line that leads from

them to us, and turn with hope and new resolve to meet the widening future.

Let us acknowledge gladly and to the full, the vastness of our fathers' labors, the peril of their lives, the high enduring courage with which they met their dangers, the sturdy spirit of their struggles to be free, the wisdom of their outlook and their forming hand. We may well thank God from grateful hearts because we come of such an ancestry and share in such a heritage. Consider what a life was theirs. Sweep from this wide expanse its roads and bridges, replace its towns and villages, its smiling fields and well-stocked farms, with swamp and forest; obliterate all trace of civilizing order and the strong encouragement of social life, and then sit down in fancy, as our fathers did in fact, to the slow siege of stubborn nature. Heap together for your wife and children a miserable shelter from the snow and storm, hoard jealously for weeks, perhaps for months, your scanty store of food with famine daily drawing near, waken at night in fear because the snapping twig may be the herald of some fierce attack, strive single-handed with the forest for an acre of clear ground, give up the joy and help and comfort of your kind—do this in fancy, but however well 'tis done, you cannot reach the measure of the sober fact. The picture is not pleasing; we see it fade without regret; it casts a shade of trouble on our comfort; but it was truth not long ago, and truth through weary toilsome years. The work seems speedy to our backward glance, but it was not so in fact. The waves of immigration rolled to our frontiers with

slowness, and their living spray was slowly, sparsely
sprinkled in this wide wilderness. Slowly the forest
and the savage yielded, each giving way with sullen
stubbornness, and only after long endurance and a
bitter warfare was a little victory won. A tiny
clearing here and there, dropped as it seemed from
the sky amid the reluctant woods, a little cluster of
rude houses at some favored spot, infrequent roads
that scarcely differed from a forest track, a ferry
where the need was pressing, rough and jagged fields
that held the promise only of a future plenty—these,
and things like these, were all that could be shown
for many years of toil and tears and danger. All
that could be shown, indeed; but there were trophies
of the struggle that did not meet the eye. Who
shall fitly tell the inner history of that time? What
pen shall thrill us with the story of its high resolve,
its fiery courage, its calm endurance, its clear look
into the future, its passion to be free? When shall
we learn how all its virtues grew with exercise, and
shamed the unfruitful earth with noble yield? No
force of nature and no shock of arms could drive
away the men who came to win this land. Repulse
might come, as come it often did, but only as a moment's check. Persistently the ceaseless toil went
on, unflinchingly the countless fights were fought,
and by and by the hope of better things grew clear.
The sparse and scattered settlers found themselves
at last in reach of neighbors, intercourse grew easier
with better and more frequent roads. the ground
once conquered paid its yearly tribute in abundance;
wants sprang into life or roused themselves from

sleep; man touched the shoulder of his fellow-man and set himself to establish social order.

In such a task the stock from which we spring demands large freedom. The German forests bred a race whose past is liberty's bright record, and whose age-long struggle has at least for partial outcome the wide embracing right to rule their neighborhood affairs. It is here that bondage bears the hardest, here that freedom is most sweet to daily life, and here that meddling by a stranger is most keenly felt. Our race knows well the power of an ordered state, yields easily to wise restraint, will bear, nay, will command, that rule be strong on fit occasion: but this is for imperial matters, its home and neighborhood concerns may not be rudely touched. The form, indeed, through which it acts in this regard is not important and may be of diverse sort, but through every form it does demand the substance of control. In the main this principle has not been shaken, and to-day it is the base on which our massive strength finds rest. We follow in the way our fathers cleared and carry on the government they framed, with scarce a change in substance and but little change in form. They began the work in rudeness as was needful; the neighborhood, in meeting, a pure democracy, declared its will and managed its affairs with little courtesy for form and little care for niceness of detail. But, speedily as every case would warrant, the township took the place of the unorganized assembly, and in this first step toward settled order is found the promise of the nation. We see it now with ample clearness,

and for them as well the seed held hope of coming
empire, although they did not dream how vast its
spreading growth would be. Look for one moment
at the township, and bear me out in finding there
the germ of all our larger life. The township is the
neighborhood in harness, its force directed to its proper ends, a compact and stubborn group of men in
full control of all their near concerns, a training-
school of citizens, a nursery of freemen. It has been
called, in happy phrase, "the seminary and central
point of democracy," and the implication of these
words is true. It deals with subjects that come
closely home, the need and care of roads and
bridges, the schooling of the young, the keeping of
the peace, the maintenance in many ways of order.
It holds the power of the local purse, affects directly
the comfort and the welfare of those within its
bounds, and handles all its proper matters in the ancient fashion, dear to freedom, of full discussion,
open talk, dispute if that may chance to follow, and
then at last of settlement by vote. Upon this stage
we see the state in miniature, the diverse clashing interests of party or of faction, the influence of motives
wide or narrow, the power of man upon his fellow,
the directing force of mind, the sober, stable element
of property, and here are found the dear results of
freedom. Here first the man becomes a citizen, per-
ceives his interest in the state's affairs, learns prudence, moderation, wisdom, sees the need of com-
promise in many matters, takes part in government
and shares its burdens, and grows to love with lasting passion the land where liberty permits to all

12

such elevating life and opens such a door to wider effort. Judge what a people trained in such a school is like to make of all its more embracing agencies. What is the county and the state and the nation, but the township multiplied, with wider ends no doubt and more complex in structure, but the same in essence and resting at the last upon the same great principle? In Lord Bacon's phrase, "the music is fuller," but the same theme is heard throughout the ampler measure.

But there are other thoughts about that early day which should be spoken. What sent that generation over sea? What kept their hearts from failing, through all the toil and trial and perils manifold which beat about their lives in constant storm? What sets that time on high to draw our reverence, make quick our love and sympathy, inspire us with a lofty zeal and kindle bright and warm the fire of noble emulation? Not suffering alone, or staunch endurance, or unswerving courage. These may awaken pity or compel our admiration, wherever seen and borne or shown in any cause, but they are not in themselves the certain sign of greatness. Nor are the wisdom and the careful foresight, the large prevision of the future, the undoubting grasp of coming empire, which marked this time, enough to justify its place upon the pinnacle of years. These qualities are great, but need not be heroic. To find the secret of our feeling as we stand before these men, our thought must go still deeper and must bring to light the motive and the purpose which made strong their lives. This it is that glorifies their

conflict and their suffering, and changes pity into
swelling wonder, that lends its splendor to their active virtues, and shines with floods of light around
their vast constructive work. This it is that sets
apart the toil, privation, battle, conquest and reward
which rise to-day at memory's call — the love of liberty and love of God, which made them possible, and
in whose name the wondrous task was taken up
and done. What other nation stands on such foundation, or sprang from such a soil?

We need not trace with careful industry the
growth of these transforming forces, or number all
the human agencies that helped or shielded them in
threatening days. Indeed, no mind is equal to such
labor. The subtle influence of race, that mystery for
which no key has yet been found, the high tradition
of all early struggles after freedom, the quickening
impulse of reviving learning, the lightning flash of
the Reformation, the welding power of persecution,
the open Bible — these at least are some among the
fertilizing agencies which greatly nourished and
brought to vigor and to rugged strength of life the
germs of liberty and free religious thought. These
impelling forces made our country possible, sent over
wintry seas the earliest handful of devoted men, sus-
tained themselves and all their followers in bitterness
of heart and failing body, shaped all their infant
policy, laid down the lines of later government, controlled the principles of social order, set rules for
daily life, and so by slow and often painful steps
worked out the peace and plenty and secure enjoyment of this free and prosperous day.

Let us not sorrow beyond measure because the steps were often painful. This is the needful course of all prevailing, fruitful effort; we recognize its law in even slight concerns, and may feel its solemn mystery, if our soul be open, in every toil and danger overpast. Our fathers shared the common lot in this, and found the common recompense. To us, how clear it shines! When at last the open struggle came which shook us free from England, how plain it is that all the past brought help. The constant stubborn fight with nature had set firm the sinews of the soldier, his ceaseless warfare with the savage had taught him prudence, compelled him to be cool, sagacious, bitterly persistent, made the new levies to consist of seasoned warriors' stuff, and, who shall doubt? won victories where else had often come defeat. So, too, with those who found the civic affairs of an infant nation in their hands. They had in truth been trained to public life from childhood. The constant meddling of the mother country, at times so hard to endure with patience or to endure at all, had forced the cause of freedom upon every thoughtful mind, roused up in every man a zealous interest, spread knowledge of his rights and duties, called out his powers to proper and to frequent play, united him to those who had like wrongs to bear, taught soberness of counsel, careful judgment, and, through slow years of injury, raised up and bred a school of statesmen. And the whole people was made stronger by its sufferings. That was no day for weakness; it searched out the joints in many a goodly armor and cast relentlessly aside the tools

that could not bear rough using. But to those sturdy
men and women whose lives were filled by the spirit
and the courage of the time, the discipline was
wholesome at the last. It brought to noble stature
capacity for sacrifice, heroic patience, unflinching
resolution, dauntless bravery and trust in the God of
nations. For such results a people may well suffer,
and with these in view our loving sympathy may
well go hand in hand with clear-eyed sight.

Why should I keep you with a longer story of this
well-known time? There is still much that might
perhaps be fitly dwelt on, much that went before and
followed the event we celebrate to-day, but you know
at least its outline, and I see those about me who
know the picture not in outline only but in all its
varied color, and whose ample learning would have
better held your interest. Need I set forth the stages
of the struggle which made us first a nation, or re-
count the part our kinsmen gladly took through all
those years of war and want and deep discourage-
ment? Need I run down the local annals, give you
incident and date, repeat the names of which we all
are justly proud, when after all such things have
little meaning and as little lasting interest, unless
they serve to illustrate the inner and the real life of
which I have already spoken? Shall I retrace the
steps of onward movement which bring us to the
memory of my youngest listener, and tell again the
wondrous tale of growth and progress? Do you
care to hear again how thrift and toil and honesty
built up our towns, smoothed out the wrinkles of the
earth, brought plenty to ten thousand homes and

gave us leisure for the higher things of life? Is
there need to speak of all the marvels which have
lent their aid—the iron road, the harnessed lightning, the countless helps to labor, the gifts of science
and the cunning hand of art? I will not tell again this
thrice-told tale, nor will I even linger at the graves
of those who died so lately in their fathers' spirit for
their fathers' cause, the cause of freedom and a nation's life. Their comrades sit around me, sure of a
place in history and sure from us, their kinsfolk and
their neighbors, of that unfailing, nobly envying,
high regard we pay to those who answer such a
summons at the hazard of their lives; but we do
not need their presence to recall the dead with
whom they fought and suffered. For these our
hearts are still in mourning, and our eyes have not
forgotten tears; the land for which they died is solemn still before their resting place. I leave to you
this past, near and remote, our past, the years that
formed us in this likeness, and turn to briefly face
the future.

Great duties wait for us to-day ; great problems
cast their shadows on our path. I cannot stop to set
them out or strive to solve them; my purpose rather
is to indicate in part the spirit and the means by
which all problems can be wisely met. We do not
aim to neatly furnish out our youth with answers to
life's questions; we cannot know the shape in which
the trial will come; our part, the part of wisdom, is
to discipline their faculties, to set their characters
aright, to make them capable and strong, and then
to commit them with God's blessing to the certain

conflict. The process does not change as manhood
brings its burdens: we must still grow strong and
capable by training, though under different teachers
and perhaps in greater and more wasteful toil.
How shall we bring ourselves to fitness for the
future's work, how qualify ourselves to look its problems calmly in the face? No man can fully answer
such tremendous question, but this at least seems
wise: it must be much to grasp as clearly as we
may the nature of the life in which we all are living
units, and to understand, so far as lies within our
power, what are its real forces and the end toward
which they work.

Our life is part of that which lies behind. Our
fathers labored and we reap a goodly harvest; but
harvests are not reaped by idle hands. There is no
miracle about the world's advance, no cause for
open-mouthed and empty wonder at the progress of
the age. Such phrases veil the truth about our life
and do much mischief. Men talk about this progress with vague declamation until they come to
feel, it may be to believe, that in some mysterious
fashion the world is moving upward and is bearing
them to triumph on its bosom. They feel as if they
must somehow be better, wiser, beings because of the
steam-engine, the cotton-gin, the railroad, the sudden marvels of electricity, and the vast spread of
prosperity and more comfortable living which has
followed thereupon. Doubtless, it would be hard to
set too high a value on the benefits which daily
come upon us from the century's advance in science
and the useful arts, and this is of course true pro-

gress. But progress of what kind? Let us regard
the plain distinction; it is progress in the handling
and control of matter and material force, and may
have as little to do with our true life as it has to do
with the movement of the stars. It may indeed
better the conditions of that life, it may bring more
wealth and larger leisure, it may soften manners
and temper by closer intercourse and thus remove
much friction, it may set us in a place of wider view
and more advantage ; but, after all, conditions may
affect us little. It is much to discover a new law of
matter, to make life less laborious by some new device, to draw closer the bonds of nations by some
easier or some speedier road, but if *we* neither invent
nor discover, how without more are we to gain
thereby? Better conditions endow us no doubt
with more and larger facilities, give us a starting-
point of more advantage, and so far we are in better
case than were our fathers. But all starting-points
are alike if the runners do not run, and much alike,
although the race begin, if the runners fail and drop
aside before the goal is won. The "progress of the
age" is much too often and for far too many of us,
other people's progress and not our own, and so far as
this is true affects us almost as little as if it passed
upon another planet. What does the steam-engine
matter to our lives, if day by day we slip farther
down the decline of mental sloth, but slightly shar-
ing in the energies which vivify the world? What
help is the railroad, if we continually care less and
less for the interlacing links of thought, and look
out on God's universe, so marvellously bound in one,

with daily duller eyes? To what end is the telegraph, if we have no answering message for the
lightning and feel a lessening thrill of sympathy
with all the subtler currents which transfuse the real
life of men? No, a thousand times no! If we are
even to retain our place in the vast throng which
surges through all the ways of life, much more if we
may hope to share in any forward movement, we
ourselves must also move with conscious effort and
make good by inward growth and outward fruit our
claim to be a part of any living progress. We have
no part in the progress of the age if we make no individual use of its conditions, whatever they may be
for each of us and differing however widely, if they
do not help us consciously to grow, if they do not
quicken our actual sympathies, make us more alive
to the human influence of to-day, yesterday and to-
morrow, lift us up to a wider range of vision, and
make more certain and more splendid the expectation of the coming sun. This is the nature of our
life, a life which feels indeed the influence of our fellows, but is at its very centre inward, personal, and
only strong when it is truly so. Nor can the
nation's life be different. The nation will be strong
and fruitful when our blood is warm, and triumph
only when its citizens are brave.

What are the forces, then, which move us? What
stirs our pulse and makes us play the part of men?
What powers have worked the wonders of the past,
and may be looked to in the troubles yet to come?
Not outward things, not wealth, or pride of life,
or lust of domination, or the nobler thirst for

knowledge, but moral sentiments and moral truths. These in the last analysis are the true, resistless forces of the world. Not to speak again of the more distant past, what lies at the very root of the age's progress concerning which I have just spoken? What builds steamships and lays down railroads, girdles the world with lightning, fills the air with the smoke and hum of industry, shakes the ground with the tread of hurrying feet, inspires the genius of the artist, and works the countless marvels of our boasted time? Most of all, an idea, a sentiment; the love of wife and child, the sacred sentiment of home. What calls a nation to its feet to dare the awful chance of war, makes it to endure hardship and sacrifice till ruin comes upon prosperity and death finds lodging in every house, sets hard the teeth of its soldiers and transforms battle into dreadful joy? A sentiment, the sentiment of patriotism, or, nobler still, the sentiment of justice to the oppressed. What sends devoted men and women to breathe pestilential airs, burn under scorching suns, face perils manifold and constant, that some poor strangers may lead better lives? What is it that builds hospitals, endows charities, restrains the license and the violence of war, diffuses gradually strengthening justice throughout the world, and surrounds so many millions with a sweeter air of kindliness and a stronger sense of brotherhood? A sentiment still, a religious sentiment, that strikes its root in moral truth. And if we turn our gaze within, and ask the cause and motive of this ceaseless inward striving these manifold activities, these anxious cares, this

beating against the bars that shut us in, this struggle upward toward the light, what other answer can
we give, than the influence still of moral truth,
made manifest in countless ways, but everywhere
and always leader and supreme?

What need to specify the end toward which these
forces work? Ask your own hearts, and let the
answer be your guide in all the doubt and stress
and pain of public trouble. The principles which
lift us up in private life, which tend to mould us in
a nobler fashion, which thrill and fill our inmost
being, these are the principles to solve the nation's
problems in the coming days. Thus we shall face
our future as, long years ago, our sires faced theirs,
with love of liberty and love of God as guiding stars,
sure that in such a spirit and with such a light we
cannot walk amiss. Let us then take courage and
go forward. This breathing-space may serve a helpful purpose. The past is full of cause for gratefulness and pride; it ought to spur us on to know we
come of such a strain; but in our children's name I
point you to the future. When the next hundred
years has run its course, and in our turn we have
changed to figures dimly seen, what shall our children's children say of us? What would we have
them say but words like these, the echo of our own
deliberate tribute to the past? " This generation
" knew the secret of the world's andvance and helped
"it onward. They looked beneath the surface of af-
" fairs and kept their steady gaze on what was true
"and lasting. Our world to-day is better, sweeter for
"their presence. Let us emulate their noble zeal for

"what was good and just, their courage in the cause
"of right, their cheerful constancy in the face of trou-
"ble, their faith in things unseen. The God they
"trusted bless their memory!"

That dear old song our fathers sang, "Auld Lang
Syne," was rendered in good style by the choir, after
which General Cameron introduced Charles Carroll
Bombaugh, M. D., the Centennial poet, as a native of
Harrisburg, who was ordered to Baltimore by the
Governor, during the war, to take charge of Pennsylvania's wounded soldiers. In that city he had
remained ever since, although, the General doubted
not, the Doctor is as strongly attached to Harrisburg
as ever.

CENTENNIAL POEM BY DR. BOMBAUGH.

We come, with clang of bells, with songs of praise,
With waving banners, with electric blaze,
With radiant hopes, and with inspiring cheers,
To crown the memories of a hundred years.

Should aliens ask us, "what is all this worth—
This centenary of a County's birth?
These simple annals, what is there to grace
Beyond the dullness of the commonplace?"
Let Dauphin's children tell them what is meant
By this display of loyal sentiment;
This evidence that time can ne'er efface
The love they cherish for their native place.
They reunite around a common shrine,
To treasure retrospects of *Auld Lang Syne;*
Some from the hearth-stone here to which they cling,
And some from distant points their tribute bring.
Howe'er their paths diverge, they still are bound
By ties that localize on common ground.
Far as they wander, differ as they may,
A kindred feeling prompts them all to-day.

Could we roll back a hundred cycling years,
And photograph the early pioneers,
How we should see in each bronzed, rugged face
The native stamp of that ancestral race
Who came to act as conscience should dictate,
Far from the partnerships of Church and State.
Stern Covenanters, Caledonia's boast,
First driven by fate to Ireland's northern coast,
And thence, worn out with Celtic broils and feuds,
Glad of a refuge in wild Western woods;
Here, too, to help to build an infant State,
Reformers from the old Palatinate;
God fearing races both; both hating wrong;
In limbs, in brain, in resolution strong.
Some English yeomen had already come,
And found at trading posts a settler's home.
But though they chose to adopt a Gallic name,
No one appeared the Gallic blood to claim.
The Jesuit Fathers sought remote frontiers;
Southward the Huguenots dismissed their fears.
How did it happen that the *fleur de lis*
Bowed the Scotch-Irish and the German knees;
That by the colonists a taste was shown
For Gallic names in preference to their own?
How could the Ferry, made a County Town,
Such homage pay to Louis XVI's crown,
And, for a season, set aside the claim
Of old John Harris and his honered name?*
Why did the County's christeners declare
That it the title of the son should wear?
Why thus commemorate, and why thus own
The heir-apparent of a tottering throne?
And why thus blazon on its coronet
The martyred child of Marie Antoinette?

They sought, tradition says—as well they should—
To give expression to their gratitude

---

*From August 3, 1785, to April 13, 1791, the town was called
Louisburgh.

To France, the ally and the faithful friend,
Through Revolution's struggle to its end ;
To LaFayette and his devoted band
Of brave compatriots on sea and land,
Who shed their blood in freedom's holy cause,
For human rights and equitable laws ;
Who helped to rescue from oppression's blight,
And give enfeebled States new life and light.

Once more, let just acknowledgments be made.
France comes again, but not to furnish aid
Where none is needed. France's Kings are dead.
Long live the new Republic in their stead !
Her people send an offering of peace
To bind old friendships that shall never cease.
O grand memento ! While that statue stands,
No hostile blood shall crimson either's hands,
And every nation's flag shall be unfurled
To "Liberty enlightening the World."

A hundred years ! How long, or short, it seems,
Depends on fruitful deeds, not idle dreams.
To sanguine vision, with its rainbow light,
Days shrink to hours in their rapid flight ;
While lagging weeks or lingering months may be
To wrong and suffering an eternity.
Sunshine and shadow, innocence and crime,
With different standards weigh and measure time.
Full twenty centuries the Pantheon's dome
Has watched the ebbs and flows of life in Rome.
Through forty centuries, survey the links
Of past and present in the silent Sphynx,
And in the stately Pyramids that rise
Until their summits pierce Egyptian skies.

Brief space compared with all this length of years,
Our Dauphin's single century appears ;
And sharply drawn, the contrasts brought to view
Between the records of the old and new.
Scan transatlantic archives, and you find
Their every page with blood-marks interlined.

Traverse each foot of Europe's wide domain,
The scars of battle are on every plain.
Where'er you turn, amid the busy hive,
"The dust you tread upon was once alive."
In age barbaric, or in feudal times,
We look for rulers saturate with crimes,
But in the royalty of later days—
Stripped of its splendors and its purple haze—
We see the chartered libertine again,
And the same scorn of all the rights of men.
Glory and Chivalry—those misused words—
Meant slaughtered subjects, ruined fields and herds ;
While Conquest trampled with its brazen heel
Faith, Justice, Truth, Humanity's appeal.

Thank God, our Dauphin no memorial rears
Of hills and valleys drenched with blood and tears ;
No broken treaties, no intestine blows,
No reign of Mars her chronicles disclose.
Not through the deeds of arms she seeks increase,
But through the triumphs of the arts of peace.
" Peace hath her victories no less renowned
Than war" with all its blood-stained trophies crowned.
And "peace with honor" gilds a storied past
Where no bars sinister their shadows cast.

Ere Dauphin's birth these hills and vales could boast
Few Indian raids or massacres at most.
' Twas fortunate exemption for our sires,   •
While others walked through sacrificial fires,
Communities less favored by the storms
Of fierce invasion in its startling forms—
The midnight foray of marauding band,
The dreadful butchery, the flaming brand.
And ever since the memorable year
That marks the County's start on her career,
Within her borders peace has spread its wings,
And given to sheltered toil the song it sings.

Unsteadfast song !   Through what chromatic change
The busy hum of industry may range.

To younger ears, the strains that once outrang
Are as unreal as songs the syrens sang.
The jangling bells of Conestoga teams
No longer rouse the villager from dreams.
The wayside juveniles no longer greet
The old-time stage-coach lumbering down the street.
On the canal, no more with tuneful splash,
Four miles an hour, ambitious packets dash.
No drowsy watchmen, with recurrent yell,
Announce the hour, the weather, and "all's well."

Once, only once, these sounds of daily life
Were made inaudible by clamorous strife;
By insurrection that, with factious will,
Shook the old arsenal upon the hill.
Lawmakers to lawbreakers were transformed;
The ramparts of the Capitol were stormed;
Statesmen who ne'er unsheathed the sword before,
Developed unsuspected thirst for gore.
What tragic fate the combatants befell,
What it all meant, let our historians tell;
And tell us what they killed each other for,
In that Falstaffian fight, the "Buckshot War."

But when, disquieted by war's alarms,
The nation summoned Dauphin's sons to arms,
Their patriot souls, responsive to the call,
Marched to the field to conquer or to fall.
When Independence flashed its beacon fires,
Prompt was the action of our strong-willed sires,
Who from the farm, the workshop and the mine,
Shed lustre on the Pennsylvania Line;
Determined men, who braved a tyrant's frown,
And plucked this western jewel from his crown.

When, with hostility still unsuppressed,
Resolved to make a second crucial test,
Great Britain's power was aimed, with vengeful thrust,
To crush the young Republic in the dust,
Clan Alpine's warriors not more quickly flew,
T' obey the mustering call of Roderick Dhu

The First Day.

Than Dauphin's sons made haste to Baltimore
To meet the invader on Patapsco's shore,
The exultant foe foredoomed to swift defeat,
To seek inglorious safety in retreat,
And leave the starry banner still to wave
O'er Fort McHenry, o'er defenders brave.

When the incursions of a neighboring foe
Provoked retaliate war on Mexico,
What mingling benedictions, hopes and fears
Followed the footsteps of our volunteers.
With what suspense we heard the whiz of balls
From Vera Cruz to Montezuma's halls;
How eager with the laurel wreath to deck
The brows of those who stormed Chapultepec;
Who, when the capital collapsed and fell,
First raised the flag upon the citadel.
Ah, Cameron Guards! small remnant left to-day!
Of those returned, how few have come to stay!

Next followed civil war, the household foe,
The family feud, the fratricidal blow.
For Dauphin's sons there was but one step then—
To meet the foe, and quit themselves like men.
And as Minerva from Jove's brain sprang out,
Full panoplied for slaughter or for rout,
So from these homes the serried ranks went forth,
To join the legions thronging from the North,
To camp and field, prepared to stand the test
Of soldier's lot, privation and unrest;
Of torturing wounds, of fever's scorching breath;
Of prison pen—to captives, living death;
Of fluctuating and protracted strife;
Of patriotic sacrifice of life.
No risk too great for faithfulness to trust
To keep the flag from trailing in the dust,
No price too high to save from worst of fates
The precious Union of the sister States.

Through the vicissitudes of four long years
Of wearying doubts, perplexities, and fears,

13

Nobly this city played a leading part
In the great drama that transcended art.
Here was the focus of the Keystone State,
The rallying point, where all could concentrate ;
Here was the camp for outfit and for drill ;
Here generous founts where all could drink their fill ;
Here soldiers' barracks and a soldiers' rest ;
Here open house to welcome needy guest ;
And here the hospitals whose tender care
Was reinforced by woman's work and prayer—
Sisters of Mercy, angels in disguise,
Whose ministrations brightened vacant eyes ;
Who to the sufferers brought grateful cheer,
And helpful hands and sympathetic tear ;
Who to the quickening of restoratives,
Added the charm that woman's presence gives ;
Who, by the couch where ebbed the tide of life,
Sat in the place of mother, sister, wife ;   '
Who whispered comfort to the parting soul,
And smoothed its pillow as it neared the goal.

Oh, womanhood ! besides this duteous care,
Who knows the burdens that you had to bear?
The aching void left by some absent one
To whom you turned as sunflower to the sun;
The saddened heart, the eye with tear-drops blurred,
The lengthened vigil, and the hope deferred ;
The anxious watch for tidings from the field,
The fervent prayer for interposing shield ?
Heroic sex ! with what strange strength endued !
What faith, what constancy, what fortitude !
Ah, we shall never know—God only knows
How much to woman our salvation owes !

And now, what rightful honors shall accrue
To those who builded better than they knew ?
The Pilgrim Fathers of the Land of Penn,
The vanguard of a line of high-souled men,
Who, with the axe and ploughshare boldly faced
A solitude, a wilderness, a waste ;

And, with decision, nothing could oppose,
Made the lone desert blossom as the rose;
And they who followed them, and here laid down
Tne broad foundations of the future town;
They who prescribed the County's boundary lines
From Mahantango's northernmost confines,
From where Swatara's peaceful waters glide,
From mountain ridge to Susquehanna's tide,
From Paxtang's banks and Derry's quaint repose,
Southward as far as Conewago flows —
What wreaths for these forerunners shall we twine?
How shall we fittingly their deeds enshrine?
Are not the best of all forget-me-nots,
These legendary, these historic spots?
Among the statues Paul's Cathedral rears,
None of its own great architect appears.
' Tis simply written on that hallowed ground—
" Seek you his monument?   Look all around."
So with our founders.   Let them rest content.
This prosperous city is their monument;
This county's records best their memories keep,
And best redeem them from eternal sleep.
We, their descendants, well may celebrate
This anniversary with hearts elate;
With pride that finds its sanction in the thought
What transformations has the century wrought;
What vast expansion everywhere appears;
What grand achievements mark the fleeting years.
Marvels and miracles—how passing strange—
Form much of life's continuous interchange.
Beneath the wonder-working hand of skill,
Submissive forces yield to regnant will;
And mighty engines move with step sublime,
Abridging space, annihilating time.
From shore to shore the ocean cables reach;
Obedient wires transmit responsive speech;
The starless night is turned to dazzling day;
Lethean vapors drive our pain away;
The magic lens infinitude unseals;
The spectroscope the universe reveals.

And with the sciences, the useful arts,
All that to enterprise its strength imparts,
What moral forces with their light illume ;
What pleasing shapes philanthropies assume;
What safeguards shield, what benefactions bless ;
Church free from State, free schools, unfettered press.
Still let us welcome every favoring chance
For moral and material advance ;
Still let us hail the providential dower
Of onward growth and of progressive power ;
Still let us not the presages forget
That greater wonders are before us yet,
That the hereafter dawning on our eyes
Gives fairer promises of glad surprise.
And, as we thus review the vanished past,
As thus the roseate future we forecast,
Let us be thankful that our light has beamed
With glow of which our fathers never dreamed,
Till, with successive brightening of the rays,
From farthing dips to incandescent blaze,
Aladdin's lamp no stranger marvels wrought
Than those with which the century is fraught.

And when, the light grown dim, life's labors o'er,
We hear our summons to the other shore,
For Dauphin's sons and daughters there is not
In all this wide, wide world, a dearer spot
Than their inheritance for that repose
Ordained for mortals when the curtains close.
Here, 'neath their own green turf, may they abide,
Here rest in peace by Susquehanna's side.

A chorus by the choir, "Hail to Thee, Liberty," from Rossini's Semiramide, followed, which was encored and repeated.

Mr. Mumma then said he had hoped to hear from General Cameron, the distinguished president of the meeting, but he says he is tired and does not feel like talking. Thus challenged, General Cameron said in a jocular way that there is nothing an old man dislikes to be told so much as that he is old. He didn't think it was kind in Mumma. "Why," he said, "Ramsey is as old as I am." Continuing, the General said that wonderful as has been the progress here, still greater has it been in Minnesota, which State has prospered wonderfully under Gov. Ramsey's care and wisdom. The General then introduced Governor Alexander Ramsey, who arose and in a voice firm and strong spoke somewhat to the following effect :

REMARKS BY GOV. RAMSEY.

LADIES AND GENTLEMEN:—I would willingly make a speech if I had one to make, but I havn't any. I came here to attend the 100th anniversary of Dauphin county, thinking to listen and enjoy myself, and also to renew acquaintances of old friends, to whom I owe so much, to whom I am indebted for my success in life. I remember the first time I beheld your city of Harrisburg. Coming along the road from Hummelstown, many years ago, young, without much ability and no money, you took me by the hand and aided me, and to you I owe my prosperity. I don't think any place so beautiful as your city by the banks of the Susquehanna, and as an old son of your city and county shall rejoice at anything that can be said for it. When far away, and wanting to hear of old friends, I used to look among the marriages (for I have been a regular reader of your papers,) but, ah ! it makes me sad to think that now to hear of old friends I first look at the deaths.

I have been away from Dauphin county for thirty-two years, and when first settling in Minnesota we organized a club of old settlers, and every time we meet we have a banquet. Last time we had a banquet we had our photographs taken in a group, and I will advise you all to have your photographs taken before a banquet—looks better than after. [Prolonged laughter.]

As the hour is growing late, I must close, but I will make a bargain with the Chairman, General Cameron, and the ladies and gentlemen present, that as I wasn't prepared to speak at this meeting of your Centennial, I will come prepared to make a fine oration at your next one. [Loud laughter and applause.]

General Cameron requested the choir to sing the Doxology and the audience to join in, which was done, and the old song which our fathers and mothers sang amid the groves and by the streams when the country was young, was sung as it rarely is anywhere by a like number of people The audience then dispersed, apparently greatly pleased with the evening's exercises. Many persons then crowded around General Cameron and Governor Ramsey, and the latter gentleman was given an opportunity to renew many acquaintances of his early manhood and form some new friendships with the rising generation.

Thus closed the first day of the Centennial celebration, which was a grand success measured by any fair standard. There were more people on the streets than anybody expected, the decorations exceeded the most sanguine hopes, and except for a little shower in the afternoon the weather was all that could have been desired.

THE SECOND DAY.

TUESDAY, SEPTEMBER 15, 1885.

COMMITTEE.

FRANK R. LEIB, *Chairman.*

HARRY D. BOAS,   THOMAS F. MALONEY,
WILLIAM H. H. SIEG, Steelton,   CHARLES A. MILLER,
JOHN A. GRAMM,   GEORGE W. RHOADS,
JOHN S. SIBLE,   GEORGE G. BOYER, *Secretary.*

THE INVITATION.

ROOMS OF COMMITTEE ON CEREMONIES OF THE SECOND DAY,
HARRISBURG, PA., July 22, 1885.

By reference to the enclosed circular, issued by the General Committee, you will note that the Celebration of the One Hundredth Anniversary of the erection of the County of Dauphin and the founding of the City of Harrisburg, is fixed for Monday, September 14th, 1885, and that appropriate and fitting ceremonies willl be held on that date.

The General Committee have named the Second Day ceremonies to consist of a parade of the Military, Grand Army, the Civic and Social Societies of this and neighboring counties, to take place at 10 o'clock in the forenoon of Tuesday, September 15th, 1885, and have appointed the undersigned committee to invite organizations of this character to participate.

The committee having in charge the ceremonies of the Second Day, hereby respectfully invite your organization to participate in the ceremonies of that day, and urge upon you the prompt acceptance of same. The committee are desirous that the parade shall excel anything of the kind ever witnessed in Central Pennsylvania, and to be such a distinctive feature of the centennial ceremonies that it will never be forgotten. With the cordial assistance of the different organizations, we can make it a red-letter day, and a credit to all who participate in making the display. It is confidently expected that the entire Eighth Regiment, Pennsylvania National Guard, under command of Colonel Frank J. Magee, will parade on this occasion.

Should your organization promptly accept the invitation herewith extended, please advise this committee how many members will probably bring and what music (if any), to enable the Committee to properly assign you in line. Special excursion trains and cheap fares will be arranged to all points. Full information will be cheerfully furnished by the Committee on application. We again earnestly urge upon you the acceptance of this invitation. Awaiting your early reply,

Respectfully yours,

FRANK R. LEIB, *Chairman*.

MILITARY AND CIVIC DAY.

The following orders and circulars are pertinent to this occasion :

GENERAL ORDERS.

HARRISBURG, PA., September 3, 1885.

General Order No. 1 :

Having been selected Chief Marshal of the Military, Grand Army and Civic Societies' Parade, to be held September 15, 1885, (being the second day of the Dauphin County Centennial Ceremonies), I hereby accept the same and announce the following appointments :

Chief of Staff. FRANK R. LEIB.

Special Aids: JOSEPH V. EINSTEIN,
GEORGE W. RHOADS,
HARRY D. BOAS,
CHARLES A. MILLER.

Aids will be announced in future orders.

Headquarters are established at No. 12 North Third street, where all communications should be addressed.

GEORGE G. BOYER, *Chief Marshal.*

———

HARRISBURG, Sept. 3, 1885.

General Orders No. 2 :

The line of procession will be composed of three grand divisions.

First Division—Military—Col. Frank J. Magee, Commander.

To be composed of the Eighth Regiment, National Guards of Pennsylvania.

Second Division—Civic Societies—John I. Beggs, Marshal.

To be composed of all societies other than military and Grand Army, and will be formed into sub-divisions to meet the requirements of organization. It is the desire of the chief marshal to place all organizations of a kind in a body by themselves.

Third Division—Grand Army Posts—Frank B. Kinneard, Marshal.

To be composed of Posts of the Grand Army of the Republic and all other War Veterans Associations.

The divisions will form at nine o'clock A. M., sharp.

First Division forming on North Fifth street, right resting on Market.

Second Division will form on North Fourth and North Third streets, right resting on Fourth and Market.

Third Division will form on North Second street, right resting on Market.

On the arrival of all trains an aid to the chief marshal will be detailed to meet the visiting organizations and assign them to their positions.

Division marshals are empowered to select their own staff and report complete list of same to headquarters as soon as possible. By order,

GEORGE G. BOYER, *Chief Marshal.*

FRANK R. LEIB, *Chief of Staff.*

HARRISBURG, PA., September 5, 1885.

General Order No. 3 ·

The following will be the route of procession for the parade on Tuesday, September 15th, 1885:

Out Market to Front, to Vine, to Second, to Chestnut, to Fourth, to Walnut, to Filbert, to North, to Pennsylvania avenue, to Broad, to Sixth, to Reily, to Third, to State, to Front, to Market, to Fifth and countermarch. By order.

GEORGE G. BOYER, *Chief Marshal.*

FRANK R. LEIB, *Chief of Staff.*

HARRISBURG, PA., September 5, 1885.

General Orders No. 4:

I would respectfully designate the following colors as the marks for the day's parade:

Headquarters will display at the head an Old Gold Flag.

First Division, Red Flag.

Second Division, White Flag.

Third Division, Blue Flag.

All Marshals and Aids will be provided with hat bands—same colors as their Division Flags.

Division Marshals will be supplied with these flags on morning of parade. Division flags to be carried by mounted Orderlies at head of division. By order.

GEORGE G. BOYER, *Chief Marshal.*

FRANK R. LEIB, *Chief of Staff.*

HARRISBURG, Sept. 10, 1885.

General Order No. 5.

The Chief Marshal of the Military, Grand Army and Civic Society parade, would respectfully announce the appointment of the following additional aids to report to him mounted, Tuesday morning, September 15th, at his headquarters, Lochiel Hotel:

Special Aid—Oliver B. Simmons.

Aids—Hon. A. F. Thompson, John Gramm, Edward Pancake, John S. Sible, W. C. McFadden, W. T. Hildrup, Jr., Jacob Faus, W. H. H. Sieg, John Tomlinson, Fred Maurer, John Horner, John Major, George W. Lutz.

Bugler—Thornton A. Bell.

Orderly—E. M. Bishop.

By order, GEORGE G. BOYER, *Chief Marshal.*
FRANK R. LEIB, *Chief of Staff.*

HARRISBURG, Sept. 10, 1885.

General Order No. 6.

The headquarters of the Chief Marshal will be at the Lochiel Hotel from 8 A. M. Tuesday, September 15th, until the line of parade moves.

By order, GEORGE G. BOYER, *Chief Marshal.*
FRANK R. LEIB, *Chief of Staff.*

HARRISBURG, PA., September 11, 1885.

General Orders No. 7.

The Chief Marshal of the Military, Grand Army and Civic Societies' Parade hereby announces the following appointments as his official staff, who will report to him, mounted, at 8 o'clock Tuesday morning, September 15th, at his headquarters, Lochiel Hotel.

Chief of Staff—Frank R. Leib.

Special Aids—Oliver B. Simmons, Harry D. Boas, Charles A. Miller, George W. Rhoads.

Aids—A. F. Thompson, John Gramm, William C. McFadden, Samuel Kunkel, John S. Sible, W. T. Hildrup, Jr., Edward Pancake, John Major, W. H. H. Seig, John Tomlinson, Jacob Faus, John J. Hargest, John Harner, Alvah H. Boyer, George W. Lutz, Jacob Whistler, M. S. Shotwell, Felix Newman, John Moore and Oliver Attick.

Dress—Black suit, silk hat and white gloves.

GEO. G. BOYER, *Chief Marshal.*
FRANK R. LEIB, *Chief of Staff.*

HARRISBURG, PA., September 5, 1885.

The following is the programme for the Military, Grand Army and Civic Societies' Day of the Dauphin County Centennial :

A salute will be fired at six o'clock A. M.

The line of procession will form at nine o'clock A. M., as follows :

Chief Marshal and Aids; General J. P. S. Gobin and staff, of the National Guard of Pennsylvania; the celebrated Third Brigade Band.

First Division—composed of the uniformed military under command of Colonel Frank J. Magee, will form on North Fifth street, right resting on Market.

Second Division—composed of all societies other than military and Grand Army, John I. Beggs, Marshal, will form on North Fourth and North Third streets, right resting on Fourth and Market streets.

Third Division—composed of the Grand Army and War Veterans' Association, Frank B. Kinneard, Marshal, will form on North Second street, right resting on Market street.

The procession will move at ten o'clock A. M., sharp, over the following route :

Out Market to Front, Front to Vine, Vine to Second, Second to Chestnut, Chestnut to Fourth, Fourth to Walnut, Walnut to Filbert, Filbert to North, North to Pennsylvania avenue, Pennsylvania avenue to Broad, Broad to Sixth, Sixth to Reily, Reily to Third, Third to State, State to Front, Front to Market, Market to Fifth and countermarch.

At three o'clock P. M. there will be a grand boat race, for gold medals, between the Harrisburg Boat Club and boat clubs from other cities.

A four-oar shell race; a double shell race; a single shell race; a canoe race; a round-bottom boat race; and to close with a tub race; to take place on the river between Reily street and the Market Street bridge.

At 4 o'clock P. M. the Eighth Regiment, National Guard of Pennsylvania, headed by the Third Brigade Band, will hold a Dress Parade on West State street.

At 7 o'clock P. M. the Mannechor and Concordia Singing Associations will give a grand Vocal Concert on Front street, near Pine, assisted by several bands.

At 7:30 o'clock P. M. the Committee will conclude the day's exercises with a grand display of Fireworks on the river from Walnut to State streets.

It is the desire of the Committee, in making up the programme for

the day, to arrange the details so as to entertain the citizens and visitors
in the best possible manner.

FRANK R. LEIB, *Chairman.*

W. H. H. SIEG,	THOS. F. MALONEY,	GEO. G. BOYER,
GEO. W. RHOADS,	CHAS. A. MILLER,	HARRY D. BOAS,
JOHN A. GRAMM,	JOHN S. SIBLE.	

ORDERS OF POST 58, G. A. R.

HARRISBURG, PA., September 4, 1885.

The Centennial Celebration of Dauphin county and the city of Harrisburg is near at hand, and Post 58 should take such prominent part therein as will convince the outside public that it stands in the foremost rank of this Department, and to this end every member is asked to use his personal endeavors to secure a full turnout at the parade of the 15th.

The Post has by resolution voted that every member in line must wear at least a G. A. R. cap; all should exert themselves to appear in full uniform, blouse, trousers, cap, white vest and black neck-tie; those who have not full uniforms will wear dark clothes, but all must wear caps, white gloves and badges, and carry canes.

The State Capital Band has been engaged to furnish music. About twenty of the neighboring Posts will take part in the parade and no effort should be spared to make the occasion one of enjoyment to all visiting comrades.

The Post will assemble at its hall Tuesday morning, Sept. 15th, at 8:30 o'clock, in the uniform above specified, all details carefully attended to, and the music engaged will report to the acting Adjutant at the same time and place.

The Post musters will hereafter open at 7:30 o'clock, and until further orders all details of the ritual fully complied with. By order of

THOS. F. MALONEY, *Commander.*

FRANK B. KINNEARD, *Adjutant.*

MILITARY AND CIVIC PARADE.

Tuesday was military and civic day of Dauphin county's grand Centennial celebration, and it was voted a success in every sense of the word. Not only in the display and number of men in line, but in the magnificent weather, the immense number in the city and the general enthusiasm.

It might have been a trifle too warm for a long march, but this was lost sight of in the general rejoicing over the fine day. Those who got up early —and pretty much everybody got up with the sun to see whether he was going to get up—congratulated everybody else that the clerk of the weather was also determined to distinguish himself.

It was along about 8 o'clock when the boom of the big bass drum, the blare of the trumpet and the steady tramp of organized bodies, began to sound on the streets. The civic societies and Grand Army men were first astir. It was going to be a big day for them. The military made its appearance later. The military is methodical and mathematically correct, and it gets there on time, but there is no hurry about it. The stranger within our gates also began his tramp about 8 o'clock, and by 9 there were so many of him present that locomotion was difficult. It is estimated that there were from twenty to twenty-five thousand strangers in the city, and along with its own citizens they flocked to the center, Market street being the objective point. It was almost impossible to get through the crowd. All the arches were up and trimmed, bunting and flags and gay-colored lanterns were displayed from every house, and what is more, some good citizens had set out tubs of ice water to refresh the weary marchers.

At 9 o'clock, Chief Marshal Boyer with his chief of staff, Frank R. Leib, made his headquarters at the Lochiel Hotel, and soon a score of aids on gaily decked horses were scurrying through the streets getting the organizations into position. The Grand Army men were the first to report and receive their orders, and were assigned to Second street, where the division formed. Soon after the tall form of General J. P. S. Gobin was seen at headquarters, and he reported that individually he was ready to move at any time. Then Marshal Beggs, of the civic division, announced that everything was lovely on his side of of the house. Shortly after him Colonel Frank J. Magee made known the fact that the Eighth Regiment was on hand and was even then marching up Market street to a rollicking tune from the Third Brigade band. Unassigned organizations reported for positions, and all were given a place, so that at 10:15 the line was ready to move. A short delay ensued unavoidably, so that it was not until 10:20 that the sound of the bugle of the Third Brigade of the National Guard, called the men into line, and the column was on the move, while thousands of spectators gave a great hearty cheer. As the head of the line reached Front and Market streets, the pro-

·cession could be seen to best advantage. It passed
at exactly 10:30 o'clock, marching as follows:

Chief Marshal, George G. Boyer.

Chief of Staff, Frank R. Leib; special aids, Joseph V. Einstein, George
W. Rhoads, Harry D. Boas, Charles A. Miller, Wilson C. Fox.

Aids,—A. F. Thompson, John Gramm, William C. McFadden, Samuel
Kunkel, John S. Sible, W. T. Hildrup, jr., Edward Pancake, W. H.
H. Seig, John Tomlinson, Jacob Faus, John J. Hargest, John Harner,
Alvah H. Boyer, George W. Lutz, Jacob Whistler, M. S. Shotwell,
Felix Newman, Oliver Attick, John Moore.

General J. P. S. Gobin; Brigade Surgeon William H. Egle; Major
Lowrie, Major W. H. Horn, Major J. G. Bobb, and Captain A. W.
Shultz, of the Third Brigade

THE PRIDE OF THE STATE.

Third Brigade Band—29 pieces, J. I. Alexander leader.

Third Brigade Drum Corps, 15 members.

Colonel Frank Magee and Staff, Eighth Regiment as follows: Lieutenant Colonel Theo. F. Hoffman; Major John F. Shaner; Adjntant J.
P. Levergood, Chaplain, Rev. Daniel Eberly; Surgeon, Samuel F.
Brehm; Assistant Surgeons, J. S. Carpenter and C. E. Jauss; Hospital
Steward, Frank Pershing; Quarter Master, Bryson M. McCool; Sergeant Major, Richardson, Drum Major, H. O. Bensinger; Bugler, Thornton Bell.

Metropolitan drum corps, 10 pieces, of Lancaster.

The different companies, all in National Guard uniform, with the
City Grays leading, then came in the following order; their military
bearing, fine marching and general appearance being much admired:

City Grays, Harrisburg, Captain T. F. Maloney, 57 men and 3
officers.

Company K, St. Clair, Captain William Holmes, 38 men and 3
officers.

Company B, Tamaqua, Captain Wallace Guss, 30 men and 3
officers.

Company G, Carlisle, Captain Edward B. Watts, 46 men and
3 officers.

Company A, York, Captain Strine, 33 men and 3 officers.

Company H, Pottsville, Captain Richard Kahn, 46 men and 2
officers.

Company I, Wrightsville, Captain George W. Seltzer, 40 men and 3 officers.

Company F, Girardville, Captain Johnson, 35 men and 2 officers.

Company E, Mahanoy City, Captain F. Wenrich, 56 men and 3 officers.

Drum Corps, eight pieces.

Company F, Fourth regiment, Pottsville, Captain Henning, 25 men and 3 officers.

Company C, Lancaster, Captain Bowers, 37 men and 2 officers.

Unassigned company, Chambersburg, Captain J. C. Gerbig, 45 men and 2 officers.

Dauphin Drum Corps.

Dauphin Guards, a volunteer military company, of Dauphin, with blue uniform and white stripes, and carrying a beautiful flag, 25 men and 3 officers, Captain William Shoop.

THE CIVIC SOCIETIES.

The second division, composed of local and visiting secret organizations, made a very handsome display. They numbered many hundreds, and their beautiful banners and regalias gave the body a very brilliant and picturesque appearance. One remarkable feature of this division was the number of aged men in line, which, considering the heat of the sun and lengthy march, showed a degree of patriotism worthy of the highest commendation.

John I. Beggs, marshal; Oliver B. Simmons, John M. Major and Wesley Fisher, aids.

W. T. Hildrup band, 25 pieces. The band wore bear-skin shakos and navy-blue uniforms. They played the original Dauphin Centennial March, by Max Vogt, the music publisher and fine composer. The march opens with "My Country 'tis of Thee," and closes with "Auld Lang Syne."

Dauphin Lodge, No. 160, I. O. of O. F., Harrisburg, J. N. O. Hankinson, marshal; aid, G. W. Jackson. Three beautiful banners and 75 members. The lodge made a handsome display. They all wore blue badges with red rosettes, inscribed. "I. O. of O. F. Dauphin Lodge, No. 160, Harrisburg, Pa."

14

Reception committee: William B. Grissinger, marshal; assistants, Charles Hambright, Samuel Wagner, W. E. E. Keene, D. H. Grissinger, B. H. Wambaugh, George W. Warden, E. M. Yeagley.

Matamoras Band, D. B. A. Mehargue, leader, 15 pieces. They wore helmet hats, blue uniforms, trimmed with red material.

Charity Lodge, No. 82, I. O. of O. F., Halifax, 33 members, marshaled by W. B. Gray. They carried a handsome Odd Fellows' flag with insignia; the members wore all the full regalia.

Marysville Lodge, No. 590, I. O. of O. F., 25 men in full regalia, W. W. Jackson, marshal. They carried a handsome American flag with blue streamers.

Paxton Lodge, No. 621, I. O. of O. F., of Dauphin, 30 members in full regalia, Wesley Clemson, marshal. Carried two pretty Odd Fellows' flags.

Lamberton Lodge, N. 708, Harrisburg, 40 members in full regalia, a handsome silk banner; P. G. A. H. Frankem, marshal, with a splendid new baton of rosewood and gilt tips presented to him by members of this Lodge, September 5th, 1885.

Juskakaka Tribe, No. 86, I. O. of R. M., of Duncannon, 25 men in full regalia, with a handsome banner of white silk, Cornelius Baskin, marshal.

Paxton Band, of Harrisburg, 20 members, Willis H. Fountain, leader.

Paxtang Tribe, No. 243, I. O. of R. M., of Steelton, J. B. Litch, marshal. 75 men in full regalia. They carried a handsome silk flag and the emblems of the Tribe.

Octorara Tribe, No. 91, I. O. of R. M., Harrisburg, John R. Cockley, marshal. They carried a handsome banner of red silk, inscribed with insignia and name of the order.

Cornplanter Tribe, No. 61, Harrisburg, Conrad Dapp, marshal, 25 men in full regalia with pretty banner of blue and red silk, inscribed in German as follows: "Cornplanter Tribe, No. 61, I. O. of R. M., and organized March 5th, 1866."

Citizen cornet band, of Hummelstown, 20 pieces, Prof. David Hummel, leader, in handsome blue cloth and gilt trimmed uniforms.

Phoenix Lodge No. 59.

Bayard Lodge, No. 150, of Harrisburg, George Diehl, of No. 59, marshal; C. R. Short, of No. 150, and George Lutz, aids. This order had 70 men in line, handsomely uniformed, displaying jewels of the order.

Mechanics band, of Bainbridge, 19 pieces, with handsome blue uniforms trimmed with bullion.

Bainbridge Council, No. 23, O. U. A. M., W. S. Smith, marshal, 60 men wearing full regalia, carrying three handsome flags in line.

Fulton Council, No. 35, O. U. A. M., of Harrisburg, 50 men, marshaled by George II. Manley.

New Cumberland Band, 23 pieces, grey uniforms trimmed with gold lace, Robert Dugan, leader.

Riverside Council, No. 87, O. U. A. M., of New Cumberland, 56 members in full regalia, with R. M. Kline as marshal, and J. M. Wisler as assistant.

Junior O. U. A. M. band of Middletown, 20 pieces handsomely uniformed.

Junior O. U. A. M., No. 156, of Middletown, 56 members, in full regalia. John Hoffman, marshal.

Wrightsville Council, No. —, O. U. A. M., 25 members with H. E Crone, as marshal. Handsome silk flag and men in full regalia.

Spring Garden band, York, Pa., 21 members wearing blue uniforms trimmed with gold lace.

Codorus Council, O. U. A. M., of York, 60 men in full regalia marshalled by S. M. Holland. They bore a handsome banner of blue silk in line.

Washington band, of Annville, 24 pieces, William Frank, leader, with neat blue uniforms and pretty navy caps trimmed with gold cord.

Washington Camp, No. 86, of Annville, 65 men in full regalia, Wm. D. Miller, marshal, and Jacob Wisler, aid.

West Fairview Cornet Band, 26 pieces, II. Dunbar, leader, with handsome blue uniforms.

Capital City Castle, K. of the G. E., with 150 members In full regalia; W. C. Gramm, marshal, and Charles A. Koler and James Mortimer, assistants. They carried a handsome blue and red banner in line. Their equipments consisted of swords, belts, white gloves, neat blue caps, etc., and they bore in line the American flag.

Mænnerchor and Concordia Singing Associations; Augustus Frick, marshal; 30 members in citizens' dress. They carried in line a large silk banner; of Harrisburg.

Liberty Cornet band, ot Middletown, 20 members, under the leadership of Prof. Val. Baumbaugh.

Ancient Order of Forresters, of Middletown; 100 members, led by II. C. Ranger. This order was instituted April 30, 1881. Three men bore a very large and splendid banner of green and red silk, with two fine hand-painted scenes in the centre. It cost $150 in England. The

Forresters wore citizens' dress, with felt hats ornamented with a white ostrich plume, tipped with green, and wore white gloves. The representations on the banner are an emblem of the Order on one side and a charity scene on the reverse.

Cornet Band, of Steelton, (colored) 20 members — John W. Campbell, leader, in blue uniforms, trimmed with gold.

Centennial committee of the Hercules Centennial Association, Wm. Howard Day, chairman; C. A. Taylor, Wm. H. Caslow, G. H. Mullin, James H. Howard and James Grant, committee.

Hercules Centennial club, of Harrisburg—Major J. W. Simpson, marshal; Henry Sophes and Richard Shaw, aids—100 members. This association wore citizens' dress, high silk hats, white gloves, and handsome white satin badges.

THE GRAND ARMY.

The third division was composed of local and visiting Grand Army Posts, and as the gallant "boys in blue" filed into view their appearance was greeted with hearty acclaim. The veterans always at the front in the performance of a duty, rallied in force on this occasion, and their number and fine appearance was an important factor in the success of the parade. Though their steps were weakened by age they never faltered, and as they countermarched on Market street and the torn flags were presented to the members of the different posts, many of the terrible scenes through which they had gone were vividly brought back.

Frank B. Kinneard, marshal. Major C. C. Davis, aid; Richard Haywood, color bearer.

Department Commander Austin Curtin and Adjutant Thos. J. Stewart. Col. Sellers, Capt. McCormick and Capt. Williams, of the staff, of Philadelphia. Captain Taylor, Q. M. G. Philadelphia.

Aids—Messrs. Floyd, Sourbeer, Gingrich, Heller, J. Diven, J. H. Santo and W. J. Adams, all mounted.

State Capital band, 30 members, Prof. Wm. P. Chambers, leader, in full uniform.

Pupils of White Hall Soldiers' Orphan school, in charge of Major J. A. Moore, principal, 17 in number. Two guidons, born by soldiers' orphan school pupils.

Post 58, G. A. R. Harrisburg, Charles A. Beaver, Marshal. Twenty-eight battle flags, torn and tattered, showing they were used in the hottest of the fight, were carried in line by 28 members of the Post.

Squad of 8 pupils of the White Hall Soldiers' Orphan School.

Post 58 G. A. R. 150 men—Comrade Thomas White, commander in charge.

Sons of Veterans' flute and drum band, 13 members, S. W. Tagg, Major Chas. Musser, leader of drum corps. They were neat drab shirts, blue pants, black patent leather belts, white leggins and notty naval caps.

Seneca G. Simmons Post, G. A. R., 175 men, handsomely uniformed. They bore in line a handsome banner of white satin, presented to tne Post by Mrs. Seneca G. Simmons, in 1878; also an old Corean ensign captured by the U. S. naval forces at Fort McKee, in Corea, in 1871, during the Corean war, when the United States government punished the Coreans for an insult offered to the United States flag. The flag was presented to Post 116 by Comrade Howard Potts, who was in the engagement. The Post was marshaled by B. J. Campbell, post commander.

Post Lieut. Wm. Child, of Marietta, S. E. Wisner, post commander, 15 men, with two handsome flags and a marker.

Drum corps of Gen. Welsh Post, Columbia, 18 members.

Gen. Welsh Post, No. 118, G. A. R., Columbia, Lancaster Co., Pa. James A. Meyers, post commander; Clayt. Hartman, S. V. C; Jos. W. Yocum, adjutant; Dr. F. Hinkle, surgeon; Benj. F. Mullen, O. D.; John H. Christy, Sgt., Maj.; Steph. B. Clepper, J. V. C.; Jas. L. Pinkerton, Q. M.; Benj. F. Dean, chaplain; Robert S. Dunbar, O. G.; John E Tyler, Q. M. S. Forty members in line, with several fine flags, one of them of yellow silk, with cannons crossed in centre.

Columbia Drum Corps; 6 members, Albert Roberts, leader.

Sergt. W. S. Lascomb, Post 351, Steelton, 11 members; Post Commander, H. B. Snyder. They had an immense bull dog as an aid. Nobody bothered that aid.

Singer Cornet Band of Mechanicsburg, Ira S. Eberly, leader; 23 men; wore blue uniforms with gold trimming.

Drum Corps of six pieces, of Soldiers' Orphan School of White Hall.

Post Captain H. J. Zinn, of Mechanicsburg, 70 men; Post commander Wm. Penn Loyd, full uniform.

Captain Caldwell Post, 201, Carlisle, Joseph Haverstick, commander, 40 men, with handsome blue silk banner.

Corporal Jerry Thompson Post, 440, colored, Carlisle, 25 men, Wm. Chapman, commander.

Kennedy Post, No. 490, Mt. Holly, 15 men, H. Wallet, commander, Drum corps of 9 pieces.

Housum Post, 306, Chambersburg, 63 men, B. F. Fahnestock, commander.

Gen. Sedgwick Post, 37, York, 50 men, E. L. Schroder, commander.

Centre View band, of Jackson township, 15 men, N. E. Snyer, commander, new blue and gilt uniforms.

Post Stephen A. Heilner, G. A. R., of Lykens, R. F. Martz, post commander, 160 members; national flag.

Grand Army Post band, of Gettysburg, 14 pieces; handsome blue uniform and helmet hats.

Corporal Kelley Post, G. A. R., of Gettysburg, W. A. Holtzworth, commander; 30 men in full uniform. Drum Corps.

Lieut. Arnold Lobach Post, of Newport; 59 men; I. C. Gessler, commander. American Flag.

Lieut. Wm. Allen Post, of Duncanon; 20 men; J. H. Bleirstein, post commander.

David Gipe Post. No. 88, of Marysville; 12 men; no officers.

Citizen Cornet Band, Millersburg, 20 members, Charles F. Miller, leader, Continental blue coats, hemlets and red plumes.

Judson Kilpatrick post, No. 212, Millersburg, 36 members, Henry Cordes, Commander.

B. F. Fisenberger Post of New Cumberland, 25 members, Dr. J. P. Orr, post commander.

Shippensburg cornet band, 19 members, S. A. Wilson, leader, blue uniforms trimmed with red.

Shippensburg drum corps, 5 members, D. Winter, leader. Handsome silk flag.

Corporal McClain Post, 423, Shippensburg, Captain Wm. Baughman, post commander, 60 members in full uniform.

Union Fire Company band of Carlisle, 16 pieces, Philip Norman, leader. Blue uniform with gilt trimmings.

Drum corps, Camp 35, Sons of Veterans, Carlisle, 16 men.

The Veteran Association of Dauphin, with 30 uniformed members.

They were all veterans of the war, and in the absence of a Grand Army post, had organized themselves into a body with the above title. They carried in the line a flag containing only 13 stars, which is believed to be over 60 years old, and was presented to Henry Bickle, of Dauphin, 40 years ago. The association made a very fine appearance in the procession. The sword carried by Capt. J. H. Steckley was worn by Capt. Geety at the battle of Pocotaligo, where he lost an eye in the battle.

Linglestown cornet band, 18 pieces in a carriage drawn by four in hand. The vehicle was handsomely draped.

Paxtang Rangers, 60 men, Captain Clement B. Care.

Councilmen in ten two-horse carriages, as follows:

First carriage.—James McCleaster, Joseph B. Ewing, S. B. Martin, I. S. Trostle.

Second carriage.— Herman J. Wolz, A. W. Weikert, J. G. M. Bay, M. H. Melvin.

Third carriage.—Jas. T. Walters, J. M. Kreiter, J. D. Weeber, J. R. Stoey.

Fourth carriage.—W. H Sible, Henry Schuddemage.

Fifth carriage.— D. E. Leighton, A. F. Fry.

Sixth carriage.— P. H. Ryan, J. W. Shearer.

Seventh carriage.—J. H. Howard, J. W. Miller.

Eigth carriage.— Edward Drinkwater, J. A. Krause.

Ninth carriage.—J. A. Fritchy, G. C. B. Swartz.

Tenth carriage.— C. P. Mason, Dr. J. Hutton.

THE NUMBER IN LINE.

First Division	666
Second Division	1483
Third Division	1294
Total	3443

THE REGATTA ON THE RIVER.

The Committee on the Military and Civic Parade, in order to add to the interest of the ceremonies of the Second Day, offered prizes to the winners of boat races on the Susquehanna. For the four-oared shells race, the only competitors were the Iola Athletic Association of Sunbury, and the Harrisburg Boat club. In the afternoon, when the grand parade was over, and refreshments had been partaken, the people congregated to the number of several thousand along the river bank, from the Water Works to the Market street bridge to witness the race. Jacob Swank represented the Iola club in the bow, and in the Harrisburg boat were C. F. Etter, bow and captain; J. D. Lemer, 2, J. C. Irving, 3, C. E. Covert, stroke. The race was started from Hamilton street, the course being from there to the Market street bridge. A few moments after the start, the ferry boat pushed out from Independence island, and before the Harrisburg rowers saw their danger they dashed into the boat, stoving in the whole end of their shell. The Sunbury men rowed over the course. When the accident occurred the Harrisburg rowers were ahead, the Sunbury crew, however, claimed the race. This was not allowed by the judge, Mr. Scheele, of Reading, who declared it "no race," because of the foul with the ferry boat. He said that if two boats rowing had fouled, or the Harrisburg had run into the bank through bad steering he would have decided in favor of Sunbury, but as the course was clear at the start, and the obstruction made while they were rowing, it was no race. If the Sunbury crew wanted the medals, they would have to row for them. He regretted the way the race resulted, but he decided in his judgment fairly. Subsequently the subject was referred to a higher authority who confirmed the decision of the referee and a time was set for a renewal of the race. The Sunbury crew, however, did not put in an appearance, and the Harrisburg Boat club received the medal.

At 3:40 the single scull race between E. C. Rauch, of Harrisburg club, and J. M. Yeager, of the Nautilus club, Reading, began. They got a good start, and Rauch went to the front. At the boat house Rauch was six lengths ahead and constantly going further away from his opponent, winning by over a hundred yards.

The canoe race began at 3:47 the contestants being H. S. Bergstresser, Frank Davies, Hugh Pitcairn, jr., Martin Fager, C. Snyder, C. E. Fink, L. E. Dare, Abr. Hughes, Frank Stevens, Harry Barnes, and Harry Vandling. They all got off in a bunch, their paddles gyrating like the sails of a windmill. It was a lively sight, and much interest was manifested as to who was going to get there first. Bergstresser settled it by going ahead, and won a good race, the others away behind.

The double scull race between the members of the Harrisburg Boat club was participated in by J. C. Irving, bow; C. E. Covert, stroke, blue; J. D. Lemer, bow; E. R. Bergstresser, stroke, red; Charles H. Chayne, bow; O. M. Copelin, stroke, white. Lemer and Bergstresser led from the start and won the race. Chayne and Copelin stopped rowing at the ferry, a row boat coming ahead and almost fouling them.

The gig race was won by E. R. Bergstresser, after a strong struggle with John D. Lemer.

The medals prepared under the direction of the

committee were as follows: For the four-oared shells the design was crossed oars on a heavy gold shield, the whole surmounted by a wreath surrounding an enameled shield with the monogram "H. B. C." of the Harrisburg Boat club, under whose auspices the regatta was held. The double scull medals had crossed oars on a wreath with a gold square containing the monogram in blue enamel. The single scull medal was "a daisy." It had the crossed oars over a wreath, and over all was a gold monogram picked in enamel. The canoe medal was a maltese cross with crossed paddles. The single gig medal was a five pointed star on a wreath, with gold center and blue enamelled points. They were all of the finest make.

This closed the races, none of them exciting, but they served to put in the afternoon very pleasantly.

How the Visitors were Entertained.

Everything was done by the Committee to entertain the visiting military, Grand Army and civic organizations. After the morning's parade, the entire Eighth regiment with the visiting companies of the Fourth, filed into the City Gray's armory. The company parlor, banquetting room, ladies' room and officers' parlor had all been converted into dining rooms, and long tables set with substantial viands made the soldiers' mouths water. After all had been cleaned up and brushed, they filed to their seats, 365 men being accommodated at one time. It required almost the entire afternoon to serve those in attendance, but the Grays were equal to the emergency and if any of the boys wearing the blue left the armory hungry or thirsty it was their own fault. The welcome was as cordial as it was sincere, and Company D will doubtless be remembered by the other companies of the Eighth regiment with nothing but the kindliest feelings.

The Grand Army guests were entertained under the management of the organizations of the city. Shakespeare hall resembled an immense dining room in the afternoon, Post 58 having selected that place to entertain their Grand Army friends. Hot coffee, sandwiches, cheese, crackers, etc., constituted the bill of fare and most eagerly were these edibles partaken of. Five hundred visiting G. A. R. members were here entertained.

Other societies, on behalf of the Committee extended similar hospitalities to their visiting brethren. And right royally were they entertained.

The City Councils were no less courteous. The Select Council Chamber presented a very inviting and refreshing aspect. A table laden with substantials and luxuries was arranged for the accommodation of members of Council and their invited guests, the borough and township officers who were in the city. George C. B. Swartz was in charge and was exceedingly hospitable in dispensing the eatables and drinkables of which there appeared to be an inexhaustible supply.

The County Commissioners had also arranged a free lunch table at which not only on this day, but during the remaining days of the displays, a large number of county officials were entertained. Berks,

Lebanon. York, Lancaster, Cumberland, Perry, and Northumberland counties were represented.

The citizens were no less hospitable than the foregoing—for every one took pleasure in making their visitors "at home," who received the "best the county afforded." It was the Centennial of the City and County, and in the general joy the strangers within our gates were heartily welcomed.

THE THIRD DAY

WEDNESDAY, SEPTEMBER 16, 1885.

COMMITTEE:

LANE S. HART, *Chairman.*

L. S. BENT, Steelton,   ANTHONY F. ENGELBERT, Wiconisco.
HENRY J. BEATTY,   D. LUTHER JAUSS,
SAMUEL A. HUMMEL,   JOHN F. KERPER,
WILLIAM J. CALDER,   JOSEPH CAMPBELL, Middletown.
                                        WILLIAM H. EGLE, *Secretary.*

COMMITTEE'S GENERAL INVITATION.

HARRISBURG, PA., August 5th, 1885.

The citizens of the County of Dauphin intend celebrating the One Hundredth Anniversary of its formation by a Grand Industrial Display and proceedings, on Wednesday September 16th, 1886, commencing at the hour of 11 A. M. It is earnestly desired that in this commemoration all the neighboring counties participate with us. In obedience, therefore, to the general wish of our community, a very cordial invitation is hereby extended to your establishment to join us on that memorable occasion. When viewed in connection with a proposed Antiquarian Display, the industries of to-day will show the great advance a century has wrought in manufactures, mechanics and the arts.

All the Railroad Companies centering at Harrisburg, have agreed to afford all establishments on their roads every facility as to transportation of freight, and low excursion rates.

We believe it will be largely to your interest to participate.

LANE S. HART, *Chairman.*

WILLIAM H. EGLE, *Secretary.*

INVITATION TO THE CITIZENS.

HARRISBURG, August 5, 1885.

The citizens of the County of Dauphin propose to celebrate the One Hundredth Anniversary of the formation of the County, by a grand Industrial Display and Procession, on Wednesday, September 16th, 1885, in the City of Harrisburg, and it is important that every town and township within the limits of the county be well represented.

The undersigned, having been appointed the committee to superintend the same, earnestly request our citizens to aid in this display, to organize for the purpose, decide upon the manner or nature of such display, and inform this committee of the same. Let each district be well represented in this grand celebration. Any information thereon desired will be given by addressing either of the undersigned committee.

LANE S. HART, *Chairman.*

WILLIAM H. EGLE, *Secretary.*

INDUSTRIAL DISPLAY DAY.

The third day of Dauphin county's great centennial celebration dawned most auspiciously. It was neither cool nor hot—just that happy half and half that makes the perfect day. About half-past eight fleecy clouds formed overhead and hung themselves over the face of the sun, shutting out his view of the festivities down here and cutting off the fierce rays he was preparing to pour out. Early—very early— the visitors began to pour into the city. They came from everywhere—from the Cumberland Valley, the Lebanon Valley, the Juniata Valley, from Lancaster, York and Adams counties, from Northumberland, Snyder, Union and Lycoming counties. From as far east as Philadelphia, as far north as Erie, as far west as Pittsburgh, and as far south as the Maryland border, the people came in vast numbers. The surrounding towns sent thousands of well dressed people to Harrisburg, and it seemed as if the whole State was doing its best to help us along. According to the Philadelphia *Times*, there were 50,000 additional people in the city, and with the strangers who remained over from the previous day about 20,000, and the citizens themselves there were fully 100,000 people to witness the great Industrial Display.

The progress of a hundred years said the *Independent*, was never better represented than it was by the Industrial parade of the Centennial celebration. It must always be conceded that in the mechanic arts,

more than elsewhere, are the improvements which
men achieve with brain and fingers displayed. A
hundred years ago the Ramage press, which required
two pulls to make an impression, was the triumph
of the "art preservative of arts," while rollers were
not thought of to take the place of balls. All kind
of machinery was in its infancy, such as was in use
a century ago being of the crude and simplest character. The application of steam was not attempted.
There was no coal discovered. Gas was an unknown
commodity. Franklin and Rittenhouse were only
dreaming about the electrical forces which were regarded as elements to be averted, not utilized for labor.
What a transformation has the progress of a hundred years made. Steam now runs all kinds of machinery, from that of the ponderous engines used in
working mines, blasting furnaces, running great trains
on railroads, to the operating of a sewing machine and
the frying of an egg. What a spectacle of grandeur,
indeed, was there made in the industrial exhibition.
Great fires glowed in process of smelting metals, ponderous hammers rang in the operation of forging;
rolls buzzed in the work of making rails; nails were
produced with the rapidity of the click of a watch;
printing presses in primitive style, and that of the
period, were running, compositors were at their cases;
the sewing machine hummed its rapid stitches; saw
mills were at work on lumber; machines making
shoes, planing boards, turning out railroad frogs, in
fact, machinery making almost every article imaginable, were in operation along the line. And to this
was added the display by manufacturers and mer-

chants, of their goods and wares in every line of each being represented in special wagons decorated according to the taste of the owners. There was originality and novelty in all of these displays. As a rule, all parades have more or less monotony in them. In that of this day the variety was endless. There were no two things alike, even in the same line. Every wagon was differently gotten up—every article displayed had a peculiar appearance; all of the work done along the monster line was different in each case. This made the display wonderfully grand in its details and overwhelmingly ponderous in its aggregation.

With so many strangers in the city it would naturally be expected that the streets would be literally packed with people at all points along the line. The previous day's parade, splendid as it was in its personnel and full of dignity and historic grandeur in its objects, had no attraction in it like that of the Industrial Display. This day's brass bands had accompaniments in steam whistles, hammers, roll and click of machinery and all the sounds which make up the notes in the anthems of labor when at its devotions. The shouts of people greeting special displays were drowned by this magnificent hum of industry. Bleating herds mingled their plaintive voices with that of neighing horses, excited by the din and confusion of the streets so unusual in their peaceful pastures at home. Swaths were literally cut through masses of people pressing on line for observation by wagons broader than those which preceded them. The weather could not have been

15

more propitious than it was. Atmosphere and
ground were in complete condition to heighten the
interest of the display.

The Chief Marshal, Joseph V. Einstein's order in
regard to the forming of the parade was as follows:

First Division form on Fifth street, right resting
on Market.

The Second Division form on Fourth street, right
resting on Market.

Third Division form on Third street right resting
on Market.

Fourth Division, comprising the Steelton delegation, on Second street, right resting on Market, facing west.

Fifth Division on Second street, right resting on
Market, facing east.

The procession will move promptly at 10 o'clock.

Chief of Staff.—Marlin E. Olmsted. Aids, Gabriel
Heister, W. Champlin Detweiler, Daniel C. Herr,
William T. Hildrup, Jr., and Penrose Dull.

Assistant Marshals.—Charles E. Brelsford, Edgar C.
Felton, Oliver P. Grove, William S. Boas, Dr. J. Ross
Swartz, George E. Hackett, Joseph B. Rife, Henry
Walters.

Aids.—William Pearson, Esq., W. M. Donaldson,
Dr. C. A. Rahter, William M. Lauman, John S. Sible,
Thomas H. McDevitt, Harry Campbell, C. West-
brook, Jr., W. L. Powell, D. C. Herr, John C. Kerper,
Wm. B. Miller, James D. Hawkins, John Croll,
Theodore G. Calder, Joseph B. Ewing, Jr., Kilburn
J. Chandler, Thomas M. Jones, Harry Stouffer, Amos

Tittle, William Hillier, Harry S. Gross, Ed. L. Wagner, Frederick C. Fink, Jr., Dr. Harry Stine, Frederick M. Ott. H. H. Hartranft, E. M. Bishop, John Y. Boyd, Samuel L. Bigler, Christian Hart, W. M. Hargest, E. K. Meyers, S. B. Martin, John Downs, Edward Lewis, A. P. Dull, W. Howard Eby, Luther R. Kelker, W. C Detweiler, Esq., George H. Irwin, Esq., Edgar C. Hummel, W. B. Hammond, W. S. Cornman, Joseph Raymond, Jacob Rife, Bert. Rutherford.

Owing to the length of some of the floats it will be impossible to make the turns below Vine street, in consequence the parade will move over the following route. Out Market to Second, to Reily, to Third, to Walnut, to Fourth, to Ridge avenue, to Reily, to Pennsylvania avenue, to North, to Filbert, to Walnut, to Fifth, to Market, to Fourth, to Chestnut, to Second, to Vine, to Front, to State, to Second, to Market square, and countermarch.

Assistant marshals and aids will wear black silk hat, dark clothes and white gloves.

In obedience to these instructions, the lines were formed. Shortly after 10 o'clock the signal was given, and the grandest parade ever witnessed, began to move in the following order.

FIRST DIVISION.

Chief Marshal, Major Joseph V. Einstein.

Following the chief marshal and his aids, the procession was headed by the State Capital Band, of this city, numbering thirty pieces. The first carriage was occupied by Mayor Wilson, City Solicitor Hargest, City Treasurer Black and Mayor Mann, of Altoona. The next carriage contained Hon. Benj. F. Meyers, S. Boyd Martin, Theo. D. Greenawalt and Joseph B. Ewing. The third conveyance was occupied by

Councilmen John J. Hargest, Harry Muehler and John C. Forney. Following these there were eleven double teams accommodating the remaining members of the City Councils.

The Shippensburg Band of seventeen pieces of brass, headed the second sub-division, marshaled by William S. Boas, aided by William B. Miller, Kilburn J. Chandler and Luther K. Kelker.

The Peipher Line, owned by Joseph Montgomery & Co., made a large and attractive display of their teams and business specialties. The first wagon was loaded with sacked peanuts, the second double team was neatly decorated with bunting and evergreen, and contained an exhibit of the grain drills and cider-mills manufactured by the Superior Drill Company, of Springfield, Ohio, and for whom they are agents. The third team carried the Jackson steel wheelbarrow. The fourth double team carried the Tiger reaper made by the Stoddard Manufacturing Company. The fifth the Excelsior self binder, in full operation. The sixth a single team carrying straw for the use of the above mentioned self-binder. The seventh team was loaded with baled twine used on the self-binder, following which was one single and one double team laden with barreled flour; the next a double team with the Junior Deering self-binder in operation. The next two teams hauled the Superior cider mills, and a large hay fork adjusted on a frame just as when in use. These were followed by five more double and single team exhibits, the vehicles containing pianos and organs, a Tiger hay rake, barreled syrups, molasses, etc. The Peipher Line dray was loaded with an immense hogshead of syrup, and was used in this business in 1859. Following was a single team, the Excelsior Light Mower. The display of Montgomery & Co. was handsomely trimmed throughout, and embraced sixteen vehicles and twenty horses. A notable fact in regard to the Peipher Line display, was that their entire stock of horses were iron greys, the superiors of which for number and qualities cannot be found in this section of the country.

The Pennsylvania Transfer Company's first team drew large wagons, beautifully decked with graceful double arches of evergreen, ornamented with bunting. These covered very pretty pyramids of exhibition plows, manufactured by the Oliver Chilled Plow Company. A very prettily decorated Oliver Chilled sulky plow followed.

The next in line was the Victor road scraper, owned and built by S. Pennock & Sons, of Kennet Square, Chester county, Pa.

The float of Forney Bros., Market street shoe dealers, was a large canopy of red, white and blue muslins, elegantly decorated and appropriately lettered. This represented a shoe factory in full operation, the machinery and men busy at work turning out shoes. In the center of the float was an old shoemaker's bench, labeled "1785, one pair a day," contrasting plainly with the busy hum of the machinery surrounding it.

Frank Hoy in his Dutch make-up, made fun for the gazers, with his little bell and a pie, from a double team carriage, scattering circulars relating to the Antiquarian exhibition.

The Singer Cornet Band, of Mechanicsburg, twenty-four pieces, I. S. Eberly, leader.

The Harrisburg Foundry and Machine Works, Martin E. Hershey, manager, as follows : First, large Paxton traction engine; second, large Paxton traction engine pulling a platform on which was the favorite Ide Automatic cut-off engine; third, two small Paxton traction engines one pulling the other; fourth, two small traction engines ; fifth, traction engine pulling the Champion thresher and huller; sixth, traction engine pulling the Champion combined thresher and huller; seventh, small Paxton traction engine. This entire display was handsomely decorated and made not only an attractive but a noisy exhibit as well. This was followed by the Citizen street sprinkler, drawn by a double team. Next came a four-horse platform wagon upon which was mounted an immense oil car tank made by the Harrisburg Foundry and Machine Works.

The next in order was a large red, white and blue float of the Harrisburg paper box factory.

The display of the Adams Express Company was headed by a man who carried an old express bag, said to have been used in 1839 by Alvin Adams, founder of the company that bears his name, when he first conceived the idea of quick and careful delivery of valuable packages. Following on a small cart was displayed an iron cash safe used the same time. Their next feature was a single wagon ladened with express packages, followed by a double team which was likewise burdened with express goods.

Fager & Maeyer, the Market street tinners, made a very creditable display of the various features of their business. Their first was a single team drawing a large variety of fine cornice designs. It was followed by a double team platform wagon, upon which a regular tin-shop was in active operation, making small tin cups, which were distributed gratis along the route of procession. The next double team hauled a unique display of parlor stoves and furnaces, followed by a platform of handsome nickle-plated parlor stoves. Then came a single team drawing an exhibit of kitchen and cook stoves. The next feature of this display was a wagon on which their roofing machinery was in full operation preparing the tin for the roofs. A very large pyramidal float contained a magnificent showing of japanned, stamped and agate wear for all uses. The whole array of exhibits by Fager & Maeyer was elaborately decorated in many styles and without any evidence of stint, or lack of labor.

O. P. Grove, dry goods merchant, Third and Verbeke streets, was represented in the procession with a large canopy float, drawn by a team of four horses. It was tastefully decorated and presented an attractive appearance. Beneath the canopy were eleven "dummys" dressed in the latest and most fashionable attire. This feature was one that particularly attracted the attention of the ladies along the entire route. The covetous eye of many a lass snapped fire as this gorgeous array of the beautiful met their gaze.

A. L. Tittle's livery display consisted of a handsome single jump seat buggy, drawn by a neat roadster; a large double flat followed with eight negro minstrels, who performed songs and danced over the entire route, creating sport and merriment for all.

The Harrisburg Burial Case Company was represented by a fine double team drawing a wagon draped in black, in the center of which, braced upright, was their business card, painted on a large square sign, in gold letters with black background.

The Duncannon Band, of Duncannon, Pa., of 20 pieces.

Bergner & Engle Brewing Company, of Philadelphia, headed their display with a barouche drawn by an elegant pair of horses. In the carriage were seated Felix Geiger, who is master brewer, at Philadelphia; B. P. Wisman, general agent; C. H. Quinzel, agent for Berger & Engle at Martinsburg, West Virginia, John C. Wieseman, their agent for this city, and Frederick P. Haehnlen, of this city. Following came a large chariot-like float, on which eight men were busily employed at the various labor in a brewery. The float had the appearance of an old stone castle, very artistically constructed and beautifully decorated. The engine, with its attached machinery, was in full and active motion. The boiler and fermenting tubs, perfect working machinery, were also in operation. From this magnificent chariot brewery the genial Felix Geiger, through his assistants, dispensed the cooling beer to friends. This costly display was drawn by four magnificent Norman horses, caparisoned in massive brass-mounted harness, that was manufactured to order in France. The horses above spoken of were brought to this country by Bergner & Engle at an expense of $600 apiece. Then followed two double teams, handsomely decorated, drawing Bergner & Engle wagons, laden with kegged beer.

George Dœhne's first wagon was very prettily trimmed with evergreen and bunting, and was loaded with malt in bags, hops in bales and twining around and through them were growing green hops and other materials used in the business. This was followed by a single team, laden with kegged beer, also handsomely ornamented.

C. A. Dressel headed his display in a single buggy. Following came a double team, preuttly bedecked in gay colors and evergreens, the wagon laden with malt in sacks, and baled hops. On each side over the display was the motto, "This is what we use."

Following came a four-horse team drawing the Louis Bergdoll Brewing Company's wagon, elaborately decorated in red, white and blue bunting and evergreen. The wheels were bound around the tires and hubs with cords of woven laurel leaves, giving the vehicle a massive appearance. This was followed by a double team drawing a handsomely ornamented wagon of the same firm, loaded with beer in kegs. John Russ, the firm's agent for this city, spared no pains to make his display attractive.

Our own brewer, Henry Fink, was represented by one of the "Keystone" delivery wagons, prettily bedecked in colors and intertwined with green hops. Following came a single team wagon, upon which was erected a high canopy, ornamented with flags and tri-colored bunting, which was also relieved by green hops entwined about the canopy.

Dan Bacon, the confectioner, sat on an artistically decorated vehicle, in front of a pyramid of his well-known cough drops, put up in pretty japanned cans, smiling all over his face, distributing small boxes of the candy gratis. The black horses that drew his display were also highly ornamented with colors and evergreens. Following came a large canopied float, drawn by two greys, constructed in faultless white. Beneath this three workmen from Bacon's establishment under the foremanship of Mr. Laubenstein, were busily engaged making stick candy, which was distributed free to the people along the route. Then came a float of like character, under the canopy of which were four men, busily engaged bottling the various drinks sold by Mr. Bacon. All the machinery was in full operation, and the exhibit in its entirety, drew forth much praise.

C. A. Spicer's display of furniture consisted of a large covered float, drawn by a double team, and handsomely trimmed in colors and evergreen. Beneath the canopy were beautiful articles of furniture, particularly among which was a handsome mahogany secretary, richly carved and mounted.

Herman R. Zeil, the Market street gent's furnisher, had a single wagon, upon which was constructed a double frame, holding almost every article of wear and underwear handled in his line. Like most of the displays, this was decorated in tri-colored muslin and evergreen.

Union Deposit Band, with twenty pieces of brass, lead the next sub-division.

II. W. Techmeyer, with the Domestic sewing machine display, then followed; one single wagon, handsomely decorated, and carrying two fine Domestic machines, above and between which was an elegantly worked cross; following them came a large double team float, one side literally covered with sample applique, embroidered and tinsel work; on the other a pretty and rich specimen of interior decoration in applique and embroidery. It is estimated that there was over $500 worth of machine work hanging upon this float. A single team came next, uniquely festooned and decorated, hauling a handsome machine.

The Singer Sewing Machine Company, Clayton Denny, manager, was represented in the line with no less than six distinct vehicles, all of which were elaborately dressed in colors and evergreens. One double float was a mass of applique, embroidery and tinsel work of most elegant design and execution.

The White Sewing Machine Company also exhibited work done by their machine and wagon covered with advertising bills.

The *Morning Call*, from this point in the line, represented by a single team, trimmed in red, white and blue bunting, distributed copies of Tuesday's issue of that paper to the people along the entire route.

Brainard & Armstrong, spool silk twist people, drove a single carriage, prettily trimmed in bunting and evergreen.

David R. Betts, city manager of the American Sewing Machine Company, represented his principals with seven single wagons, each bearing a pretty machine, and prettily trimmed in colors and evergreens.

W. W. Boyer, coach-maker, of South Third street, appeared with a large float, upon which he displayed an old sulky bed, built in 1832, and two handsome pleasure carriages, built at his own shops. The whole was tastefully bedecked with flags and bunting.

Lewis Gastrock, coal dealer; two teams, drawing single wagons, were burdened with coal screens and other yard utensils, handsomely decorated with bunting, flags and Chinese lanterns.

SECOND DIVISION.

The second division formed on North Fourth street, right resting on Market street, and was headed by the Harrisburg butchers.

Chief Marshal, Henry Walter.

Aids—William Kyle, Adam Kreig, J. L. Koons, John Kyle, Harry S. Stouffer, and John Shaffner, all well-known butchers.

William T. Hildrup Cornet Band, Prof. Herman Newmeyer, leader, 25 pieces. The men wore their blue fatigue dress uniform.

Carriage containing four of the oldest butchers in the city, "Knights of the Cleaver," of the olden time, whose pleasant countenances indicated that they were highly honored by the younger and more vigorous men of the trade by taking the advance conveyance in this novel and highly creditable display. These four old men were Michael Newman, John Young, Martin Waltzer and Frederick Sweitzer, old and highly respected citizens, in a barouche drawn by a pair of bays.

The Cow Boy, Daniel Elliot, colored, employed by Messrs. Hemler & Delone, Harrisburg cattle dealers, mounted on his mustang.

William Bricker's team of four-in-hand drawing a butcher shop on wheels, with live stock (calves, sheep, hogs and a live ox) on wagon. This wagon was handsomely trimmed with evergreens and bunting, and labeled: "We as butchers represent our home trade." In the rear of the wagon were six well-known, live, progressive Harrisburg butchers, in clean linen and spotless white aprons, and James R. Dixon, a well-known Carlisle butcher and Democratic candidate for sheriff, as their guest.

Wm. T. Hildrup's team of four Norman horses, driven by Wm. Merkley, tugged another butcher shop on wheels. The wagon was handsomely draped, and on it a sausage machine in full operation, with butcher George M. Hiller handing out excellent bologna sausage along the route. On this wagon were representative butchers, Messrs. George

Marzolf, George Koser, John R. Sellers, David Wenrick, Martin Waltzer, jr., and Augustus Miller. The wagon was labeled, " The old and the new way."

P. D. McNeal's two-horse wagon, handsomely draped, containing 24 butcher boys, from 7 to 12 years of age, nicely uniformed, with white caps, white shirts and blue pants.

Forty-four butchers, on horseback. These were from the city and surrounding towns, all doing business in the Harrisburg markets.

Wm. E. Machlin's rag warehouse was represented by a four-horse team and two two-horse teams, with bales of colored rags, assorted rags, white rags, all sorts of rags, and a number of the employees at work.

Two two-horse teams laden with Stouffer flour of Royal Oak brand, in barrels and sacks.

Luther R. Kelker, two teams, representing the N. Y. Enamel Paint Company, with a pretty design of the company's business house in the city of New York.

Colonel Geo. F. McFarland's floral display was a miniature green house on wheels, filled with flowers, plants, &c. On the sides was a large floral inscription, in letters 21 inches long, made of zinna's,—"George F. McFarland." On the rear was an immense floral bell. Following this, came a horse team with a pyramid of fruit—sixteen varieties of grapes, with apples, pears, &c., representing, " The offering of Pomona."

The next four-horse team represented the Hydraulic Cement Pipe Works of Henry J. Beatty, Herr street and Pennsylvania canal. This followed by a one-horse team of the same establishment—with six men working along the line of march.

Hart's Printing and Publishing House, South Third street, was well represented. The display was in charge of Samuel E. Murphy, the foreman of the office in the line, and fifty-eight employees. The outfit was conveyed along the route on three four-horse and three single teams The printing office was represented by an old Washington press, made in 1785, and a Hoe cylinder of 1885—making the contrast an interesting as well as a striking one. The bindery was also represented with paper-cutting and book-back finishing apparatus, and the electrotype foundry was fairly represented. Even the stalwart engineer, William Williams, and the "devil" of the office, an apprentice rigged up in a harlequin suit, with the horns of the "imp" sticking out in prominence from the sides of his smutty phiz. "That is a devil.

as is a devil," remarked an enthusiastic admirer, standing on the curb-stone at Fourth and South streets. Messrs. Frank B. Kinneard, J. N. O. Hankinson and others assisted Mr. Murphy in this attractive display. The wagons were handsomely decorated and the horses covered with white muslin covers, ornamented in attractive red letters—"Hart's Printing and Publishing House."

The *"Daily Patriot"* printing house was represented as follows: Peter Wilson, colored, an office attache, drove Mr. E. K. Meyers' "Flying Sam," 36 years old, in the *Patriot* business wagon. Team of two horses, representing the *Patriot* printing house, equipped with two pairs of cases, a Washington hand press of the "long ago" pattern, and a Gordon jobber at work. Herman J. Wolz, the city route agent, had his ten carriers handsomely equipped with blue uniforms and white caps, and wearing buttonhole bouquets. They distributed half sheets of the *Patriot* along the route.

Mr. George Houser's two-horse team conveyed the well-known printing house of the "Estate of Theo. F. Scheffer." There was a Gordon press working, and compositors setting type. This was one of the first printing offices in America to print oil color toy books. It is located at 21 South Second street, and was established in 1832. Pressman—Geo. W. Scheffer; compositor, Lewis G. Poulton; foreman, Louis K. Scheffer.

Harrisburg *Independent* Printing House, conveyed on a float drawn by Lauer's team. There was an old style Washington Hoe press on the wagon, a pair of cases, etc. The employees distributed a historical sheet of the *Independent* printed in red, white and blue colors.

Next came the *Sunday Morning Telegram*—James M. Place, Esq., manager. Their wagon had a modern Gordon jobber and a pair of cases. The rig was in charge of William G. Boyer. Fac-simile copies of the *Sunday Telegram* were distributed along the route, not more than 6x8 inches in size.

Citizen's Cornet Band of Millersburg, 20 pieces—Charles L. Miller, leader.

The Saddlery and Harness House of S. A. Hummel, Market street, was represented by Noah A. Walmer, foreman; on one of Neely's two-horse wagons. The display attracted much attention. It was a perfect saddler's shop on wheels.

Edward Boyer's coach shop, East Market street, represented on three one-horse floats, handsomely trimmed, with five fine carriages on exhibition—one of them being a handsome two-seated Surry wagon.

A double team float represented J. Laverty & Co's., furniture, carpet and store house.

Wagon representing Philip M. Ditzler's harness, trunks, &c., with a man dressed in Indian costume at work.

George W. Meily's shoe house, Market street, was represented by a beautifully draped wagon, drawn by two horses. The wagon was handsomely fitted up, resembling the interior of a large shoe house.

A one-horse conveyance represented Stern's Market street shoe house, with cases of shoes exposed to view.

Edward L. Wagner's cigar manufactory was represented by a two-horse float, with men at work in the factory.

Matamoras Band, 18 pieces, J. W. Mahargue, leader.

Team drawn by two horses, and a wagon loaded with barrels of flour, sacks of flour, etc., representing the Lochiel Mills.

Wilson Bros. works, East State street, were represented by a one horse team, on which was an improved cider-mill, and a "Telegraph fodder cutter," two of their specialities.

D. W. Gross & Son's drug house was represented by a mule team drawing a wagon containing an immense gilt mortar.

The Eureka Fabric Hose interest was represented by a pyramid of fabric hose, on a wagon drawn by two horses. Mr. C. W. Wales is the agent.

J. A. Kramer, plumber, North Third street, a one-horse team with plumbing material on exhibition.

Fred. W. Yingst, carpet dealer, one-horse team, with a display of Turkish rugs, arranged in the form of a pagoda, on which sat a boy dressed in clothes made of carpet.

John T. Ensminger, of Second and Chestnut streets, had a one-horse and a two-horse wagon in line, representing a display of parlor and other furniture, with a folding bed in operation.

J. W. Koons, of East Harrisburg, a four-horse wagon, with a display of stoves, sheet-iron work, etc., with six employees at work along the route.

Thomas Liken, the Ridge Avenue grocer, had a one-horse fancy wagon and a one-horse business wagon in line.

Cement N. Studebaker, grocer, Second and State, had a two-horse and one-horse wagon in line, representing the "Snow Flake Flour" of the Studebaker mills.

J. L. Knox, the tinner, of South Ninth street, a two-horse team, with stoves, spouting, etc., representing the Lebanon stove works.

Linglestown Band, 20 pieces, in band carriage.

Four-horse wagon from Linglestown, with a settler's Log Cabin of 100 years ago—the smoke issuing from the chimney, and the iron pot suspended from a tripod. On the top of the cabin a live fox was chained. Eight or ten men, dressed in homespun, represented the "settlers" of a century ago.

Frank L. Hutter, book-binder, had a novel turnout. It was a triangular-shaped car, covered with canvas, on which was the inscription : "We push our business." There was no horse in front of the car, but behind was a horse giving force to the legend on the canvas. A horse under the canvas was the moving power.

A four-horse wagon, on which rode twenty farmers from Manada Hill.

Mount Pleasant dairy wagon, drawn by one horse.

George H. Sourbeer, the Broad street undertaker, a carriage drawn by a pair of bays ; a two-horse hearse for adults ; a white enameled hearse for young people, drawn by a pair of horses, and a one-horse business wagon.

John H. Staub, carpet weaver, was at work at an old loom built seventy-five years ago.

G. W. Reese, farmer for David Fleming, had a two-horse team, with a display of vegetables on wagon.

Henry M. Kelly, the coal and wood dealer, had several wagons in line. In one was a brawny young fellow with a saw and buck, manipulating a cord-wood stick.

Thomas Egenrider, bakery wagon.

THIRD DIVISION.

Chief Marshal, O. P. Grove, with four aids.

Citizen's Cornet Band, Hummelstown, 26 pieces.

W. L. Powell & Co., were represented as follows: A two-horse wagon, piled with bannanas and other trophical fruits.

Float drawn by six Norman horses, with an extensive display of barrels, hams, and other dried meats, etc., with a banner inscribed: "1785 —1885."

Powell & Cos.' delivery wagon, distributing Centennial souvenirs along the line.

Steelton Flouring-Mills, four-horse float, with mill in operation, driven by a small steam engine.

Float drawn by four Norman horses, wagon piled with flour in sacks in a pyramid shape, 15 feet high. On the top was a sheaf of wheat the apex being an immense bouquet of natural flowers.

Two-horse wagon, containing "Our Boys." 12 lads dressed neatly and wearing white caps, representing the sons of the millers.

Two-horse wagon, filled with flour sacks, variously illustrated.

Team of four mules, with a cooper shop on wheels, with men at work making barrels. The Steelton Flour-Mill Company had hundreds of sacks of flour done up, and these were distributed amongst the crowd. The part taken by this company was equal to the best.

A. B. Dunkle, a two-horse team, drawing wagon laden with parlor furniture.

E. Daron & Son, team drawn by two horses, representing their music house, organ discoursing sweet music along the route.

J. G. Keller, painter, grainer, and wall paperer, made a display in a one-horse wagon.

The Acme cultivator, represented by W. B. Dale, agent, was drawn by a pair of stylish sorrels, which attracted much attention. The farmers were delighted with the beautiful and very popular agricultural implement.

William F. Neely represented his furniture interest in a handsome one-horse outfit.

FOURTH DIVISION.

The grand display from "Birmingham-on-the-Susquehanna," the Pennsylvania Steel Works, was simply immense, and reflected great credit on the manager of the works for the public spirit he displayed in permitting the employees to take part in the great Centennial demonstration. The 1,000 or more employees were under the charge of Edgar C. Felton, as chief marshal, with five aids or assistants.

First came a six mule team, with a representation of the Bessemer mill in full operation, converting steel into ingots.

Steelton Band, Harry I. Newlin, leader, 23 pieces, men in gray fatigue uniforms.

Two hundred and fifty workmen of the Bessemer department, George H. Blake, foreman of "turn." Edward J. Grunden, foremen of second "turn," 150 men. The first "turn" was equipped with white caps, blue shirts, white neck-ties, dark pants, each man with a clean white towel around his neck, and wearing a button-hole bouquet. The second "turn" wore a uniform of dark pants, duck leggings, blue shirts and white neckties.

The engineers and firemen, 28 in number, were in charge of James E. Galvin, chief engineer. They were uniformed in neat, dark blue suits. Mr. Galvin carried a beautiful and very valuable cane, the wood from which it was made having lain in the bottom of the Delaware for about 100 years. It is a portion of the English war ship "St George," which was sunk in Delaware bay in 1776. The cane was made from wood taken from the sunken ship in 1876. It has rich, dark color, and is polished up handsomely.

Cornet Band, of Steelton, colored, 22 pieces, James Johnson, leader.

Pennsylvania Steel Company Blooming-Mill and Hammer Department in operation on wagons drawn by four stout mules. There were ten men at work.

Four men in red uniforms, wearing neat white caps, followed the Blooming-Mill outfit.

Liberty Cornet Band, of Steelton, 25 pieces, A. M. Landis, leader, in neat blue uniforms.

Eighty-five Blooming-Mill hands, wearing neat uniforms, red shirts, white caps, etc. They were marshaled by Jacob H. Snell and John Reeme.

Employees of University Mill, 40 men, wore neat blue uniforms, with white caps and red ties. They were marshaled by S. M. Guss.

The Pennsylvania Steel Company's Rail-Mill department was represented on a float, drawn by six powerful horses. There were nine men at work running rails through miniature rolls.

Citizens' Band, of Churchville, 24 pieces, Jacob Strite, leader, blue uniforms, with gilt trimmings.

Employees of the Rail-Mill, 187 men, marshaled by John Kirk, uniformed with blue shirts, white caps, linen pants and red belts.

The steam machinery in the Rail-Mill was represented by 42 men in uniforms of blue flannel shirts, dark caps, white belts and white neckties.

The Interlocking Switch and Signal department was represented by 125 men. On a float, drawn by four horses, was a group of men at work; the signal being manipulated by Vesser E. Powell. The men were uniformed in white shirts, black pants and blue belts, marshaled by Owen T. Cummings.

Two-horse wagon, with forge and four men at work.

A four horse team, with a wagon handsomely draped, interlocking switch department, a man working the leaver of an interlocking apparatus.

The merchant mill employees came next.

New Cumberland Band, 23 pieces, Rush Dugans, leader, uniformed in grey suits.

Two hundred and sixty men, dark uniforms white belts, and duck leggings.

Float drawn by six stout mules. On this was a small steam engine, with rolls in operation, manned by a group of busy workmen.

FIFTH DIVISION.

William M. Donaldson, chief marshal, with six aids.

Jr. O. U. A. M. Band, of Middletown, 16 performers, H. Brehm leader.

One of the most interesting features of the grand procession was the delegation of Indians from the Carlisle training school, in charge of one of the gentlemanly attaches of the institution. It was an exceedingly appropriate display, and excited the most favorable comment. At the head of the Indian sub-division, the center of attraction, was a powerful Indian, over six feet in height, wearing the full costume of a mighty chief. His make-up was a profusion of paint, feathers, fringes, trinkets, embroidered buckskin and other trappings. He walked with head erect and with a springy step, looking neither to the right or left, his eagle eye fixed on some object away up the thronged street, as if he meant to march toward it with mathematical precision. This was "Big Bear" of the Sioux tribe. At his side were two Indians who arrived at Carlisle only the Saturday previous, on a visit to their friends. One was "Le-me-go," a Crow Indian, and the other "Big Belly," a Sioux. They wore the dress they don in the wilds of the far west, in the land of the setting sun—and their appearance contrasted strikingly with those of their well-dressed intelligent children and relatives marching behind them. These two Indians had long, dark hair, and marched bareheaded, which gave them a wierd appearance. They were followed by 34 well dressed young Indians, representing about fifteen tribes. The pupils all wore gray uniforms, trimmed with red cord. They all had folding slates in their hands, and the entire delegation seemed to be delighted with the attention which was being bestowed upon them.

Wagon drawn by two greys, with six Indian boys employed at baking, printing, and carpenter work.

Two-horse team, with six Indian boys at work at harness and shoe making.

Two horse-wagon, containing six Indian boys at blacksmithing and tin smithing.

William H. Lawser's sportmen's supply house was represented by a two-horse wagon, on which an immense wooden gun and a big wooden key were conspicuously displayed.

A lad riding on a Mexican burro.

The leather firm of Rife Bros., Middletown and Harrisburg as represented in a barouche, with three gentlemen and a lady. Fine specimens of finished leather were displayed in this vehicle.

On a float following was an exhibit that did them no little credit. All the business of manufacturing leather was gone through with. Their motto was "Nothing Like Leather."

Raymond & Campbell's Middletown stove works were represented as follows : Pair of ponies drawing a fancy wagon with three pretty nickle-plated models of stoves; two horses, with a handsome display of nickle-plated improved stoves; two horse wagon, with improved cook stoves; two-horse wagon with ranges; two-horse wagon, with large bell and steam radiator, all in charge of Messrs. J. F. & D. E. Raymond.

L. Poulton representing his picture frame works, had a two-horse wagon fitted up, with four men at work making frames.

D. H. Kauffman's dairy was represented by four handsomely decorated milk wagons.

Wm. F. Hurley's undertaking establishment was represented with a carriage drawn by a pair of bays with black plumes.

A one-horse team represented the house of W. L. Gardner's Star Grocery, 310 Sixth street.

The Harrisburg Provision Company (Jacob Dold, of Buffalo, N. Y., doing business in this city, at Buffalo, N. Y., and Kansas City,) was represented by a large wagon drawn by a pair of horses, the vehicle loaded down with barrels of "Royal Hams," dried meats, etc.

The B. &. E. Goodman clothing house had a two horse team in line, with a fine display of fashionabe clothing on their wagon.

Johnson & Co.'s paper warehouse was represented by a two-horse wagon filled with bales of wrapping paper.

The Great Atlantic and Pacific Tea Company was represented by one two-horse and two one-horse teams, the wagons gaily decorated and filled with their specialties.

The Milwood Cliff Cracker Company of Ridge avenue, had a team and wagon in line, manufacturing goods.

Harry Berrier's book bindery was represented on wheels, an immense book filling up the wagon.

John Killinger, Market street grocer, had his business wagon in line.

P. Vaughn, gas fitter, had a wagon laden with hydrant stocks, etc., in the display.

W. H. Yinger's steam laundry was represented by a neat one-horse wagon, neatly trimmed.

Moeslein & Reiber, carpenters and builders, had a two-horse wagon in line, with a force of carpenters at work.

Philip Weaver, grocer, South Second street, a one-horse business wagon, filled with goods.

Conrad Seeger had a business wagon in the display with a handsome assortment of fancy rugs and carpets.

Benj. F. Umberger, grocer, Herr and Cumberland streets, a business wagon with a display of goods.

John F. Kerper, grocer, had a three-horse team, with a fine display of goods.

Sons of Veterans Drum Corps, Harrisburg, 13 pieces, led by C. Musser.

Fleischman & Co's compressed yeast firm had their nobby business wagon, and a very stylish tandem team in the procession, and the outfit attracted considerable attention.

John C. Nutt, grocer of North and Spruce streets, had his business wagon in the display.

J. F. Mayer, confectioner, display of sham ice cream, etc. Popcorn balls, manufactured in line, were distributed along the route.

W. H. Walkemeyer, Court avenue, ice dealer, had several wagons in line.

D. H. Coffin, milkman, four wagons in line, covered with evergreens and flags.

Patrick Russ, a team of mules drawing a load of peanuts in sacks.

The J. X. Quigley Medicine Company, State and Third streets, a business wagon.

Philip Hess, of Susquehanna township, had a two-horse truck wagon, filled with some of the products of his farm, and also a one-horse team loaded down with fresh vegetables.

John Loban's truck wagon filled with garden produce.

S. W. Oyster & Bro., commission goods, South street, flour, feed, etc., with a neat business wagon.

Harrison & Co., Dauphin Spice Mills, Chestnut and Third streets, made a neat display with two wagons containing a number of their employees, and a line of goods.

West Fairview Cornet Band, Hiram T. Dunbar, leader, with 22 pieces.

Jacob Hess, grocer, North Third street, had a handsome business wagon in line.

The Baltimore One Price Clothing House, a pony team and business wagon and a one-horse wagon, with a number of figures dressed up grotesquely.

Knull & Co., hatters, of North Third street, had a wagon in line on which was placed "Jack the Giant," ten feet high, and an immense fancy colored shirt, large enough for an awning over the deck of a steamboat.

John G. Gruber, a broom factory on wheels.

J. L. Dipner & Bro., grocers, Market square, a business wagon filled with choice goods.

N. Russ' oyster bay was represented by a wagon with barrels of oysters and a man opening bivalves along the route.

Rogers Bros., grocers, Front and Market streets, a business wagon filled with goods.

Oliver Attick, North Eleventh street, a float containing a handsome carriage.

Emanuel Brown, carriage maker, 628 North street, had a handsome wagon in line.

Thomas Lego, huckster, had his business wagon in line.

J. H. Cragwell, 646 Broad street, a neat barber shop on wheels, in full operation.

The Keystone Electric Bell Company, represented by S. W. Entrekin, had 16 bells rigged on a wagon.

Joseph J. Oglesby, furniture dealer, team with furniture display.

Andrew A. Hoak of Allison's Hill, a large float representing a stone quarry scene, with men at work.

The Paxton Cornet Band, Willis H. Fountain, leader, 21 pieces, with stylish uniforms, headed the last sub-division of the procession.

J. S. Sible, Ice and Coal dealer, eight large ice wagons handsomely decorated, fourteen coal carts, and several lumber wagons.

As the last display passed those who had timed the procession said that it took two hours to pass a point. It was certainly the grandest affair Harrisburg ever witnessed in her history, and the admirable manner in which it was managed reflected great credit on Chief Marshal Einstein, Chief of Staff Olmsted and the large staff of efficient aids. The procession marched all over the route as published, and at the close was reviewed by the chief marshal. The parade was about six miles miles in length.

GENERAL SUMMARY OF THE PARADE.

Vehicles, - - - - - 238
Horses, - - - - - 491
Bands, - - - - - - 20
Musicians, - - - - - 409
Estimate number of men in line. - - 5,000

Of all the displays made, none were of a more complete kind, and none so large as that from the Pennsylvania Steel Works. Apart from its imposing character, it was thoroughly representative. There were over one thousand men in line, and their hand-

some appearance and good marching elicited rounds
of applause. The immense machinery that the
heavy wagons carried along was in full and noisy
operation, and the rattle of the Bessemer mill mingled musically with the heavy thud of the powerful
hammer. The rail mill department was splendidly
represented. Representations of hot rails run
through the rollers in the manner followed at the
great works at Steelton was shown, and the men
labored as earnestly as though they were really
making the rails. The machinery used was most
complete, and the sight was appreciated by all the
crowd that saw it. The display of the railway sig-
nals from the steel works was an especial feature, a
full working model being in line. Nothing so plainly
demonstrated the growth and progress of the county
as did the Steelton display, and no part of the great
procession will be remembered with more vividness.
Major Bent who was justly proud of the part taken
by the Pennsylvania Steel Works, issued the following circular to the heads of the various departments
which were represented in the Industrial Parade:

STEELTON. Sept. 17, 1885.—I desire to express to
you, and through you to the employees in your department, the gratification I felt in witnessing the
parade yesterday. It was most certainly a creditable
display, both of men and material, and beyond that
the spirit manifested to make the demonstration a
success is but an additional proof that the past success of the Pennsylvania Steel Company is largely at-
tributable to that loyalty of purpose which charac-

terizes its employees, in putting forward at all times their best efforts to further the interest of the company.

Personally, I thank you, not only for the courtesy which you extended to me yesterday, but which at all times you evince it your pleasure to bestow.

L. S. BENT,

V. P. and General Manager.

In referring to the trades day of the celebration, the *Telegraph* said: The exposition of industry in the procession of Wednesday last will live in the memory not only of the citizens of Dauphin county, but be noted and dwelt upon for a long time in the distant cities and country round about. As an evidence of growth, even for one hundred years, it was astounding. The whole population of the county in 1785 would have had to be multiplied by at least five to make up the numbers participating in the demonstration of yesterday as proprietors and employes alone, while the spectators lining the sidewalks, and all the doors and windows and even roofs of the elaborately decorated buildings throughout the long route, were variously estimated from thirty to fifty thousand. All the great industries of the city, and many in the country, were represented by working exhibits; the machine shops, the furnaces, the rolling-mills, the steel-works, the agricultural implements, the brewers, the merchants, all the almost innumerable interests that go to make up a live, enterprising, and prosperous people. The undertaking was entered upon with some misgivings, but as the time drew on one after the other determined that they would do what they could individually to make the affair as creditable as possible. The result was the grandest pageant of the kind ever seen in a city of our class; not only astonishing our citizens, but inspiring the unbounded admiration of visitors. One gentleman exclaimed enthusiastically, "Had I not been here to see, no possible description could have given me any idea of this magnificent demonstration. No more talk of slow coach in this population. Harrisburg has covered herself with glory." Besides the cause for gratulations, we have in the evidence it gives of sturdy progress in the utilitarian arts, the general good order in so large an assemblage of people, the prevailing self-respecting dignity of deportment; as illustrating the character of the population which thus celebrates its Centennial, shows a growth in moral health greater even than our material progress, or our increase in population. With the city full of visitors, and excitement every day in the week, and fifty special policemen on duty; not one arrest for violence or offenses against property, and less than a dozen for intoxication, tells a story at which we may truly rejoice. All in all then, Harrisburg is a proud, and we may hope and believe a grateful city. Proud of her achievements, and grateful that her people give such evidence of deserving the respect of the world.

THE FOURTH DAY.

Thursday, September 16, 1885.

ADVISORY COMMITTEE.

Francis Jordan, *Chairman,*

Charles L. Bailey,	Peter K. Boyd,
W. W. Boyer,	Richard Hogan,
David Maeyer,	Andrew K. Black,
Jacob F. Haehnlen,	Henry B. Buehler, M. D.

THE FIREMAN'S UNION—1885.

Who had complete control of affairs.

President,
JAMES N. BLUNDIN, Good Will.

Vice-President,
CHARLES P. MECK, Citizen.

Treasurer,
WILLIAM K. ALRICKS, Washington.

Recording and Corresponding Secretary,
SAMUEL H. ETTLA, Hope.

Financial Secretary,
JOHN J. ZIMMERMAN, Paxton.

Executive Committee—L. R. Keller, Mt. Pleasant, Chairman ; Wm. H. Lynch, Friendship; Jacob Houser, Hope; George Weitzel, Citizen ; H. F. Young, Washington ; John Barry, Mt. Vernon ; Miller Mailey, Paxton ; C. M. Davis, Good Will; Michael Drawby, Susquehanna.

REPRESENTATIVES.

Friendship—Wm. H. Lynch, Wm. E. Barnes, Edward Crostman.

Hope—Samuel H. Ettla, Jacob Houser, E. L. Tittle.

Citizen—Chas. P. Meck, Thos. J. Earnest, George Weitzel.

Washington—Levi Wolfinger, William E. Brodbeck, Henry F. Young.

Mt. Vernon—John Barry, John Barr, John Fitzpatrick.

Paxton—John J. Zimmerman, James Walters, Miller Mailey.

Good Will—Jas. N. Blundin, George W. Lutz, Chas. M. Davis.

Mt. Pleasant—Luther R. Keller, John Fitting, Al. Meredith.

Susquehanna—John Keiser, J. B. Sparrow, Michael Drawby.

FIREMEN'S DAY.

In September, 1884, the State Firemen's Association were invited to hold their convention in 1885 at Harrisburg. The action taken by this body struck the key-note for the time of celebrating Dauphin County's Centennial. An earlier period had been suggested, but in deference to the volunteer firemen of the city, the week of the holding of their State organization was selected for these imposing exercises. From that time onward, the firemen worked to secure success, and the result no doubt exceeded the expectations of the most sanguine. Early in the year, the Firemen's Union was formed, and they proved the great power which made failure an impossibility. So fully impressed were the citizens of the city and county with what the firemen would and could do, that until almost the last moment, many had an idea that the Centennial celebration would be merely a "firemen's jollification," and nothing more. Those who knew what herculean efforts were being made to make each day's ceremonies grand and imposing, and spoke hopefully of the week's displays, had little sympathy. As each day passed with renewed Centennial splendor, the mass of the people only began to realize the crowning success which ever awaits the efforts of united and energetic association.

The firemen's display was no mere "jollification."

It was the representation of usefulness, bravery and honor, and came as a fitting close to the great Centennial week. The men who have no fear in time of danger turned out strong. Pennsylvania was not only represented, but from New Jersey, Maryland and the Virginias came the flower of volunteer firemen, alike a credit to themselves and the States they represented.

The magnificent weather, like that of the entire week, served to keep up the general joy, and it was the subject of remark that the clerk of the weather had a choice, and selected a lot of sunshine on hand, manufactured expressly for Harrisburg's Centennial week.

All Wednesday afternoon, that night, and Thursday morning the visiting firemen began to pour into the city. They came in all colors of uniforms—but they had on their business clothes, and could fight fire in them. They meant business, too, as was shown by the many ways in which they went about getting their line in order for marching. Their apparatus was in perfect condition, and only needed a little shine here and there to make them veritable pictures. The city was crowded, and it is not putting too high an estimate on the number to say that 40,-000 strangers were here. The railroads all ran extra excursion trains, which were crowded. Large special excursion parties were organized in near-by towns, which came early and thronged the streets. As on previous days, it was almost impossible to move, so dense was the crowd. All the fire companies were accompanied by many friends.

All night long the cling and clang of preparation went on, and the boom of the drum was heard every minute in the night. As the visitors reached the houses of their guests they were received with cheers and the ringing of bells. Many people did not go to bed at all, but roamed the streets, following bands and seeing companies received. With all the excitement there was no disorder. The firemen were early on the move in the morning, and Chief Marshal J. N. Blundin had his hands full receiving reports and giving directions to his large staff of officers.

At 10 o'clock the companies were formed into line and marched to their respective assignments. They were sturdy men in those lines, ready for duty when duty called, and fully deserving of all the homage that the city could tender them. And there remained no doubt that the people observed and appreciated these facts. The display of apparatus was of a high order of excellence. Every engine and hose carriage shone and glinted in the rays of the sun, while order and care were apparent from one end of the line to the other. Especial attention was paid to the older firemen or those who had done duty in the past. Among these were the splendid body of men from Philadelphia known as the Volunteer Firemen's Association. They were veterans without a doubt, and showed up in elegant style. The Bradford Exempt Fire Company was one of the most notable in line, their exceedingly handsome personal appearance causing the ladies to follow them with admiring eyes in every street. There was not a man among them

who was not well-built and good looking; all were
big, stalwart gentlemen, among them being fifteen,
none of whom weighed less than 200 pounds. While
here the latter were entertained by the Hope company of this city, a banquet being given to them on
Tuesday evening and other especial attentions paid
them. They were accompanied by the L. Emery, jr.,
band of twenty-three pieces, with Prof. P.
M. Black, leader. This was one of the best bands in
the line; and during their stay they serenaded a
number of prominent citizens, among them being
Governor Pattison, Gen. Simon Cameron. Mayor
Wilson and Col. Francis Jordan. Among other
notable companies, were the Altoona men, whose evo-
lutions while marching were loudly applauded. Too
much praise cannot be bestowed upon the excellent
appearance and management of our own firemen.
Not a company among them was lacking in any particular. They were all composed of fine, sturdy men,
neatly arrayed, and with apparatus that reflected the
highest credit upon their attention and usefulness.
They covered themselves and the city with glory,
and to them is gladly given the credit of furnishing
a beautiful and memorable *finale* to the centennial
celebration. The route of procession, as directed by
the marshals, was—Countermarch on Second street,
down Second to Chestnut, to Front, to Paxton, to
Second, to Meadow Lane, to Third, to Market, to
Fourth, to Reily, to Third, to Boas, to Two-and-a
Half, to Briggs, to Third, to State, to Front, and dis-
miss.

Chief Marshal Blundin, with Assistant Marshal

Walters, was at Second and Market streets, and received the division marshals and others as they came to report. It was fifteen minutes after 11 when the order was given to "forward march!" and the procession moved off in the following order:

Chief Marshal, J. N. Blundin.

Aids, James Walters, Paxton; James B. Floyd, Friendship; John P. Rupley, Hope; Frederick J. Cleckner, Washington Hose; Frederick J. Gastrock, Citizen; Charles F. Dawson, Mount Vernon; C. M. Davis, Good Will; Henry M. Kelley, Mount Pleasant; Amos Maley of Susquehanna, Blair Bollmer and Ed. Crossman; markers for the first division.

Following the marshal and aids was a four horse barouche, in which was seated the old veteran ex-Chief Engineer George C. Fager. The Citizen Fire Company, of which he is a member, presented him with a very handsome floral offering before leaving their house to join the procession.

First Division.

This division was composed of the guests of the Friendship Fire Company of Harrisburg. No labor had been spared to make a fine display, and the efforts of the company were amply rewarded, as will be seen by the array of visitors appended. It was headed by a platoon of chief and visiting engineers, as follows:

E. Zitzelman, chief engineer of Scranton fire department; John P. Dillinger, chief engineer of Allentown fire department; J. W. Harberson, chief engineer of Lebanon fire department; John Welsh, chief engineer, and Thomas Magee and Wm. Grimwood, first and second assistant engineers, of Harrisburg. A platoon of ex-chiefs of our own department followed: Albert Welper, of the Hope, Andrew Schlayer, of the Friendship, George V. Corl, of the Friendship, Isaiah Reese, of the Good Will. and ex-Chief John Mayer. of Altoona fire department. The division was marshaled by W. E. Barnes. In almost every case the visiting chiefs and ex-chiefs carried elegant silver horns, with elaborate floral decorations.

The Spring Garden Band, of York, with twenty pieces.

The Vigilant Fire Company of York, Harry Smallbrooke, foreman; Joseph Butt, assistant foreman. The men were equipped with regulation black hat, blue flannel shirts, black pants, white tie and gloves. Black fatigue caps were worn on their belts. Their elegant Button steamer, glittering in nickled splendor, was drawn by four magnificent Percheron greys, driven by A. K. Keever, of this city, and in charge of Assistant Engineers Michael Spangler and Edward Strine, of the Vigilant.

Ironville Band, of Lancaster county, with sixteen pieces of music, under the leadership Aaron Eshleman.

The Vigilant, No. 2, of Columbia; marshaled by Martin Smith, Edward Beck and Patrick Moriarty. Men equipped in red regulation hats, red shirts, white scarfs and black pantaloons. Attached to belts were white duck fatigue caps; headed by four pioneers, four men bearing branch-pipes and four with handsome silver lamps. Their pretty Clapp & Jones steamer was drawn by four elegant bays, driven by B. Houser, of this city. The Vigilant boys are a fine looking set of men, and were much admired for their gentlemanly deportment.

Worth Infantry Band, of York, Pa., 20 pieces, led by P. A. Waltman.

Union Fire Company, No. 3, of York, Pa., marshaled by James Reeling, assisted by Foreman Samuel Fruett. The men were equipped in black regulation hat, with silver shield, black pantaloons, red shirt and black fatigue caps. The company drew their beautiful parade carriage, which was handsomely trimmed and much admired. Beneath the carriage, with red, white and blue collar, was their favorite Newf Foundland dog, " Jacket."

Millerstown Band, of Millerstown, Pa., 22 pieces.

Vigilant Fire Company, No. 2, of Altoona, under the control of Chief Marshal William Westfall and Assistant Marshal Joseph Bennett. The company had no apparatus. It carried in line an elegant American flag, presented to it in 1881, at Reading, by the citizens, for having the second finest steamer in the line. Alderman B. F. Rose, one of the oldest firemen in the state, accompanied the Vigilant. As a marching company it took high rank. The men were equipped in dark blue overcoats, green regulation hats, with silver shield and gold letters, green belts and fatigue caps.

Citizen's Cornet Band, of Hummelstown, under the directorship of Capt. David Hummel, with 27 pieces, preceded the next sub-division who came in the following order :

Eight representatives of the Friendship Fire Company, No. 1, of Wilmington, Del., in citizens attire, with white and gold badges on lappel of coats.

Preceding the Friendship was a four-horse barouche, in which were seated Alexander Ramsey, ex-governor of Minnesota; A. E. Kapp, of Northumberland; Bucher Ayers, of Philadelphia, and Chambers Dubbs, of Harrisburg; this was followed by a carriage, drawn by a pair of greys, occupied by C. A. Landy, of Chicago; C. M. Anstett, chairman of the fire committee, of Bethlehem; S. Charles Seckelman, ex-chief of the Bethlehem fire department, and G. W. Wales, of this city, agent for the Eureka Hose Company, of New York. Then followed another barouche, drawn by a handsome pair of blacks, with visiting representatives of fire departments. The next vehicle, drawn by a fine pair of black horses, was occupied by James A. Green, vice president of State Firemen's Association; W. W.

17

Wunder, of Reading, secretary of the State Association; D. A. McCullen, assistant engineer of the Wilmington, Del., fire department, and John McCaffery, ex-assistant engineer of same department.

Friendship Fire Company, No. 1, of this city, marshaled by William H. Lynch, assisted by John Faerster; equipped in dark blue pantaloons, black regulation hats, with red shields, red flannel shirts, and white gloves. The column was flanked by two men bearing red silk guidons lettered in gold, and headed by a platoon of eight pioneers, and one of eight, bearing branch pipes, decorated with flowers. The hose cart, drawn by two dark greys, was decked in floral beauty and finished with a very pretty star of flowers and evergreens, carrying Coroner George F. Shindler. Their steamer, "Marion Verbeke," drawn by four blacks, driven by C. A. Kitzmiller, was also beautifully bedecked with floral designs, and shone with polished splendor. The company deserved great credit for the division under their care.

SECOND DIVISION.

The visiting companies of this division were the guests of the Hope Fire Company, No. 2, of this city. From the fact that two especially well-drilled companies, competing for the elegant gold marching medal, were guests of the Hope, this division attracted marked attention.

A platoon of visiting marshals headed the Hope's division.

The Altoona band, 32 pieces, lead by Jule A. Neff, furnished the music for this section of the procession.

Altoona Fire Company, No. 2, headed the column with an elegant large banner of blue silk, with their company motto lettered in gold, supported by four of their number. The men were equipped with regulation red hats with white shields, red shirts, black pantaloons and white duck leggings, white neck scarf and white gloves. Every man was armed with a highly polished pioneer ax. Drill commander Col. Malden Valentine took his men through a manuel of arms that was peculiar and new. The manœuvring and drill of this company was exceedingly fine and attracted marked attention. At every turn of the procession the company's superb drilling elicited rounds of applause.

Metropolitan Band of Philadelphia, twenty-five pieces, under the directorship of Thomas Lachell.

Philadelphia Volunteer Fire Association was headed by an elegant silk banner, elaborately painted, and four blue silk guidons. This fine body of old "timers" was well handled by Chief Marshal William Delaney, with William Kidd as aid and James Hood, George Young and Thomas Moore as assistant marshals. This company, composed of eighty men, drew their elegant parade carriage, of white, picked in gold and carmine, with reel of linen hose, and handsomely ornamented with floral designs. The men were equipped with grey overcoats, black regulation hats, black fatigue caps, black pantaloons and belt, and carried United States flags, presenting a pleasing and attractive appearance.

Friendship Cornet Band of Winchester, W. Va., with twenty-one pieces, led by T. H. Hoffman.

Friendship Fire Company of Winchester, W. Va., marshaled by Capt. Hardy, were equipped with dark blue pantaloons, white regulation hats, with silver front lettered in gold, white shirts with large red collar. Each man carried an ax or branch pipe.

Williamsport, Maryland, Band, twenty-one pieces, under the leadership of McHenry Steffey.

Independent Junior Fire Company, of Hagerstown, Md., was marshaled by Alexander M. Roberts, assisted by George Freidinger; men equipped in black pantaloons, red shirts, white scarfs, green regulation hats with gold shields, and white caps. Eight pioneers, with white ties and olive collars, headed the column. Their pretty Silsby steamer, a perfect mass of emblazoned nickel, was drawn by four magnificent greys, driven by T. Born, of Hagerstown. Following was a neat parade spider, painted in pea green, with handsome silver mountings, drawn by a pair of black steeds.

Lewis Emery, Jr., Band, of Bradford, Pa., with twenty-two pieces, under the directorship of P. N. Black.

Bradford Exempts, of Bradford. A great deal had been said of this organization long ere it reached the city, and when the people caught sight of Drum Major J. J. Lane they breathed a sigh of relief, inasmuch as they realized that the long-expected Exempts were close at hand. The reputation that preceded this company was fully supported by them in the elegant appearance they made in the pageant. They were equipped in grey overcoats, white belts, regulation black hats with white frontis-pieces, black pantaloons, white scarfs, and buff gloves. They presented an elegant appearance, and were the recipients of marked attention.

Liberty Cornet Band of Middletown, twenty-four pieces, led by Valentine Baumbaugh, followed by the Sons of Veterans' Drum Corps, Camp 15, thirteen men.

Hope Fire Company, No. 2, Harrisburg, marshaled by the President, Al. T. Black, with John Wells, William McCoy, and Jacob Kohler assistants. Three beautiful flags, one State flag, one national colors, and the other a new company flag, elegantly painted and edged with bullion fringe. The column was headed by a platoon of eight pioneers. The entire company numbered seventy-seven men, equipped with regualation hats, dark blue pantaloons, white gloves and scarfs, and black fatigue caps. Almost every member of the company was supplied with a tastefully arranged bouquet. Company drew their beautiful parade carriage, which was apparently a mass of solid silver. Their service carriage was drawn by two greys. The steamer was drawn by four blacks, driven by Dennis Dougheny.

The St. Thomas Cornet Band, of St. Thomas, Franklin county, twenty pieces, led by John Kessel.

Junior Hose Company of Chambersburg, marshaled by Captain George Pensinger. Uniform—blue shirt, trimmed with white, white leggings. Each member carried a branch pipe, and they were much admired for their marching. The Juniors are all young men, their uniform was handsome, and their splendid appearance gained them much applause. It may be said here that the Altoonas were given the right and the Juniors the left of the line because of their fine marching.

THIRD DIVISION.

Charles P. Meck, chief marshal.

Thomas Earnest, assistant marshal; Capt. H. C. Krebbs, marshal of the Sarah Zane; Chas. F. Gilmore, marshal of Washington Company, of Coatesville, Pa. The guests of the Citizen.

Sarah Zane Cornet Band, of sixteen pieces, with Edgar F. Snapp, leading.

Sarah Zane Fire Company, No. 3, of Winchester, W. Va., were equipped in dark blue pantaloons, shirt, regulation hat and white gloves.

The company had a handsomely decorated parade carriage. The head of this column was lead by two pioneers and three men carrying branch pipes. The Sarah Zane carriage had an arch upon it, on which could be plainly read " Pride of Sarah Zane," the same having been presented by the Citizen, of Harrisburg, about a year previous.

Star Band, of Coatesville, with twenty-one pieces, under the leadership of George Russell.

Washington Fire Company, of Conshohocken, Pa., marshaled by John A. Harrold. Uniform—long blue overcoat, regulation fire hat ; no apparatus.

Washington Fire Company, of Coatesville, also marshaled by Capt. Harrold, were equipped in regulation hats and dark blue overcoats. No apparatus.

Washington Hose Company, of Coatesville, Mordecai Markwood, chief marshal; chief engineer, George W. Brooks. Sixty men entered the parade, drawing a pretty bedecked spider. The vehicle was painted in green, with gold relief. The carriage was certainly beautiful, and it is doubtful whether it was equaled in the entire line.

The New Cumberland Cornet Band of twenty-two pieces, under the direction of Rush Dugan. Following was a double teamed barouche, in which was ensconced Daniel A. Kepner, John B. Tomlinson and C. F. Coates, old veteran firemen. A notable fact in this connection is that Messrs. Coates, Tomlinson and Geo. C. Fager are the last remaining members of the original Citizen organization, and Mr. Kepner was a member of the old Harrisburg Fire Company, from which sprang the Citizen company.

Citizen, No. 3, marshaled by Chief Thomas J. Earnest, assisted by T. F. Townsend. The men were attired in regulation uniform from top to toe, having regulation black hats, black pantaloons, red shirt, black belt and white tie, with buff cuffs and gloves. The column was headed by a platoon of four pioneers and four pipemen. The members of the company drew their handsome parade carriage, beautifully decorated with floral designs. The service carriage was drawn by two iron greys, driven by W. J. Meck. The steamer was drawn by four stout iron greys, driven by Peter Scrivner. The apparatus was prettily decked in flowers and bunting.

FOURTH DIVISION.

The fourth division was one of much excellence. The members of it were the Washington Hose and their guests, who were the Good Intent, of Pottsville. The division was headed by Frederick J. Cleckner, aid to the chief marshal. They marched without faltering, and everything that could be was done to insure the success with which they met.

The Third Brigade Band, of Pottsville, one of the best in the state, in strict military style, thirty-two men, under the leadership of J. I. Alexander.

Good Intent Engine Company, of Pottsville, marshaled by Peter White, assisted by Chief Engineer Fred. Meisninkel, of Pottsville. The men wore a peculiar, yet attractive, uniform. The overcoats were black, pants black and hats black, yet there were features that made them attractive. White frontispieces decked the hats, and fine red badges filled an appropriate place on their breasts. They numbered sixty-five men, and had with them a fine hose carriage, decorated, on which was seated a boy fireman. Their large engine was drawn by four plumed horses.

Elizabeth Band, twenty-one pieces, L. Sheetz leader, gave fine marching music.

Washington Hose Company, of Harrisburg. George W. Simmers was marshal, assisted by others. The men wore bright red shirts and handsome fire hats, the frontispiece of which flashed in the sunlight like bayonets. They had twenty-five men in line, and were followed by their hose carriage, upon which were seated David F. Jauss and Levi Wolfinger, old members of the company, with John Brown as driver.

FIFTH DIVISION.

The fifth division was made up of a fine hook and ladder display, under the charge and the guests of the Mt. Vernon Hook and Ladder Company, of this city. They handled their division in a manner highly creditable, and had as their guests the Pioneer, of Hagerstown; Empire, of Carlisle; and Good Intent, of Sunbury. E. B. Hoffman was marshal of the division, and with him marched W. H. Armstrong, of Hagerstown; J. D. Einstein, of Carlisle; W. H. Adams, of Sunbury, representatives of the various companies in line.

Hagerstown Band, of seventeen pieces, John Lockbaugh, leader.

Pioneer of Hagerstown, Md., marshaled by George H. Fisher and W. C. Lane. The men marched well for an undrilled organization. Grey shirts and white hats with red trimmings, and the usual black pants made up their uniforms. Their hook and ladder truck was drawn by four greys, the only decoration being a handsome wreath.

Carlisle Brass Band, L. C. Faber, leader, and twenty-one pieces.

Empire Hook and Ladder Company, of Carlisle, headed by James Durnin, George Ramsey, James Martin and Wm. Shrom. Michael Minnich, marshal. The men wore red shirts, red hats with black frontispieces and white badges. Truck in line drawn by four horses covered with light red blankets lettered in black. The "Hivers," as they are familiarly called at home never looked better. Their truck was decorated in an attractive manner.

Sunbury Cornet Band, twenty-three members, under the leadership of Joseph Kline.

Good Intent, of Sunbury. Blue badges, surrounded by old gold, adorned handsome blue shirts that added to the beauty of helmet hats worn by the members. William H. Adams, marshal, and Peter Rockafellow and William Hoffman as assistants; while Messrs. Dietz, Simpson, Shipman and Sinsox led the line. They made a fine showing. Four plumed bays pulled their truck.

State Capital Band, of Harrisburg, thirty-one pieces, W. P. Chambers, leader, and, as customary, excellent music was rendered.

Mt. Vernon, of Harrisburg, George Huston and Ross Blosser, marshals. A handsome silk banner carried in line which bore the mottoes, "Veni, Vidi, Vici," of the company, presented by their lady friends July 4, 1879. Black firemen's hats, red shirts, doe skin gloves, white badges and white ties adorned the persons of the Mount Vernon boys; and as the men are large, well formed and somewhat handsome in appearance, they did not fail to cause much admiration and draw enough commendation from the ladies to place a bouquet in the hands of almost every member. The unique, handsome and valuable Hayes truck, drawn by four handsome horses, was decorated in fine style. The Mount Vernon never looked better.

SIXTH DIVISION.

The sixth division had the Paxton company for its proper management, and well did they sustain their reputation as a company that looks after details to please the public. Their guests were the Rolla Engine Company, Elizabeth, N. J.; Vigilants, of Roanoke, Va.; and Union, of Carlisle. This division was admired as much as any in the line.

Drake's Veteran Zouave Band, of Elizabeth, N. J., nineteen men, William Drake, leader.

Rolla Engine Company, No. 2, of Elizabeth, N. J. This company had a mixed representation. J. Madison Drake, editor of the *Sunday Leader*, was marshal, and they had as their guests twenty-five veteran firemen dressed in citizen clothes with white helmets. These men invariably accompany the Rolla when away from the city. The pioneers of the Rolla were captained by John Benjamin. They wore fire red shirts, white hats with gold and red frontispieces, and marched like veteran soldiers. N. G. Smith was foreman, George Delvin first assistant, and H. Rudolph second assistant. They wore blue frock overcoats, and helmets. Forty men drew a handsome steamer, decorated and ornamented with a wreath and a pair of white doves.

J. M. Smith, with Wm. Baker and B. F. Kramer, as assistants, marshaled the Vigilants of Roanoke, Va.

Roanoke Machine Works Band, twenty-four pieces. N. J. Russel, leader.

Vigilant Steam Fire Company, of Roanoke, Va. Green shirts with white trimmings and white hats was the majority uniform, yet green hats with red fronts were worn by the linemen. Without apparatus. It was a company of which Roanoke may well be proud. A finer body of men never paraded the streets of this city. They were marshaled by W. F. Baker, his assistants being F. D. Shade and B. F. Kramer; captain of the company, J. M. Smith.

Union Fire Company Band of Carlisle, J. Dysert, leader, with sixteen men. They made excellent music and wore a full military dress suit.

Union Steam Fire Engine of Carlisle, E. J. Krause, carrying the handsome silk banner presented to them a few days prior by Mrs. James Bosler. Masters Reily and Shaeffer supported the banner. The marshal was Edward Brindle, and James Richards, assistant. The men wore a novel shirt. It was red trimmed with blue on the breast, while the hats were black with red frontispieces and red inlaid letters. Sixteen file men led off. Their handsome new parade carriage, valued at $1,500, and one of the handsomest seen in line, was drawn by the men. A spider carriage, labeled "Union, 1784," drawn by a mule with a blanket inscription "Loco Gets There," was in charge of a boy. This company, both in number and bearing, was a fine body of men, and greatly admired.

The end of this division was the only historical portion of the entire parade. Ten men dressed in all the costumes characteristic of the Indians and representing the tribes of John Harris' days, headed the division. Dan. Weaver was chief of the squad of imitation red men.

Paxton Band, twenty-one members, Willis Fountain, leader.

Paxton Fire Company of Harrisburg, John W. Lyne, marshal, and Samuel Dickey and James Banford, assistants. They were followed by A. E. Schreadly and John Lyne, as guidon bearers, and O. A. Griffith with a stand of colors. Reuben Bender, president. Eight men with axes and pipes and all carrying bouquets came next. They were followed by sixty-one men with new blue shirts, handsome hats and gold satin ties. They presented an attractive appearance and came in for a liberal share of favors from the many spectators. On their hose carriage were a number of small boy firemen, while their steamer, "John Harris," was drawn by four gray horses.

SEVENTH DIVISION.

The seventh division was composed of the Good Will and their invited guests, the Liberty Steam Fire Engine Company, of Allentown ; the Shawanee Hose Company, of Columbia ; the Columbia Steam Fire Engine Company, of Columbia ; the Nay-Aug Hose

Company, of Scranton; the Washington Independent Steam Fire Engine Company, of Sunbury, and the Reily Hose Company, No. 10, of this city. The head of the seventh was made up of George W. Lutz, president of the Good Will, marshal, and Peter Rhoads, John Porter and Aug. Steinman, assistant marshals. Chief Engineer Isaiah Reese, of the Good Will steamer, in full uniform, carrying silver fire horn, followed by a platoon, in which was W. H. Albright, of the Liberty Steam Fire Engine Company, of York; Alfred B. Reichenbach, chief marshal of the Liberty Steam Fire Engine Company, of Allentown, with his assistants, John D. Murray, John Huffort, and Oscar Mink, all wearing attractive and handsome uniforms. A. S. Steinmetz was in charge of the division marker. George W. Mumma, ex-first assistant chief engineer of the Good Will company, was also with the officers on the right of the division; the companies in the following order:

The Allentown Cornet Band, twenty pieces, led by Prof. Martin Klinger. The band wore a neat military uniform of blue cloth with gold trimmings.

Liberty Steam Fire Engine Company, Allentown. President Geo. Kline, foreman ; William Morrel and assistant Chief Engineer Muench, of the Liberty, of Allentown, each carrying a silver horn, and preceded by the officers, forming a platoon. They were equipped with blue shirts, enameled leather belts with company's name, regulation fire hats, white neck ties, gauntlets, and light linen fatigue caps. The Liberty were on their way home from a visit to York, and brought no appatus with them. This company was made up of good material, had many fine looking young men, and marched admirably.

Columbia Cornet Band, eighteen pieces, led by J. D. Slade. They wore neat blue cloth uniforms, trimmed with gold, making a very attractive appearance.

Shawanee Fire Company, No. 3, of Columbia, thirty members, mar. shaled by Charles C. Cassidy, assisted by J. Kauffman and Thomas Tuley. At the front were twelve pioneers, eight carrying branch pipes and four axmen. The Shawanee boys wore handsome uniforms— black pants, red shirts, New York regulation hats, white neck ties, monogram and "3" in green figure on breast. The steamer, a Clapp & Jones build, was drawn by a pair of horses, and the bright work of the machine shone like a mirror. Fireman George H. Lutz had charge of the apparatus.

The Newville Keystone Cornet Band turned out seventeen pieces, Charles Householder, Jr., leader. They wore handsome blue cloth uniforms, trimmed with gold, and blue cloth caps, navy pattern.

Cumberland Steam Fire Engine Company, of Carlisle, had forty-five handsomely equipped men in line. At the front of the column was President James A. Green; Vice President Frank E. Spahr; Secretary Fred. Treibler, and Treasurer Peter A. Spahr. The company was marshaled by William Gephart. Third-class Button steamer, "Geo. B. McClellan," drawn by four horses. The steamer was handsomely burnished, and made a fine appearance.

Nay-Aug Hose Company, No. 1, of Scranton, thirty-five members, handsome silk flag inscribed "Nay-Aug Hose Company, Scranton, Pa., organized 1858." The Nay-Aug had among its make-up many splendid looking young men. The officers were James Gilhool, foreman, F. W. Deitzelman, assistant. They had in line twenty-five members, wearing regulation fire hats, fine blue cloth coats, white enameled leather belts with "Nay-Aug" in raised letters, gauntlets and white neckties. They had no apparatus, having just returned from a visit to the New York firemen.

Washington Steam Fire Engine Company, of Sunbury, thirty members, were led by Ed. S. Young, foreman; Julius Moesleme, first assistant engineer; William H. Miller, treasurer. Uniformed in new red shirts, black pants, regulation white hats, white tie and black patent leather belts. Their third-class Silsby steamer was drawn by four-in-hand, very fine horses, adorned with red, white and blue cockades.

West Fairview Band, twenty-six pieces, H. J. Dunbar, leader.

Eight pioneers, four axmen and four branch pipemen of Reily Hose. G. W. Reily Hose Company, No. 10, had sixty-four equipped men in line. This was their first appearance in public, and they made an excellent display. They were uniformed as follows: Black pants, red shirts, white fatigue caps, and black silk ties.   Reily hose carriage handsomely decorated, and drawn by the members.   The company was officered as follows: John Peifer, marshal, assisted by Albert Sible, Charles De-Haven and Stanley Marshall.

Following the Reily Hose was an old time hand engine one hundred years old, which came originally from Philadelphia, and has been used at Pennsylvania State Lunatic Hospital since 1854.   On the top sat a young lady, under a canopy of red silk, representing the Goddess of Liberty.   She was attired in red, white and blue, with a wreath of golden wavy hair falling over her shoulders, and attracted much atten-tion along the route.

William T. Hildrup Band, Prof. Herman Newmyer, leader, turned out twenty-six pieces, in full uniform.

Good Will Steam Fire Engine Company, George Kautz, chief mar-shal, Martin L. McComas and William Smith, assistants.   Sixteen pioneers, bearing branch pipes and axes.   The company turned out seventy-five men, wearing black pants, red shirts, regulation hats, black neck ties, gauntlets with monogram on shirt.   They wore badges of white silk, tipped with blue, with a steam engine under monogram. Good Will hose carriage, drawn by a pair of cream-colored horses. William K. Verbeke, present City Controller, and the first president of the company, rode on this carriage over the route.   Good Will steamer, "Wm. K. Verbeke, No. 7," drawn by four handsome greys.   The steamer was literally covered with flowers, natural and artificial, and profusely decorated with bunting.

EIGHTH DIVISION.

The eighth division comprised the guests of the Mount Pleasant company, the lively and vigorous organization on "Allison's Hill." It was headed by A. C. McKee, of the Mount Pleasant Fire Company, as marshal; C. Frederick, of the Friendship Fire Company, of Chambersburg; Ira W. Kline, of the Hope, Manheim; and H. D. Cushing, of the Martins-burg Fire Department, as assistants.

The Junior Band, of Chambersburg, seventeen pieces, led by C. W. Eyster, handsomely uniformed and wearing helmet hats.

Friendship Steam Fire Engine Company, of Chambersburg, fifty members; William Miller, marshal, and William Henneberger and Henry Reby, assistants. They wore regulation fire hats, red shirts, pants, and gauntlets. Eight pioneers, four pipemen, and four axmen preceded the column. The rest of the members, except the officers, carried parade axes. Their steamer was an Amoskeag, and was drawn by four grey horses, with covers, on which " Friendship, of Chambersburg," was conspicuous.

Mechanics Band, of Martinsburg, twenty-five pieces, led by Jacob Watson. Their uniform consisted of handsome navy blue coats, with gilt trimmings, and navy caps.

Martinsburg, West Virginia, Fire Company, uniformed in red shirts, white caps, black pants, and white duck caps; C. O. Lambert, marshal, and Charles Diffenbach, assistant. Their Silsby steamer was drawn by Wm. T. Hildrup's four Norman horses.

Manheim Cornet Band, led by Clarence H. Young, had nineteen pieces, the members wearing blue cloth coats, gilt trimming, navy pattern caps and grey pants.

Hope Hose Company, of Manheim, numbered forty-one men, C. Bear, marshal, with Messrs. Behm and Houser, assistants. They wore red hats, red shirts, dark pants and white neck ties. They had in line an old hand engine of one hundred years ago. A transparency on its top read: "Hope No. 1, of Manheim," "Our first apparatus, organized A. D. 1825, incorporated, A. D. 1874." Two old fire buckets labeled "Hope, 6 and 7," and "Farmers Bank, 8 and 9," were on the platform. The levers were two iron contrivances like pump handles, one on each side. The old chuck-frames are still kept in the quaint looking little box.

Citizens Band, of Churchville, Jacob Strite, leader, twenty-five pieces, was uniformed in handsome new swallow-tailed coats, trimmed with gold, and caps of navy pattern.

Mt. Pleasant Hose Company, No. 8, was marshaled by John Fitting, and paraded forty-four men. The head of the procession was led by eight pioneers. The men wore regulation hats, red shirts, white cuffs, gauntlets, with white enameled belts with figure " 8 " in raised letters on them. Their carriage was handsomely trimmed and drawn by a pair of grey horses.

NINTH DIVISION.

This division comprised the guests of the Susquehanna Hose Company, of South Harrisburg. As the company was a new one, they were given few guests, but they treated them most royally. The marshal of the division was George Drawby.

Middletown Cornet Band, Valentine Baumbaugh, leader, with twenty-eight pieces.

The Liberty Steam Fire Engine Company, of Middletown, had seventy-five members in line, led by Harry Hipple. They were uniformed in black pants, red shirts and regulation fire hats, neckties and gauntlets. Their steamer which is the oldest in the State, was drawn by four black horses.

Paxton Cornet Band, of Linglestown, nineteen pieces, Joseph F. R. Lingle, Leader. They wore handsome blue cloth coats, swallow-tailed pattern, trimmed with gold lace, and white plumes on hats.

Susquehanna Hose Company, No. 9. The uniform consisted of red shirts, black pants, white caps and white enameled leather belts with figure "9" on front. Their carriage was drawn by the members. It was decorated with a double arch of evergreens, interspersed with flowers and bunting. On the apex of the arches was a large figure "9" in the top center of which swung a blood-finch. There were also a number of other pretty birds, notably a white heron, a South American parrot and other birds among the decoration. One year ago to the day the Susquehanna Hose Company was organized and this was a big celebration of the anniversary. The company turned out sixty-five men, all handsomely equipped. Martain Kain was marshal and Lawrence O'Connell, assistant. Their hose carriage was as bright as a new dollar.

SUMMARY OF THE PROCESSION.

Total in first division, . .	. 405
Total in second division, ...	652
Total in third division, . .	. 302
Total in fourth division, .	143
Total in fifth division,	. 269

Total in sixth division, . 382
Total in seventh division, . . . 395
Total in eighth division,. . 257
Total in ninth division. . . 177

Grand total. 2982

The parade moved over the route as published, and was greeted on every hand with manifestations of the greatest pleasure by the thousands who witnessed its marching. Many of the firemen were presented with bouquets and banners and flags, and every man who carried a trumpet had the mouth of it closed by a huge bunch of flowers. It took an hour and a half to pass a point, and then the marching was rapid. At two o'clock the parade was dismissed, and the various Harrisburg companies took their guests to large halls and gave them a substantial luncheon, at which there were many speeches and much merrymaking. So ended the big firemen's display of the Harrisburg centennial celebration. alike a credit and an honor to those gallant men who planned it and so successfully carried it to a magnificent ending. It was fitting that the event should go out in a blaze of glory, and we do not think any body of men are more capable of giving it that aspect than the firemen.

THE FIRE COMPANY DECORATIONS.

In this historical record of the celebration, the following description of the artistic decorations made by each company, who so royally entertained their guests, is worthy of preservation :

The Friendship company's double arch was a picture of artistic skill and graceful elegance. It was trimmed with spruce, liberally punctuated with miniature flags. The arch at the top was peaked, and this projection was occupied by a gilt globe, and three handsome flags arranged in fan shape. Beneath the arch were graceful festoons of bunting, amid which was suspended a flower-covered frame in the shape of a " Keystone" a large figure " 1 " indicative of the rank which the company holds in the department. Tri-colored flags were tastefully arranged on the sides, near the bases of the four posts of the arch, and at regular points along the curves of the arches themselves hung cylindric Chinese lanterns. Beautiful rustic fountains were located at each base of the four posts. The cupola of the house was trimmed with flags and flag bunting. The large gilt eagle under the cupola held in its beak a wreath of spruce and flowers, and the large gilt figure "1" on the building was surrounded with a similar decoration. The end pilasters of the building were draped with flag bunting, gathered and confined in the center with rosettes. A strip of flag bunting ran along the building between the first and second story, in the center of which was the word "Welcome." A gas jet star surmounted the central door, while flower wreaths and the figures " 1785 " and " 1885 " occupied places just above each of the side doors. There were a few minor decorative features, which, with those above described, combined to form a very handsome representation of artistic adornment.

The Hope decorations were of a very elaborate nature, and commanded universal admiration. The arch was a double one, and was trimmed with flags, bunting and small shields. It was surmounted by a statue of Liberty, holding a shield in the left hand and a folded American flag in the right hand. Above the head was a gas jet star, and directly below the feet a shield and anchor. The arch was festooned with bunting and laurel, well sprinkled with Chinese lanterns. Directly under the arch was the words "Hope,"—"1814"—"Welcome," in gas jets, the latter word being flanked with star gas-jets. On the pillars supporting the arches were pedestal-shaped brackets, each containing life-sized "dummy" firemen, the one dressed in modern and the other in ancient fireman's dress. At the base of the pillars were pots of exotic plants, and a few feet distant on either side of the street were two very handsome rustic fountains. The decorations of the house were profuse and beautiful. The apex of the cupola was surmounted with four flags in an upright position, while many other smaller flags occupied positions near them. Directly over the top of the cornice of the building was a large arch of looped red, white and blue bunting, in the center of which was a small shield, and the word "Hope" in large gilt block letters. At either side of the arch were beautiful double stars. Directly beneath the cornice was a large American flag, reaching across the entire building. This was gathered up in the center, and at the loop a large gilt eagle, supporting in its beak a long

18

piece of bunting which fell on either side, in graceful curves, to the beaks of smaller gilt eagles over each of the two end windows. Below the large central eagle were wreaths and double stars, with a handsome picture of a young fireman. The pilasters of the building were covered with narrow red and white striped muslin and decorated with wreaths and shields, the latter containing the State coat of arms. The large arch of the central door-way was draped in pleated blocks of red, white and blue bunting, so arranged as to convey the idea of a sunburst. The two side entrance doors were arched with spruce, thickly sprinkled with miniature flags, and the brick panels between the pilasters above and at the sides were draped with white and blue striped muslin. There were many other embellishments of a minor nature on the house and the premises. Enough, however, is here stated to give the reader an idea of what the Hope achieved in the way of handsome decorations. We have only to add that in performing their pleasant labor the derived very valuable assistance from the lady friends of the company.

The Citizen Fire Company had two arches — a double one at the intersection of Fourth and Walnut, and a single one on Fourth street, opposite their building. The double arch was of spruce and miniature flags, loopings of bunting and Chinese lanterns. A "dummy" fireman stood on the top and attracted much attention. The single arch, opposite the company's building, was likewise covered

with spruce and miniature flags, and festooned with
bunting. Beneath was suspended a handsome banner of blue silk, containing the words: "Welcome to
the Visiting Firemen." A supplementary banner of
white muslin was attached to this, containing the
words: "Citizen, No. 3." Both of the arches were
connected together by long strips of bunting with
very pleasing effect. The building was handsomely decorated. The cupola ornate with flags,
streamers and shields. Each of the windows and
central doorway were draped with flag bunting. A
gas jet star, with the letters: "Welcome Firemen,"
also in gas jets, surmounted the central doorway.
Above these was a handsome picture representing a
startling fire scene. Beautiful wreaths and Chinese
lanterns completed the decorations.

The Washington Hose Company's arch was of
striped bunting, gathered in at the sides, thus forming an opening suggestive of a tent entrance. The
apex was surmounted with a large figure "4," flanked
on either side with small flags. A second and smaller
arch fronted the main entrance to the house. This,
however, was formed of spruce and miniature flags.
From the center dropped a wreath of small flags,
a string of globular Chinese lanterns was suspended
across the street. The decorations of the building
were beautiful in their simplicity. A large United
States flag occupied the apex. Draperies of bunting
and spruce festooned with flags occupied suitable
points, and there were two shields on the upper front
of the structure, each bearing the word "Welcome."

A picture of Washington surmounted the central door of the building.

The arch of the Mt. Vernon Hook and Ladder Company was trimmed with flag bunting, and wreathed, screw-like, with laurel and spruce. At the parts where the arch sprung from the posts were shields and pedestal-like projections, containing pots of choice exotic plants. Handsome Chinese lanterns hung below the sweep of the arch, and on the top over the center were shields and small flags. The pilasters of the building were draped with simple as well as flag bunting, and further ornamented with wreaths of laurel. Over the large central doorway on a piece of flag bunting, was the word "Welcome,", surrounded by a wreath of laurel. Altogether the decorations were very handsome.

The double arch of the Paxton boys was a very handsome combination of bunting, spruce and miniature flags. Suspended beneath were graceful loops of bunting, and from the center depended a small wreath surrounding a stuffed "shitepoke," the tutelar divinity of the district in days "lang syne," when to be a "shitepoker" was esteemed an honor of no little degree, and as if to remind the present generation of that fact, directly beneath the "bird" was a label bearing the words "It never dies." At the four bases of the arch were pots of choice exotics. A smaller arch, parallel with the sideway, fronted the main doorway of the company's building, and was likewise tastefully trimmed with spruce and miniature flags The building itself was replete with decorative drapery. The cupola of the structure was artistically dressed with small flags, and alternate lengths of red and white bunting arranged vertically. The front pilasters of the main structure were covered with flag bunting. Curtains of flag bunting were looped gracefully at each of the windows. Above the principle door, the space between the pilasters was occupied with red and white bunting draped in the shape of an immense sun-burst. Below this was a framed picture of the attempt to burn John Harris. Smaller sun-bursts occupied a place over each one of the two side doorways. Altogether the decorations of the building and its surroundings formed a picture that gave the spectator a very enlarged view of the liberality and good taste of the Paxton company.

The Good Will Fire Company were commended for the variety and beauty of their decorations. Their large double arch was trimmed with spruce and miniature flags. The bases of the poles were wrapped with red, white and blue muslin, which formed a very pretty contrast with the green of the arch. The arch was handsomely festooned with bunting, and Chinese lanterns gave additional attraction to its appearance. The steeple of the building was thick with small flags, bunting and spruce wreaths. Long guy cords reaching from the two front corners of the building to the summit of the flag staff, were also strung their entire length with small flags, with very pleasing effect. A large United States flag, spread across the front of the building, was looped up in the center and trimmed with spruce. Long pieces of red, white and blue bunting, lozenge shaped and expanded in the center, occupied a large portion of the front pilasters, and were alike pretty and novel. A belt of white and blue bunting was stretched across the building below the second story windows, and there was an arch of spruce and bunting above the main entrance door, underneath, which, in large letters, was the word "Welcome." Arches of flags, bunting and spruce were also over each of the side doors, and these inclosed large stars, within which were portraits of Lincoln and Washington. The Calder street side of the house was also replete with flags, bunting and wreaths of laurel and spruce.

The Allison' Hill boys of the Mt. Pleasant, No. 8, put their best foot forward. They erected two fine single arches near their handsome new house, which were tastefully decorated with evergreens, bunting, flags, etc. From three flag-staffs, planted at the three corners of their house, floated beautiful streamers lettered "Chambersburg," "Martinsburg," and "Harrisburg,"—the first two names in compliment of their guests from the places designated. Around the top of the west front of their house, and around the corners of the belfry Chinese lanterns and flags were secured, and a beautiful flag floated from the tall staff on the cupola. The interior of their house was handsomely decorated—all kinds of devices being used for the purpose. On the Howard street side of their house the Mount Pleasant company made a very handsome triangular plot, nearly the entire length of the building, in the center of which was a mystic fountain and beautiful ferns.

The Susquehanna Hose Company, one of the youngest in the department, and occupying an unpretentious small frame structure, gave evidence that in matters of taste they were quite equal to their brother firemen. The arch in front of their building was very handsomely trimmed with flags and spruce, and the building itself was covered with tri-colored and flag bunting, arranged in loops and otherwise, with a very handsome effect.

The headquarters of the youngest company in the department—the Reily Hose, of West Harrisburg—was not behind the rest in decorations, circumstances considered. They had erected a handsome arch, trimmed it with taste, and displayed a profusion of flags, bunting and appropriate designs. The front of their house was draped in holiday attire.

ANTIQUARIAN DISPLAY.

EXECUTIVE COMMITTEE.

HENRY McCORMICK, *Chairman.*
JOSHUA M. WIESTLING, *Vice-Chairman.*

RUDOLPH F. KELKER,
HENRY McCORMICK,
JOSHUA M. WIESTLING,
CYRUS J. REES,
ELIAS Z. WALLOWER,
SAMUEL McILHENNY,

JOSEPH MONTGOMERY,
LUTHER M. SIMON,
ADAM K. FAHNESTOCK,
CHAS. S. SEGELBAUM,
AUGUSTUS R. SHELLENBERGER,
WILSON ELDER, *Secretary.*

LEBANON COUNTY AUXILIARY.

Mrs. G. DAWSON COLEMAN,
Mrs. JOHN B. McPHERSON,
Mrs. DAVID S. HAMMOND,
Mrs. WILLIAM M. GUILFORD,
Mrs. JOHN W. KILLINGER,
Mrs. GEORGE W. KLINE,

GRANT WEIDMAN, Lebanon,
ROBERT H. COLEMAN, Cornwall,
E. R. ILLIG, Millbach,
ISAAC HOFFER, Lebanon,
J. H. REDSECKER, Lebanon,
J. P. S. GOBIN, Lebanon.

SPECIAL COMMITTEES.

China—Old and New.

Miss Hannah Ianthe Johnson, Miss Sarah Beatty Egle,
Miss Sarah Esther Harris,   Miss Jane Irwin, Middletown,
S. Bethel Boude.

Church Furniture—Ancient and Modern.

Mrs. James McCormick,   Mrs. Warren A. Zollinger,
Miss Caroline Pearson,   Miss Emma Brady,
Miss Matilda Cox,   George R. Fleming.

Ornaments—Jewelry, Silver, &c.

Mrs. Charles A. Kunkel,   Miss Fanny M. Eby,
Miss Susan Wierman,   William P. Denehey.

Wearing Apparel—Before 1840.

Mrs. Francis Wyeth,   Mrs. F. Asbury Awl,
Mrs. John C. Kunkel,   Mrs. Eliza Espy Sergeant,
Mrs. J. Montgomery Forster, William Sayford.

Wearing Apparel—Since 1840.

Mrs. Chas. L. Bailey,   Miss Martha Orth Seiler,
Mrs. Robert E. Pattison,   Mrs. Joseph Strouse,
Miss Lavinia Dock,   E. Jay Jones.

Books of all Kinds—Old and New.

Miss Anna C. Weir,   William A. Kelker,
Mrs. H. O. Witman,   John B. Seal, Millersburg,
Mrs. John W. Simonton,   Miss Julia Snyder,
Miss Bertha Witman.

Glass—Old and New.

Mrs. George Bergner,   Miss Regina G. Calder,
Miss Martha Buehler,   Miss Elizabeth Bergner,
Edwin M. Haldeman.

Musical Instruments—Ancient and Modern.

Mrs. John R. Shoemaker,   Alexander Roberts,
Miss Georgiana Huston,   Charles A. Bigler,
                    Leonard H. Kinneard.

Needle Work—Silk, Wool, Linen.

Mrs. Richard J. Haldeman,   Miss Jane J. Dull,
Mrs. M. W. McAlarney,   Miss Mary Whitman, ·
Mrs. C. H. Brelsford,   Miss Jennette Cameron,
                    James M. Lamberton.

Relics of Indian Wars ; those of 1776, 1812, 1846, and 1861, including, Arms, Flags, Accouterments and Clothing.

Louis W. Hall,   Edmund Mather,
George Garverich,   W. J. George,
George E. Reed,   Wilson C. Fox,
                    Frank Kinneard.

Implements of Early Husbandry.

Leander N. Ott, Rockville,   Gabriel Hiester, Estherton,
J. J. Milleisen, Lower Paxtang,   Dr. Thomas G. Fox, Hummelstown,
J. Ed. Rutherford, Lochiel,   John Motter, Harrisburg,
                John H. Backenstoe, South Hanover.

Miscellaneous.

Mrs. T. Rockhill Smith,   Miss Emma Boas,
Miss Isabella M. Hays,   Mrs. Edward H. Hickok,
Miss Rebecca Brown,   William F. Bailey.

Household and Kitchen Furniture, Bedding, Linen, &c., of the Early Settlement.

Mrs. George W. Reily,   Miss Martha Orth Alricks,
Mrs. William K. Cowden,   Miss Mary Sergeant,
Mrs. James Calder,   Edward Z. Gross.

Pottery—Old and New.

Mrs. Joseph B. Ewing,   Miss Ann Hackett,
Mrs. Thomas Hammersly,   Miss Margaret I. Boas,
Mrs. Thomas Elder,   Miss Helen Espy,
                    Miss Mary Berghaus.

Works of Art—Portraits, Engravings, Photographs, Crayons, &c.

LeRue Lemer,
Miss Bella Fager,
Miss Martha Pollock,
Miss Sarah B. Chayne,
Miss Cora Martin.

Indian Relics—Stone, Wood, Iron.

W. E. Kirk, Lochiel,
W. W. Geety, Dauphin,
John Ringland, Middletown,

Decorations.

Mrs. Susan B. Ray,
Mrs. George C. Bent,
Mrs. D. L. Jauss,
Mrs. B. Frank Etter,
William T. Hildrup, jr.

Coins, Currency, &c.,—Old and New.

Mrs. Henry McCormick,
Frank Deitrich,
Jeremiah Uhler,
Naudain Hamilton,
Newton H. Davies,
Benjamin M. Nead.

Harris Memorial.

Mrs. Isabella S. Kerr,
Mrs. Elizabeth H. Kerr,
Miss Nellie Pearson,
Miss Mary W. Kerr.

Grandmother's Room.

Mrs. Seneca G. Simmons,
Miss Myra Simmons.

THE ANTIQUARIAN DISPLAY.

To the Dauphin County Historical Society is due the credit for originating, what has been conceded on all sides the most unique, as it was the most successful, exhibition of the kind ever held in this or any other country—the Antiquarian Display of the Centennial of the City and County. Early in 1883, the subject was suggested by the Editor of this volume, at a meeting of the Society. And in fact, when, at a subsequent date, a committee was appointed to take charge of the Centennial ceremonies, it was not then the intention that this committee should direct the entire ceremonies—but simply to control the exhibition and to prepare for the literary exercises. The message of Mayor Wilson, (previously referred to,) however, and the prompt action by the City Councils in appointing a similar committee to confer with the former, completely changed affairs, and before the members of the Historical Committee were aware—of their number A. Boyd Hamilton, Esq., was the president, and William H. Egle, M. D., general secretary, of the joint organization. The Antiquarian Display, however, was not lost sight of in every preparation made looking to a grand and successful celebration, and it may be here stated that to the individuals named, in connection with George Wolf Buehler, Esq., also of the Historical Committee, were the people of our goodly city and county indebted for that marvelous exhibition, which not only gave eclat to the Centennial proper, but added to its financial success. Few have the remotest idea of the difficulties encountered, and it is not to be wondered at the agreeable surprise universally acknowledged, when the display was arranged and opened to the public.

It is certainly not the intention to forget the efforts made by the citizens of our neighboring county of Lebanon,—of the indefatigable labors of the committee, of which body Mrs. G. Dawson Coleman was president, nor of the munificence of the loan of Robert H. Coleman, Esq., of Cornwall, which added so much to the splendor of the exhibition. Our gratefulness to them is not forgotten in our self-glorification, and all our citizens who witnessed the wonderful display, fully appreciated whatever was done by them to insure the success thereof. Few of any of these committees may be here in Anno Domini 1913, when Lebanon county shall celebrate, with all the "pomp and circumstance," the glory of her centennial, but those who come after us, will remember the disinterested labors of those of A. D. 1885, and redouble every energy to make that future celebration overshadow the one which has now passed into history.

At the first, the greatest difficulty encountered, was the securing of a proper place for holding the exhibition. There seemed to be but one building large enough, but so great was the rental asked that the committee looked further. The erection of a temporary structure was suggested, but this did not meet with much favor. At last, when a fairer offer was made by the manager of a rink located on Chestnut street, near Fourth street, it was decided by a unanimous vote to accept the offer, and every arrangement made to place the building in the best possible shape for the reception and display of the articles for exhibition. This was an herculean task, but the various committees, without exception, were so earnest and enthusiastic that within the period of forty-eight hours, the Palace Wonderful rose up in all its uniqueness and beauty.

On the day of the opening of the exhibition, Thursday, September 10, 1885, "ye local of the *Telegraph*" rhapsodied in this wise: "The sound of the hammer and saw had almost ceased at the State Capital rink to-day, and by noon it was announced that all the rare and quaint old articles would be in position for the opening this evening. The vast room is a regular old curiosity shop, and the antiquarian as he wanders through it is filled with delight. The lover of the curious will find here all that he is looking for, while the idle looker on, who has no object in his visit beyond that of curiosity to see what is here, can while away several hours and be astonished at every turn.

"The entrance will be from Chestnut street, the exit on Blackberry avenue, at the rear of the hall. Turnstiles at the entrance will prevent anything like a rush, and it is expected that everybody who enters will have the even change—a twenty-five cent piece.

Samuel W. Fleming, Treasurer, with Hother B.
Hage, A. J. Youlin, and O. L. Stackpole as assistants,
will oversee this part of the building.

"To particularize in a description of the exhibits
would simply be impossible. It would take a dozen
reporters, working ten hours a day, two weeks to note
everything within these four walls. It would be a
stupendous task—so great is the number and varied
the articles to be seen. Dauphin county has re-
sponded nobly to the appeals of the various committees, and from almost every township there have been
sent relics of ye olden time and curious things. Lebanon county has covered herself with glory, and
occupies a large space with the exhibits of her citizens.

" Three rooms are partitioned off and given up to
the collections of antique furniture. One of these
contains relics of the Harris family, the old-style
furniture and household implements, and, if you care
to, you can look in a mirror wherein the great and
only George Washington once surveyed himself.
The display of old furniture all the way through is
good. Of old spinning wheels and rare clocks there
are many and handsome specimens. Old books, in-
valuable, from the beautiful volumes of manuscript
written by the monks on vellum, and the ponderous
Bibles of pre-reformation days, down to the first
rudely illuminated pamphlet ever made in America,
(in Harrisburg, by the way,) can be seen in great
numbers. In this respect the exhibition is a gigantic
success, and the bibliopole can spend hours looking

at what to him is a perpetual delight. The collection
of Indian relics comprises all that has been collected
for years by men who made the hunting of such
things a specialty. There is an especially fine collection of Indian relics found in the vicinity of Harrisburg by our local collectors. There are besides
collections of modern Indian curiosities from the
Far West, which are exceedingly interesting. The
whole world has paid tribute to the miscellaneous
exhibition. India, Japan, Europe, Africa, and countries too numerous to mention, contribute their curiosities, which are placed in good position for visitors
to see. Even old Pompeii and Herculaneum have
given up of their buried treasures, and from the first-
named buried city comes a chair that is of peculiar
value. The collections of Mrs. G. Dawson Coleman,
Robert H. Coleman, and Mrs. Horace Brock, of Lebanon, are simply superb. They comprise the most exquisite and rare silver work, gold work, old clocks,
laces, Gobelin tapestries, pictures, china, bronzes, old
furniture, and a thousand different things that to
enumerate and describe would cover a page of the
largest newspaper in this city. In ancient needle-
work there are rare clothing, household articles,
pretty trifles, quilts, comforts, towels, etc., all tastefully arranged and properly labeled. This department will be a source of perpetual delight to the
lovers of ancient needle-work. A quaint exhibit is
that of the costumes of years ago. Dress a man or
woman in some of the costumes on exhibition and
put them on a Harrisburg street, and a big crowd

19

would be attracted in a short time. All the clothing is arranged on dummies, and shows to excellent advantage. Perhaps the most curious in the men's department are the old-time military and dress suits. In the ladies' department there is the figure wearing a huge bonnet, called a calash, very tony a century ago, but one wonders how, when Jonathan wanted to kiss Jerusha he ever could get far enough inside that calash to reach her pretty mouth. Of old pictures and engravings there is a large and wonderful collection. Chiefly interesting are the portraits of old Dauphin county people—family portraits that have been transmitted from generation to generation, and are regarded with veneration. Then there are quaint old silhouettes and pen portraits, side by side with the oil portrait and photograph, and the really splendid modern paintings, the work of Harrisburg artists. The collection of coins at this exhibition cannot be duplicated in America. Everything may be seen here from the widow's mite to the modern $20 gold piece. Chinese razor and bird money, coins found in Pompeii, bullet money, India money, Japanese money, coins of Europe, Asia, and Africa, old Roman coins, copper coins that weigh over a pound, silver coins fifteen ounces in weight, old Continental and Colonial money. In fact, the collection is indescribable. The china and glassware department is complete, and wonderfully beautiful are the exhibits. Old china that is looked upon as almost sacred by its owners, may be seen here, magnificent vases in profusion, rare specimens of early

American china and cut glass, old tea-sets, curious silvered china and beautiful Bohemian glassware. The decorated china is elegant and tasteful, and some of the finest collections in the country have contributed their rarest gems to this exhibition. All in all, the varied collections at the exhibition are worth going a long distance to see. They are instructive and interesting—they are, as it were, educators. We have not mentioned all that may be seen, reserving for future issues to give prominence to them. Everybody in Harrisburg should go. The doors will be opened this evening, and no doubt the building will be crowded."

The *Independent*, in its issue of the same date stated: "From the people of judgment and cultivated taste, who had an opportunity to examine the exhibits now arranged in the rink, where the Antiquarian Exhibition will open this evening for the public, the general expression was this morning that it is the most wonderful and magnificent display in antiquity they had ever seen. To describe it in detail would occupy all and more of the space we devote in one issue to reading matter, and to make special selections for description would be invidious in distinction and unfair in personal mention. We therefore confine ourselves in this first notice of the exhibition to generalities and in calling attention to what some people from a distance have brought to the rink. To the right of the building, from the Chestnut street entrance, are the Coleman exhibits, those of Robert Coleman, of Cornwall, Lebanon county, and those of Mrs. G. Dawson Coleman, of North Lebanon, Lebanon county. To name the articles in both these exhibits would faintly give an idea of what they consist. In wealth of volume, splendor of each article, magnificence of construction, variety of design and use, and antiquity of origin, they are dazzling and wonderful. The bulk of the Coleman exhibit is of historic interest, covering epochs in French and English history, identified with the reign of Napoleon I. The splendor of some of the courts of Bourbon Kings in jewelry, dresses, gems, furniture, silver and gold ware, paintings and other rare curiosities is here shown. These two collections alone will afford a student in art and antiquity hours of gratifying study. Running along the same side of the rink, on tables, shelves, and hung on the walls, are piles of every imaginable kind and class of products in art and mechanism, the work of skilled hands and artistic fingers, of genius and cunning, which the people of the last and those of the early part of the present century used in household and personal adornments, showing the taste, refinement, and culture of two generations that have been gathered to their graves. In this stately collection are dresses a century old, bonnets worn when Washington was in Harrisburg, chairs on which revolutionary heroes rested, tables and dishes used one hundred and one hundred and fifty years ago, rare old paintings, delicate needle work, the output of the carding machine and the spinning wheel, and the anvil beat by hammers which rang a century ago. We repeat, that to describe these

articles is impossible, and to study them all in detail
will demand patience, care, and judgment, and the
visitor to the exhibition who can bring these qualities to bear on the exhibits certainly has a rich treat
before him.

"On the left side of the rink, from the Chestnut
street entrance, and down the three aisles formed by
the placing of rows of cases and tables, are collections of articles, all of more or less antiquity, many
of them gems of art and triumphs of mechanical
skill, and aggregating such huge displays as are well
calculated to overwhelm the visitor. The general
expression is, how could so much wealth, such novelty in antiquity and in history be so long hidden
from public view? The collection, in its historic interest, will give character to Dauphin and Lebanon
counties, as containing relics showing the culture of
the early settlers in each, the aids which furthered
their industry, and the machinery which lightened
their toil. It shows, too, how the homes of the ances-
ters of the present citizens of these counties were em-
belished, the cradle at which their great-grandmothers sang their lullabys, the platters from which their
ancestors ate, the chairs on which they sat, the Bibles
they read, the hymns they sang, the clothes they
wore, the covers under which they slept and the
stoves at which they were warmed.

"In this collection of antiquities of domestic use
and personal wear, in industrial appliance and home
adornment, we repeat, are articles which it is impossible to enunciate in a notice like this, which is

designed merely as a general direction to the public
to examine the collection in detail. The reader who
fails to do this will miss a rare opportunity to famil-
iarize himself with the past by means of the antiquities thus handed down, as well as to behold in these
mute relics of by-gone days the progress we have
made since living men and women used them in
their every day life."

An editorial in one of the daily newspapers of the
same date says: "The collection of antiquarian exhibits is a surprise and source of gratification to even
the most sanguine of its projectors. The beauty of
the exhibit is in the unexpectedly large number of
contributions and contributors, and still more in the
interesting character of the articles, and the very
small proportion of no particular interest. In the
items of ancient furniture and garments, the old man
or woman may stand lost for hours in reminiscences
of his or her childhood, recalled by the dresses the
father or mother wore. Grandfather's wedding coat
of fine broad cloth and antique cut; grand-mother's
wedding dress of richly embroidered and beautiful
satin; or, at the bonnet stand, attracted by a collection of calashes, those coquettish little head coverings
in silk, rigged like a gig top, he stops, and memory
travels back over the waste of years until he seems
to stand again in the presence of the sweet, bright-
eyed, and merry girl, who, when she met him would
pull the top forward by its ribbon, and peep with
roguish eyes, demure and tantalizing, from under it,
and then let it fall back, and with joyous frankness

laugh in his face. The sensations produced by contact with the old things which recall our youth, and the still older, which would recall the youth of our fathers and mothers could they come back from the mysterious land to see them, are worth all the trouble and cost of the collection. Beside these are books printed in the year the art of printing was discovered; manuscript books written in exquisite beauty upon fine vellum, so long ago that their date can only be guessed at; table service brought across the sea long before the struggle for independence, and even while the first colonists on the coast were building block-houses to shelter them against the attacks of Indians; bed clothing woven by the great-grandmothers of the old people of to-day; wonderful relics of the Indians who were found here when our ancestors first came: beautiful specimens of gobelin tapestry; articles of furniture, among them a metallic chair found in a tomb in the ruins of old Pompeii; a charming portrait painted on a cobweb. But why try to give an idea by mentioning the details; the keenest observer will require two days to get a satisfactory idea of the exhibit, and still go away wishing you had more time. The exhibit is now open to the public, and is to continue open all next week. There are none to whom it will not prove of interest, and more to those who stay long enough to study it, than to those who only take a running look through it, and then leave without more than a passing view of it."

"The Antiquarian Display in the rink," said the

Sunday Telegram of the 13th, "which was thrown open to the public on last Thursday evening, is an important and charming feature of the Centennial celebration. The managers having charge of the collection of the exhibits, spared no pains to secure valuable articles of all kinds, possessing the attributes of age. And they have been eminently successful in their endeavors. They have gathered from this and other counties one of the most elaborate, interesting, and valuable collections of articles ever seen in this State, with the exception of the great Centennial at Philadelphia. After an infinite amount of labor, and a demonstration of fine taste, all the articles have been splendidly arranged in the commodious rink building. It is impossible to enumerate even any noticeable portion of the exhibits. They include rare and ancient furniture, clothing, and specimens of art, exquisite in workmanship, and of almost incalculable value. The display from Lebanon county is most notable, and is a part of the fine curiosities of the wealthy Coleman family. Among this display is an elegant piece of gobelin tapestry of wonderful workmanship. It is, in fact, one of the most beautiful specimens of that work owned by any family in the United States. Then there are rich and elegant court dresses, costly antique clocks, and a handsome display of delicate needlework. Along one side of the room are three apartments furnished in the style of ye olden time. There are pieces of quaint old furniture, staid working chairs, and hoary spinning wheels in abundance.

The Harris memorial room attracts general attention. In it is furniture once used in old John Harris's home. There are old books in abundance, and rare Bibles that have come down through four centuries to their present owners. The display of carved wood, ivory, chinaware, Indian relics, and ancient wearing apparel are all of a first-class order. One of the most curious articles in the rink is a metal chair, dug from the ruins of Pompeii, and supposed to be many centuries old. It is in the Coleman collection. A double row of electric lights have been placed in the rink, and there will be turnstiles at the doors. The admission fee has been placed at twenty-five cents. One of the features of the exhibition is the register placed near the entrance by F. L. Hutter. It is an elegantly bound volume with advertisements upon each page and place for the visitors to subscribe their names."

Other newspapers, at home and abroad, spoke in terms of the highest commendation of the value and extent of the exhibit, expressing at the same time wonder and surprise at its marvelous character. Over and above these considerations and the lessons taught thereby, was the financial success of it. By and through it the General Committee, as well the people of the city and county, were spared the mortification incident to a depleted treasury, and an indebtedness which might have been difficult to liquidate.

Owing to the failure in preserving a full record of every article loaned, notwithstanding the efforts of

the General Committee to secure this, the lists which
follow may not give that fair showing which they
ought to do. Many of the exhibitors prepared be-
forehand, which all should have done, a list of every
article loaned. This will account for the completeness and accuracy of some. We believe we have the
names of all contributors, and these are arranged
alphabetically, whether loans are given with them
or not. We have endeavored to prove faithful to the
trust confided in us, and no one can say that we
have not performed our duty conscienciously. We
can not be held responsible for the short-comings of
others, and only give what we have got.

LEBANON COUNTY EXHIBIT.

BROCK, MRS. HORACE, Lebanon:

Old Venetian clock five hundred years old, and entirely made by
hand. This was the first style of clock ever made for private use.

Old Austrian watch, which repeats the quarters of the hour with two
bells.

A collar of Venetian punto in aria, which was the first point lace ever
made, and is all of the geometric design, probably taken from Greek
models. None of this lace has been made since the latter part of the
sixteenth century.

A piece of early point de Venice, called Stellata. Made in the seventeenth century, and no longer produced.

A very fine specimen of the "queen of lace"—the famous Rose point
de Venice. Made in the seventeenth and eighteenth centuries, but not
now.

Modern copy of old Rose point.

Modern point de Venice. The finest lace now made.

Point de France lace of the eighteenth century.

Flemish lace of the seventeenth century.

Valencienne lace of the seventeenth century.

Mecklin lace of the eighteenth century.

Genoise lace of the eighteenth century.

English lace of the seventeenth century.

Point d'Elençon lace of the eighteenth century—Rococeo style.

Modern point d'Alençon.

Modern Mecklin.

Modern Brussels point a l'Aiguilles. The finest Brussels lace.

Modern Brussels point applique.

COLEMAN, ROBERT H., Cornwall:

Two old paintings of Venice, by Vetunhe.

Two old clocks, time of Louis XIV.

Table cover owned by Marie Antoinette.

Piece of green velvet, embroidered in fleurs de lis and gold stars, used as a rug by Marie Antoinette at Trainon.

Two gilt chairs, with imperial eagle in a crown on the back, belonging to a set owned by Napoleon I.

Three old Roman statuettes.

Bronze group, Farnese bull.

Pair of old bronze knockers.

Gilt fire set (five pieces) used by Napoleon at Elba.

Pair of andirons used by Napoleon at Elba.

Old majolica inkstand.

Carved walnut bellows, Italian, of the sixteenth century.

Breast pin—antique Grecian work—turquoise, cameo, bacchanalian scene.

Three gold Etruscan rings, from tombs near Betolle.

Child's bronze chair, buried in the tomb of a young Prince, near Naples, 2,500 years ago. (This is the only perfect chair of its kind ever found.)

Bottle from the tomb of Chiusi.

Six vases, &c., of curious shapes, from Cortona.

Three Chinese mummies, from Cortona.

Three Roman lamps.

Two old Etruscan terra cotta panels.

Old terra cotta—St. John preaching in the wilderness.

Six old Etruscan vases.

Old Dutch inlaid table, containing writing desk, chess board, &c.

Three ribbons of the Order of the Legion of Honor, worn constantly by Napoleon, and afterwards given by him to his brother Jerome.

Report, addressed to General Napoleon Bonaparte, Commander-in-chief, and containing his signature.

Old ebony box, inlaid with ivory, and representing mythological subjects.

Head of scepter of an Etruscan high priest, very rare, from a tomb at Corneto.

Etruscan bronze specular mirror, very fine, from tomb at Orvieto.

String of Etruscan beads, from tomb at Chiusi, near Naples.

Bronze bracelet from same tomb.

Two old Grecian capitals.

Silver frontlet—antique—tomb at Corneto.

Set of necklace and armlets, from same tomb. Of great interest and value.

Pair of ear rings, from tomb at Orvieto.

Pair of Venitian ear rings, (A. D. 1550.)

Carved wooden chair, from San Donato palace.

Case of small jewelry, found in tombs at Orvieto, Sarteano and Chiusi.

Ancient Roman comb, for hair ornament.

Pair of ear-rings from Sarteano, with marks of fire on them, the corpse having been burned.

Bronze rings from Chiusi.

Writing desk, in gold and silver gilt, given by the Queen of Westphalia to her husband, King Jerome, brother of Napoleon Bonaparte. In the center are the initials J. N., with the royal crown, and are also on the other parts of the desk. There are secret springs which open places where the king kept many private papers.

Marble bas relief, A. D. 1550. Subject: Faun, satyr, &c.

Terra cotta bas relief, of old Florentine school Jupiter.

Two old rebel flags.

Embroidered picture, very valuable.

Knives, spoon, and fork, gold; belonged to Marie Antoinette.

Two pieces of Persian metal work.

Stiletto, belonged to Corsini de Medici, A. D. 1540, with the arms of the Medici family engraved on one side and the initials of Corsini on the other. The sheath is silver mounted. The knife itself is hollow, and serves as a sheath to a very fine stilletto, with a notched point for poison, to which the great duke used to treat (?) his friends when he wished to quietly dispose of them. The silver chain was worn around the waist and attached to the belt by a large silver clasp, on which are the head of Jupiter and the arms of the Medici in high relief.

Jeweled box, with the eagle of France and the arms of Westphalia and Wurtemburg in gold. Belonged to Catharine of Wurtemburg, Queen of Westphalia.

Knife, fork, and spoon (silver) used by Napoleon at Elba.

Music stand, designed by Louis XVI, when Dauphin, for Marie Antoinette, with monogram in the center.

Silver and gilt chalice, ornamented with medalions which represent the portraits of Peter the Great, Catharine and Alexis, the Russian eagle and two inscriptions, (Russian.)

Hexagonal tea caddy.

Pair of Japanese bronze candle-sticks.

Crown of Madonna in silver.

Tankard, silver and gilt, (1707.)

Tankard, silver, (1705.)

Tankard, Russian work. On the cover the head of Peter the Great, around the tankard, a subject from the Old Testament, Isaac and Rebecca.

Tankard, German work of the seventh century.

Tankard, Holland.

Vase, with portrait and arms of Napoleon, presented to him by his brother.

Coleman, Mrs. G. Dawson, Lebanon:

Tea pot, a specimen of the earliest English plated ware. Part of Captain George Dawson's camp outfit in the Revolution.

Repeating watch in blue enamel. The figures on the face strike the bells every hour.

Very old Swiss watch.

Antique enameled watch. The chatelaine a rooster with its tail of rubies, diamonds, and emeralds, and the body formed of one large pearl.

Antique enameled watch in an enameled stand. Italian.

Old enameled pendant. Italian.

Order of St. George. English.

Old enameled Venetian ear rings.

Tankard of 1700.

Pair old silver beer mugs.

Pair old silver goblets.

Pair silver drinking cups, from Russia.

Old silver baptismal cup from Norway.

Silver rose water sprinkler from Constantinople.

Scissors of Damascus steel, inlaid with gold, from Damascus.

Silver necklace from India.

Silver necklace from Algiers.

Silver lamp from the Holy Sepulchre at Jerusalem.

Gold sugar bowl and spoon and cream pitcher from Russia.

Two large spoons, in gold and enamel, from Russia.

Pair old silver coasters for decanters. English.

Nubian necklace set with uncut stones.

Pearl shell from the Red Sea, carved at Bethlehem, in the Holy Land.

Book of pressed flowers gathered in various parts of the Holy Land and bound in Jerusalem in olive wood from the Mt. of Olives.

Antique lamp. Rome.

Ornament cut from Jade, the holy stone of China.

Picture painted on a cobweb.

Old silver lamp made in Jerusalem.

Presse papier, ornamented with the various stones of Russia.

Very old plate. Vienna.

Old Delph china ornaments set in silver.

Screen of very old Chinese tiles.

Antique fan of 1780.

Antique cloisonne ornaments—various colors. Chinese.

Specimen of the first china made near Philadelphia.

Specimen of glass cut at Pittsburgh early in this century.

Antique bellows of the sixteenth century. Venice.

Very old bronze knocker. Italian.

Silk dress, embroidered by hand, and worn at the Court of Queen Anne—1706.

Antique medicine case, in sections, of gold and lacquer. Chinese.

Six antique spoons, marked in Hebrew. Jerusalem.

Two large antique Apostle spoons.

Four very old spoons from Holland.

Antique Swiss spoon of the Canton Berne.

Twelve very old silver Apostle spoons.

Six gold tea spoons, enameled with views, very old. Russia.

Eight gold tea spoons, enameled in colors. Russia.

Two very old Apostle spoons, with bowls of wood.

Three silver Nubian bangles.

Silver necklace from an Arab Sheik.

Silver ornament worn by the women of Bethlehem on the top of the head.

Silver ornament worn by the Bethlehem women under the chin, and fastened to the head piece.

Dutch spoon marked 1590.

Pair of silver ornaments worn by horses in Arabia.

Saddle cloth used by an Arab Sheik.

Specimen of very old India embroidery.

Old Russian embroidery.

Two pieces of silk woven with gold thread at Damascus.

Two silk sashes woven with gold thread at Damascus, Syria.

Silk sash worn by Arab runners at Cairo, Egypt.

Two pieces of old embroidery from Cairo, Egypt.

Piece of ancient embroidery from Bethlehem in the Holy Land.

Turkish towel embroidered in gold.

Old bouquet holder. Chinese.

Antique set of enamel.

Articles dug from the ruins of Pompeii.

Very old Turkish silver coffee set from Constantinople.

Pair antique bracelets, in silver and enamel, from Syria.

Pair old English spoons.

A very old English spoon, with a coin in the bowl.

Antique vinaigrette in enamel. Italian.

Old spoon from Norway.

Silk pieces worn by Arabs wound around the fez.

Holy Bible, illustrated—1690.

Two books printed by Benjamin Franklin in 1742.

Book printed by Benjamin Franklin in 1755.

Book printed by Benjamin Franklin in 1757.

Book printed by Benjamin Franklin in 1764.

History of York, printed at York, in 1834.

Book published by John Wyeth, at Harrisburg, in 1811.

The conduct of the Paxtang men—1764.

New England Rarities—1672.

The Chronicles, written in Latin and illustrated.

Book by Dr. Martin Luther, printed at Jena, 1562.

Pennsylvania Chronicle and Universal Advertiser, printed in Philadelphia, 1768.

New Discovery of a Vast Country in America, extending about 4,000 miles between New France and New Mexico. Printed in London, 1698.

Principall Navigations, Voiages and Discoveries of the English Nation. London—1589.

EMBICH, JACOB, Lebanon:

German Bible. Printed at Gosslar, 1615. This Bible was for a time the property of Johann V. Strop, secretary to Queen Christina at Stockholm, Sweden, who presented it to Peter Riehl, on the 4th of August, A. D. 1663, with the wish that he will "keep the same to his memory, and not part with it knowingly as long as he lives."

German Bible. Printed at Runeberg, 1733.

Picture of Mrs. Samuel Reinhard, deceased, taken when six years old, at Manheim, Lancaster county, Pa., 1811.

Picture of Mrs. Hannah Swarr, deceased, taken when twenty years old, at Manheim, Lancaster county, Pa.

Picture of Samuel Ensminger, wife and child, taken at Manheim, Lancaster county, Pa., 1790.

Walnut corner cupboard, with date 1785, made at Hummelstown, Dauphin county, Pa.

Original minutes of Cedar Fire Company, of Lebanon, Pa., organized July 17, 1773.

German Reformed Hymn Book, with music, printed 1747. (Old Hundred, page 197.)

Old chest, name of Jacob Welcker, 1768. P. PB. on front.

GERDSON, H. A., Lebanon:

Record book of Hebron Moravian church, beginning in 1750.

GLONINGER, MRS. CYRUS D., Lebanon:

Broom from Sandwich Islands.

GLONINGER, MRS. JULIA, Lebanon:

Jar of mace, nutmegs, and coffee.
An advertisement of 1787.

GUILFORD, MRS. W. M., Lebanon:

Two reticules, or bags, of 1830.

GREENAWALT, P. S., Lebanon:

The Martyr Book, published at Ephrata, by the Brotherhood, 1748.
Pistol used by Col. Philip L. Greenawalt, of Lebanon, during the Revolution.

HAMMOND, MRS. DAVID S., Lebanon:

Carved ivory chess men.

David Hammond's certificate of membership Society of Cincinnati, signed by George Washington at Mt. Vernon, October 31, 1785.

Commission of Lieut. John Steel, signed by George Washington March 19, 1793.

Fan, painted 1742.

Original grant from Thomas and Richard Penn to George Steitz for land upon which the town of Lebanon is built, May, 1753.

* Seal of George Steitz.

Scales and weights used by George Steitz, 1749.

Apron, worked by Margaret Steitz, 1730.

Warrant and commission to George Reynolds, descendant of George Steitz, to raise a company in the First battalion, May 7, 1756.

The muster-roll of Captain George Reynolds' company of foot, stationed at Fort Allen, 1756.

Stone pitcher, marked with initials "G. R.," with crown above. Belonged to George Steitz.

Old blue Canton china.

One pair cut-glass decanters and castors, one goblet, one wine glass, one cordial glass ; very old.

Charter and acts of Assembly of the Province of Pennsylvania from 1700 to 1759. Two volumes in one.

HONAFIUS, CYRUS, Lebanon:

Book on Magic, printed in Weimar in 1505.

KILLINGER, MRS. JOHN W., Lebanon:

Painting on velvet.

REINOEHL, ADOLPHUS, Lebanon:

Naturalization papers of 1761.

UHLER, R. R., Lebanon:

German Bible of the seventeenth century.

WAGNER, C. B., Lebanon:

Specimen of early German printing.

20

CONTRIBUTORS TO ANTIQUARIAN DISPLAY.

Abele, Rev. John G.
Abel, Lewis.
Albert, Rev. John N., Union Deposit.
Alleman, Mary.
Allen, Mrs. Martha J.
Alricks, Hamilton.
Alricks, John.
Alricks, Miss.
Alter, John.
Altmeier, Harry.
Amos, Mrs. A. E.
Anderson, Mrs. Mary.
Armstrong, Mrs. II. J.
Aughinbaugh, Mary E.
Baab, Jacob.
Baer, A. E.
Baker, E. S., Middletown.
Ball, Mrs. Joseph.
Balsbaugh, Henry.
Barnitz, Mrs. Jerome T.
Barr, Isaac, Middletown.
Barringer, Mrs. Mary.
Barry, Mrs. Eliza J.
Barth, John.
Baum, Adam II.
Beard, Mrs. Henry.
Beck, J. Augustus.
Beidleman, Mrs.
Bell, A. II., Union Deposit.

Bellman, Mrs. Oliver.
Bellman, William.
Berghaus, Miss Mary.
Bernheisel, Peter.
Bertram, Peter R.
Bickel, Henry.
Biery, Mrs. Fred.
Bingaman, Charles.
Bintner, Peter.
Black, Mrs. Joseph.
Blessing, D. F.
Block, Mrs. J.
Blumenstein, Conrad.
Boas, Mrs. Charles A.
Boas, Mrs. Daniel D.
Boas, Mrs. Harry D.
Boas, Mrs. Irvin S.
Boas, Miss Margaret I.
Boas, William D.
Bombaugh, Mrs. Julia D.
Boone, Mrs. Annie F.
Boude, Mrs. Catharine J.
Boude, Miss Emily.
Bousman, Mrs. William, Middletown.
Boyd, Mrs. Eliza.
Boyd, Mrs. Jacob M.
Boyd, Mrs. James.
Boyd, Mrs. Peter K.
Brandon, Mrs. W. B., York Springs.
Brestle, Mrs. Michael, sr., Middletown.
Briscoe, Mrs. John.

Broadie, Annie.
Brooke, Mrs. Mary E.
Brooks, Mrs. Emily D.
Brown, Mrs. Jacob D.
Brown, Mrs. Phœbe.
Brown, Mrs. Susan M.
Bryan, L. Clinton.
Buehler, Mrs. George Wolf.
Buehler, Mrs. Jacob.
Buehler, Miss Martha.
Buehler, Mrs. William.
Buffington, Mrs. Thomas W.
Calder, Rev. James.
Calder, Mrs. James.
Calder, Miss Mary.
Calder, Miss Regina C.
Calder, Mrs. William J.
Cameron, Mrs. James.
Cameron, General Simon.
Carmony, J. E., Middletown.
Carpenter, Mrs. E.
Carroll, J. S.
Carroll, May.
Cartwright, Mrs. Jacob.
Cassel, David, Hummelstown.
Cassel, John, Hummelstown.
Chayne, Miss Sarah.
Chester, Mrs. Jane M.
Clark, Mrs. Elizabeth S.
Cline, John.
Clyde, Mrs. Eliza.

Cohen, Harris.
Collins, Mrs., Steelton.
Conrad, John B.
Cooper, M.
Coover, Dr. Joseph H.
Coover, Dr. William H.
Corbett, Mrs. Mary M.
Cornwall, H. C.
Cowden, Mrs. William K.
Cox, John B.
Cox, Mrs. John B.
Cox, Miss Kate.
Cramer, Mrs. Nathan, Millersburg.
Criswell, Frank.
Criswell, Mrs.
Critson, Mrs. C., Middletown.
Croll, William A., Middletown.
Croll, Mrs. William A., Middletown.
Crull, F. P.
Crutchley, Mrs. Mary.
Dace, Mrs. J. F. C.
Dare, Mrs. Nora P.
Davidson, D. M.
Day, William Howard.
Davis, A. J.
Delaney, John C.
Delaney, Mrs. John C.
Deller, Mrs.
Demmy, Mrs., Middletown.
Dent, Thomas A., Steelton.
Detweiler, Mrs. E. P., Halifax.

Dick, Mrs. J. L.
Dietrich, Frank.
Dietrich, Mrs. H.
Dietrich, Rev. W. R. H., Newport.
Dipner, Charles D.
Dipner, Jacob L.
Diven, Mrs. Samuel N.
Dock, Mrs. Clara.
Dock, Miss Laura.
Dock, Miss Myra.
Dœhne, Mrs. George.
Donecker, Mrs. Catharine.
Dorsheimer, Sallie, Mechanicsburg.
Drahil, Elizabeth.
Dubbs, Chambers.
Dull, Mrs. A. J.
Duncan, Maggie, Churchville.
Dunkel, Mrs.
Dunlap, David.
Dunlap, Robert.
Dunott, Mrs. J. D.
Early, D. S.
Earnest, George.
Ebersole, Henry.
Egle, Miss Catharine Irwin.
Egle, Mrs. Hiram.
Egle, Miss Sarah Beatty.
Egle, Dr. William Henry.
Ehling, Catharine.
Elder, Mrs. Nancy Brown.
Elder, Mrs. Rebecca O.

Elder, Mrs. Thomas.

Emaus Orphan Home, Middletown.

Emminger, David.

Ensminger, George, Strinestown.

Ensminger, John T.

Espy, Miss Helen.

Espy, Mrs. James S.

Espy, Mrs. Josiah.

Eshenauer, Jacob J.

Etter, Mrs. B. Frank.

Etter, Mrs. Catharine.

Etter, Mrs. H., Middletown.

Etter, Mrs. G. W., Middletown.

Fackler, Benjamin, Progress.

Fackler, Miss Elizabeth, Hummelstown.

Fackler, Miss Emma, Hummelstown.

Faerster, Mrs. G.

Fager, Miss Bella.

Fager, Dr. Charles B.

Fager, Mrs. John H.

Fahnestock, Adam K.

Fahnestock, Miss.

Faunce, L. A.

Felix, Mrs. E.

Fenn, Miss Julia.

Fenn, Samuel M., Lykens.

Ferguson, T. J., Silvers Spring.

Fertig, Elias, Dauphin.

First, Mrs.

Fisher, Adolphus, Middletown.

Fisher, Frank D.

Fisher, Miss Rebecca.
Fleming, Samuel W.
Flender, Mrs. James M.
Foote, Mrs. B. J.
Forster. Benjamin Law.
Forster, Mrs. Benj. L.
Forster, Mrs. J. Montgomery.
Forster, Mrs. Margaret S.
Forster, Mrs. Robert H.
Fortney, David E.
Foster, Robert J.
Fox, Mrs. M. A.
Fry, Matthew B.
Gaitor. Mary.
Gardner, Mr.
Garman, Mrs. J., Lykens.
Garverich, George.
Gastrock, F. J.
Geety, William-Wallace, Dauphin.
George, William J.
German, William.
Gilbert, Mrs. Spencer C.
Gingrich, Mrs. E. S.
Gingrich. Miss Mary.
Gipe, Mrs. Catharine.
Glover, John W., & Son.
Goldsmith, Abraham.
Goodyear, Milfred S.
Gorgas, William R.
Gotshall Richard, Dauphin.
Graffen, Henry N.

Gratz, Miss Ella.
Gray, Mrs. John,
Graydon, H. Murray.
Graydon, Mrs. H. Murray.
Greenawalt, J. &. J. K.
Greenawalt, Theodore G.
Gross, Mrs. E. B.
Gross, Edward Z.
Grove, John W., Steelton.
Hackett, Mrs. Ann E.
Hage, Mrs. Mary A.
Hagan, Dennis.
Haines, Mrs. Mary.
Hake, Daniel J., Middletown.
Haldeman, Mrs. Richard J.
Hamill, Mrs. Kate.
Hamill, Leila.
Hamilton, Adam Boyd.
Hamilton, Adam Boyd, jr.
Hamilton, Benjamin Wallace.
Hamilton, Dr. Hugh.
Hammersly, Mrs. Thomas.
Hankinson, J. N. O.
Harris, Miss Sallie E.
Hart, Lane S.
Hartin, C., Dauphin.
Harvey, Mrs. John C.
Hays, Miss Margaret.
Hayes, Mrs. M. R.
Heiker, Truman, Highspire.
Heiney, Miss Barbara.

Hellerman, Mrs. Hiram.
Hench, Mrs. N. J.
Hendrickson, Mrs. J. R., Middletown.
Hepperle, Mrs. B.
Herr, Mrs. David S.
Hess, Jacob.
Hickok, W. Orville.
Hickman, Mrs. Eliza.
Higgins, Josiah.
Hinckel, George.
Historical Society of Dauphin County.
Hoerner, Miss Elenora, Hummelstown.
Hoerner, Miss Lucy, Hummelstown.
Hoerner, Peter, Hummelstown.
Hoffman, Mrs. L. M.
Hogan, Mrs. Richard.
Hollinger, Elias.
Hoover, James W.
Horstick, A. W., Progress.
Horstick, Isaac, Progress.
Houser, George H.
Houston, Miss Georgiana F.
Houston, Mrs. W. H.
Howard, K.
Hoyer, B. F.
Hoyer, Mrs. George.
Hoyer, Mrs. Josephine.
Hummel, Mrs. Albert.
Hummel, Mrs. Eliza Bucher.
Hummel, Miss Emma.
Hummel, John F.

Hummel, Mrs. Valentine.
Hurley, Mrs. Wesley F.
Hursh, Mrs. Caroline.
Hutchinson, Mrs., Middletown.
Ingram, Mrs. Samuel D.
James, Mrs.
Jauss, Mrs. Christian E.
Jauss, Mrs. David F.
Jauss, D. Luther.
Johnson, A. P. W.
Johnson, Miss Clara, Middletown.
Johnson, Miss C. F.
Johnson, Frederick.
Johnson, Miss H.
Johnson, Miss Hannah Ianthe.
Johnson, Miss Martha Alricks.
Kahnweiler, Joseph.
Kapp, Amos, Northumberland.
Kearns, Mrs. Martina.
Keenan, Mrs. Jane.
Keener, Mrs. E.
Keffer, Mrs. John J.
Keister, Mrs. Mary.
Kelker, Frederick.
Kelker, Henry A.
Kelker, Mrs. Henry A.
Kelker, Luther Reily.
Kelker, Rudolph F.
Kelker, Rudolph F., jr.
Kelker, Mrs. Rudolph F.
Kelker, William A.

Keller, H. B.
Keller, M. J.
Keller, John P.
Keller, Mrs. John P.
Kemerer, B. F.
Kemp, Mrs. Agnes.
Kennedy, Mrs. S. H.
Kepple, Mrs. John.
Kerr, Mrs. Elizabeth.
Kerr, Harris.
Kerr, Mrs. Isabella S.
Kerr, Lydia, Highspire.
Kerr, Miss Mary.
Kiefer, Andrew R.
Killinger, Mrs. John W.
Kirby, Daniel.
Kirby, William C.
Kirk, William E.
Klaiss, Frederick, Steelton.
Klein, Mrs. Eliza D.
Knight, Harry W.
Knox, J. Lewis.
Kreider, Mrs. Margaret.
Kuhn, John R.
Kunkel, Mrs. John C.
Landis, George, Middletown.
Lantz, Mrs. Anna.
Lathe, William.
Lauman, Miss Maria, Middletown.
Lee, Mrs. Charles A.
Lee, John F.

Leib, Mrs. Kate.

Leibrick, Miss Hannah.

Lemer, LaRue.

Lenhart, Mrs. George H., Middletown.

Leonard, Martin C.

Lingle, John.

Linn, Mrs. Erasmus.

Livingston, Jacob, Fort Hunter.

Lloyd, Mrs. F.

Longenecker, Mrs. Elizabeth.

Low, Johnson.

Lowe, Mrs. Anna Fenn.

Lowengard, Mrs. Joseph.

Lusk, A. Penn.

Lutz, Henry F.

McAllister, Mrs. D. S.

McAllister, James H., Rockville.

McCammon, Mrs., Middletown.

McCarrell, Mrs. Samuel J. M.

McCarroll, Mary.

McCarroll Mrs. William.

McCauley, Mrs. Gilbert M.

McClelland, Mrs. S. E.

McClure, Mrs. Robert.

McCormick, Mrs. Henry.

McCormick, James.

McCormick, Mrs. James.

McCreath, Mrs. Andrew S.

McCreery, George J.

McCrone, Mrs. John A.

McDaniel, James Sawyers, New Cumberland.

McDowell, Mrs. Thomas Crawford.
McFadden, David.
McFadden, William H.
McGaghey, Bud.
McGaughey, Miss Addie.
McGee, Miss Nancy.
McGonigal, Mrs. W. A.
McGuire, W. W.
McKee, Miss K.
McLaughlin, A., Enterline.
Mahaney, Mrs. W. E., Steelton.
Mahon, Mrs.
Maloney, Mrs. M.
Marks, Herman.
Martin, Harry J.
Martin, William D.
Martz, Mrs., Millersburg.
Mather, Mrs. Edmund.
Mason, William.
Maurer, Mrs. Daniel C.
Maurer, Frederick C.
May, Nathan.
Meese, Jacob W.
Meily, Mrs. Middletown.
Meisenhelter, Maria.
Meredith, A. E.
Mersereau, Mrs. James S.
Metzgar, LaRue.
Middaugh, Fitch K.
Middaugh, Israel.
Midlam, John F.

Milleisen, Mrs. J.
Miller, Miss Annie.
Miller, Abraham C.
Miller, Mrs. D. J.
Miller, Mrs. F. X.
Miller, G. M.
Miller, George W.
Miller, Jacob A.
Miller, Mrs. Jacob R.
Miller, Joanna.
Miller, Joseph, Fisherville.
Miller, Shelley E.
Mitchell, Mrs. William.
Moore, Mrs. C. J.
Morley, Mrs. Hiram P.
Morley, Winfield Scott.
Morrow, Mrs. Mary.
Morton, Annie.
Moyer, Henry, Campbellstown.
Muench, Mrs. Robert L.
Mullen, Miss Fanny.
Mullen, Mrs. Thomas F.
Mullen, Lydia.
Mumma, David.
Musgrave, Mrs. Sarah N.
Napier, Mrs. Eliza.
Napier, John.
Napier, Mrs. Robert.
Neidig, Mrs., Rockville.
Nead, Benjamin M.
Nieth, Miss Kate.

Nicholson, Mrs. Mary.
Norman, P. A.. Carlisle.
Null, Samuel.
O'Connor, Dr. Mortimer.
O'Donnell, Mrs. Ellen.
Olewine, Mrs.
Ort, Peter M.
Orth, Mrs. Barbara.
Orth, Mrs. John G.
Orwig, Mrs. Louisa II.
Orwig, Joseph R.
Orwig, Miss M. M.
Orwig, Ralph.
Ott, Frederick M.
Ott, Leander N.
Oyster, Mrs. Simon.
Page, Jacob.
Painter, Mrs. Henry.
Park, J. F., Middletown.
Parker, Mrs. Sarah R.
Parthemore, E. Winfield Scott.
Pearson, Miss Carrie.
Pearson, Isaiah.
Pennsylvania State Library.
Peters, Mrs. Benjamin G.
Peters, John D.
Phelps, Mrs. Anson II.
Pilkay, Joseph J.
Poffenberger, Dr. A. T., Dauphin.
Poffenberger, Miss Margaret, Dauphin.
Pollock, Miss Martha.

Pollock, Miss Rachel.
Poulton, Lewis G.
Poulton, Mrs. Susan A.
Power, Mrs. Louisa Kean.
Pratt, Mrs. Capt., Carlisle.
Pretz, Mrs. Elias.
Price, Harry.
Pritchard, Mrs. William T.
Rawn, Mrs. Charles C.
Ray, Mrs. Susan Bucher.
Raymond, C. W., Middletown.
Reckord, Thomas J.
Reed, George E.
Reel, Mrs. Adam.
Reel, Charles.
Reese, Cyrus J.
Rehrer, Miss C. M.
Reinhard, Albert.
Reinhard, Miss Jennie.
Rhine Bros.
Rhodes, Mrs. Catharine.
Rice, George H.
Ricker, Mrs. Rebecca.
Rife, John W., Middletown.
Ringland, Dr. John, Middletown.
Ringland, Mrs. John, Middletown.
Ringland, Miss Louisa B., Middletown.
Roberts, Alexander.
Rodfong, Miss Grace, Middletown.
Rodgers, Mrs. S. L.
Rohrer, Mrs. S. E.

21

Romich, Mrs. E.
Rupp, A. B., Middletown.
Rutherford, John A.
Rutherford, John B.
Rutherford, Mrs. L. B.
Rutherford, Miss Margaret.
Rutherford, Mrs. W. Frank.
Rutherford, William Swan.
Rutherford, Mrs. William Wilson.
Ryan, E.
Sargeant, Mrs. Eliza Espy.
Saul, J. M.
Saunders, Mrs. M.
Sayford, William.
Schaffner, Miss Carrie S., Hummelstown.
Schaffner, Daniel, Hummelstown.
Schaffner, Mrs. Martin, Hummelstown.
Scheffer, Frederick W.
Scheffer, Theo. F., estate of.
Scheffer, Mrs. Theo. F.
Schellenberg, Elsie.
Schmidt, Joseph.
Schmidt, Mrs. L.
Schraedly, F. B., Middletown.
Scott, Miss Bertie.
Scott, Frederick.
Scott, Miss Lizzie.
Scott, Margaret.
Seeger, Augustus.
Segelbaum, Mrs. Charles S.
Sellers, Miss.

Selser, Samuel, Middletown.

Shanahan, Rt. Rev. J. F.

Sharp, Albert R.

Sheaffer, Miss Carrie.

Shearer, Mrs.

Shenk & Eicker, Marsh Run.

Shields, Mrs. James D.

Shindler, George F.

Shoemaker, Frederick.

Shoemaker, Mrs. George J.

Shoop, Mrs.

Shoop, N. P.

Showers, C. F., Carlisle.

Shriver, Mrs. B. F.

Shunk, Miss Elizabeth.

Shunk, Miss Mary.

Shunk, Mrs. William Findlay.

Siegfried, Mrs. Charles W.

Sides, Michael, Middletown.

Simmons, Mrs. Seneca G.

Simon, Mrs. John B.

Simonton, John Wiggins.

Simonton, Mrs. John W.

Simpson, John W.

Slaughter, David.

Sloan, Alexander.

Small, Mrs. Charles H.

Small, Mrs. George H.

Small, John Kunkel.

Small, Miss Mary.

Smeltzer, William, Oberlin.

Smith, Jacob.
Smelz, Mrs. D. W., Middletown.
Smith, Mrs. T. Rockhill.
Smull, William Pauli.
Snyder, Agnes.
Snyder, Mrs. E.
Snyder, Frank, Steelton.
Snyder. Miss Kitty.
Snyder, Rev. William H. H.
Sohn, John.
Soper, Mrs.
Sourbeer, Henry S.
Stouffer, J. H., Lower Paxtang.
Steinmetz, William B.
Stevens, Mrs. Kate.
Stevens, Thomas H.
Stevens, T. J., Mechanicsburg.
Stewart, H.
Stewart, Mrs. Henry.
Stine, George W.
Stoey, Mrs.
Stofer, Mrs. J. W., Middletown.
Stoner, Miss Mary A., Highspire.
Stoner, M. J., Highspire.
Stormfeltz, Mrs. E.
Strock, Mrs. Joanna.
Stroh, William B.
Strouse, Mrs. Joseph.
Stuart, Henry.
Swartz, Abraham.
Swartz, Mrs. Charles.

Swartz, S. L., Highspire.
Taylor, Miss Mary.
Theilheimer, Philip.
Thomas, Findlay I.
Thompson, Miss S., Middletown.
Tittle, John C.
Tomlinson, Mrs. John B.
Tompkinson, Joseph.
Tompkinson, Miss Martha M.
Towsen, Harry H.
Towsen, Mrs. James A.
Trewick, Walter.
Trewick, Mrs. Walter.
Trostle, Isaac D.
Uhler, Miss Margaret.
Ulrich, Mrs. A., Middletown.
Ulrich, Mrs. John, Middletown.
Unger, Mrs. Susan.
Updegrove, Mrs. L. V.
Utz, Miss Annie M.
Utz, Mrs. Sarah.
VanAsdlen, Jacob.
Vandling, John S.
Vaughn, Mrs. George.
Vaughn, Mrs. Robert.
Voght, George J.
Wagner, Martha A., Steelton.
Walters, Harry.
Ward, Mrs. Silas.
Watson, Amy M.
Watson, Harry S.

Watson, Mrs. J. A.
Watson, Mrs. Mary.
Weand, Hiram B.
Weaver, Mrs. J. S.
Weaver, Uriah M.
Weills, Dr. William M. L.
Weimer, Jerome.
Weir, Miss Annie C.
Weir, Miss Sybil M.
Wellinger, Mrs. Susan.
Wenger, Amos, Progress.
Wertz, Catharine.
Whinery, William B.
Whisler, Jacob.
Whiteside, George A.
Whiteside, Miss M.
Widner, William K.
Wierman, Mrs. Thomas T.
Wiestling, Mrs. Jacob G.
Wiestling, Joshua Martin.
Wiestling, Mrs. Joshua M.
Wiestling, Miss E. R., Middletown.
Wikel, Mrs. John.
Wikel, Mrs. Peter G.
Williams, Mrs.
Williamson, Mrs. Mary E.
Wilson, Mrs. Thomas L.
Wilver, John.
Winters, Mrs. George.
Wise, Mrs.
Wise, Susan.

Witherow, Mrs. John G.
Witman, Mrs. Henry Orth.
Wolfersberger. Mrs. Catharine.
Wollerton, Charles.
Woodward, Lewis B.
Wyeth, Mrs. Francis.
Yeoh, Mrs., Millersburg.
Yingst, Mrs., Middletown.
Yingst, Minnie, Hummelstown.
Young, John.
Y. M. C. A. of Harrisburg.
Zimmerman, Mrs. A.
Zimmerman, Mrs. Conrad O.
Zimmerman, Mary E.
Zollinger, Mrs. Elizabeth.
Zollinger, Mrs. Julia B.
Zollinger, Warren A.
Zollinger, Mrs. Warren A.
Zortman, Daniel.

DAUPHIN COUNTY EXHIBITS.

As stated elsewhere, no one regrets as much as the Editor the imperfect record here given. He is not responsible for the failure in this respect. Fortunately some of the exhibitors handed in at the time a full list of all articles they loaned, which will account for the completeness and accuracy of a portion of the valuable collection exhibited, and not simply to give those persons any undue prominence. At the last moment the several committees endeavored to make out lists of articles in their respective classes. Owing to this fact many articles are duplicated, which, of course, is excusable under the circumstances. Those we also give, although not with the idea that they are complete. The number of exhibitors exceeded six hundred, while the articles numbered nearly ten thousand separate and distinct items. The people of the county did well.

BERRIER, HENRY, Harrisburg:

Natural Obligations to Believe the Principle of Religion. In sixteen sermons. By John Long, D. D., rector of Bedington and chaplain in Ordinary to his Majesty. 1719.

The Accomplished Practiser in the High Court of Chancery. By Joseph Harrison. 1750.

The History of the Empire. By the Liens Heiss. 1729.

The works of John Sheffield, Earl of Mulgrave, Marquis of Normandy and Duke of Buckingham. The Memoirs of His Grace John, Duke of Buckingham. Written by himself. 1729.

Book-keeping Methodized; or a methodical treatise of merchant accompts, according to the Italian form. By John Mair, A. M. The seventh edition. 1763.

CALDER, MISS REGINA C., Harrisburg:

Book of Poems. 1789.

Homer's Illiad, translated by Alexander Pope. Philadelphia, 1795.

Fruits of Solitude in Reflections and Maxims; also, Fruits of a Father's Love, being advice of William Penn to his children, relating to their Civil and Religious Conduct. Benjamin Johnson, Philadelphia, 1794.

CAMERON, GEN. SIMON, Harrisburg:

Works of Flavius Josephus, in 2 vols. Frankfort-on-the-Main,1581.

Works of Rev. John Flavel, late minister of Dartmouth in Devon. 2 vols., London, 1716.

The works of John Locke in 3 vols. London, 1722.

The Columbiad; a poem by Joel Barlow, minister to France. Philadelphia, 1807.

A New Law Library, 8th edition; Giles Jacob, Gent. London, 1742.

COOVER, DR. JOSEPH H., Harrisburg:

German Bible, by Martin Luther, printed in Frankfort-on-the-Main, in the year 1596, A. D., and supposed to have been used in the translation of King James' Bible.

Commentary on the Epistles of the Galatians and Hebrews, by Nicholas Hemmingio, in the year 1570 A. D., (Latin.)

Ovid's Metamorphoses, with English translation. Printed in the year 1790 A. D.

Literary magazine of England, for the years 1811 and 1812, (four volumes.)

Book of Daniel. Printed in the Chinese language with wooden blocks, known to the Chinese as early as 400 to 500 A. D., or 1400 years ago.

Tang Kaing daily newspaper. Printed in Japanese and Chinese characters, in the 7th year, 9th month and 6th day of Ming Che, the sovereign of Tang Kaing, the eastern city of Japan.

Piece of Marble, inlaid with Mosaic, from the Palace of the Cæsars and Emperors of ancient Rome, built over 70 years B. C., and excavated in the year 1869 A. D.

Piece of marble from a Sarcophagus in the Catacombs of St. Caliytus, Rome, Italy—a burying place for early Christians.

Pen holder and pen used by General Garibaldi in the Italian Parliament at Rome.

Piece of marble from the fountain, in the atrium of the supposed house of the Athenian, Glaucus, in Pompeii, built 300 years B. C., and destroyed by the memorable eruption of Mt. Vesuvius, on the 24th of August, in the year 79 A. D., which buried the city and most of its inhabitants for nearly 800 years.

Lava and scoria from the different eruptions of Mt. Vesuvius, from the memorable eruption of August 24, 79 A. D., to the eruption of 1872 A. D., (the white,) which hurled stones and lava to the height of 4,000 feet and covered an area of twenty-five square miles, twenty feet deep.

Medallion head, carved out of the lava of Vesuvius.

Two pieces of gold mosaic, taken from the church of St. Mark, the tutelary saint of Venice, built in the year 916 A. D., and decorated with oriental magnificence, and contains 45,790 square feet of gold mosaic, representing Scripture scenes.

Coins from England, France, Belgium, Holland, Germany, Austria,

Hungary, Italy, Greece, and Switzerland, half-penny of King George I and II. 1714 and 1727 A. D.

Letter of credit showing the manner of drawing money in the different countries of the world.

Relics from the battlefield of Gettysburg July 1, 2, and 3, 1863, and presented to the contributors of the Memorial church:

Piece of shell from Tawneytown road.

Wood from Culp's Hill.

Eagle made of fuse—case of bombshells.

Bullets from Culp's Hill.

Marble from Soldiers' National Monument.

Granite from Round Top.

Shrapnell, grape, and shot from shells.

DAUPHIN COUNTY HISTORICAL SOCIETY.

MSS. Original roll of the Pennsylvania Society of the Cincinnati, December 6, 1783.

MSS. Original deed of Frederick Hummel and Rosina, his wife, to Anthony Dœbler, for lot in Fredericks-Town, dated Jany. 25, 1763.

MSS. Supervisor's account book for Paxtang township, from April 5, 1768, to April 13, 1846.

MSS. List of taxable dwelling houses within the borough and township of Lebanon, in the county of Dauphin, for the year 1800.

MSS. Statement of the expenses of erecting the Poor House and other buildings and improvements on the poor house farm, of Dauphin county, for the support and employment of the poor of said county, exhibited to the Commissioners and Auditors of the county, at their annual settlement in January, 1811.

MSS. Constitution and proceedings of the Harrisburg Library Company, instituted September, 1795. 1795–1809.

MSS. Names of members of the Harrisburg Library, 1800–1804.

MSS. Constitution and proceedings of the "Harmonical Association of the Borough of Harrisburg." 1818–1821.

MSS. Harrisburg lot-book.

MSS. Notes of Sermons by Rev. John Elder. 1760–1770.

MSS. Roll of members of Harrisburg Greys. 1831.

MSS. Commission of George Buehler, of Dauphin county, as collector of the Direct tax. September 23, 1800.

Invitation to cotillion party in 1828.

Burlesque "shin-plasters" of 1837.

Band worn by Parson Elder, found in his pulpit Bible.

Web-stool of ante-Revolutionary date.

The draft-wheel used during the civil war.

Carlisle Gazette from 1787 to 1817. The first newspaper published West of the Susquehanna.

Parson Elder's copy of Atterbury's sermons, containing the family record of Rev. John Elder, on the fly leaves.

Pocket almanacs from 1760 to 1783, belonging to Rev. John Elder. and containing notes of marriages, &c.

Trial of McManus and others for the murder of Francis Shitz. Harrisburg. John Wyeth. 1798.

The practical distiller, by Samuel McHarry, of Lancaster county, Pa. Published by John Wyeth, 1809.

History of the American Revolution, by Bernard Hubley, Vol. 1, (all that was published.) Northumberland. Andrew Kennedy, 1805, Evening Chronicle, or Philadelphia Advertiser, for 1787.

American and Commercial Daily Advertiser, Baltimore. 1807 and 1808.

Pennsylvania Reporter and Democratic Herald, Harrisburg. 1828 and 1829.

Bucks County Messenger, Doylestown. 1821.

New York National Advocate, (for the country.) 1825-6.

National Intelligencer, Washington, D. C. 1826.

National Journal, Washington, D. C. 1825 and 1826.

Political Sentinel and Lancaster County Democrat, Lancaster. 1829-30.

The Lancaster Republican and anti-Masonic Opponent, Lancaster. 1830-31.

Gazette of the U. S., (for the country.) 1801 and 1802.

The Philadelphian, Philadelphia. 1829 to 1831.

Pennsylvania Intelligencer, Harrisburg. 1820 to 1826.

Daily Times, Harrisburg. 1853.

Harrisburg Chronicle. 1831 to 1833.

The Whig, Baltimore. 1808-'09.

Independent Journal, Downingtown. From 1827 to 1830.

View of Harrisburg. About 1840.

Two views of old Derry Church.

DETWEILER, MRS. EUNICE P., Halifax:

Lace cap, knit. 1779.

Lace cap, embroidered. 1801.

Piece of lace of 1798.

Sword presented to a British officer for gallantry at the battle of Louisbourg. 1745.

Cane made of wood from the U. S. ship Constitution.

Cane made of wood from the first Masonic Temple in the United States.

Holy Bible, translated from the Latin vulgate, diligently compared with the Hebrew, Greek and divers other languages, and first published by The English College at Douay, Anno 1605. (This volume is published in 1796.)

Dryden's poems. 1776.

Astronomical and geographical essays by George Adams, mathematical Instrument maker to his Majesty and optician to the Prince of Wales.

DIETRICH, FRANK, Harrisburg :

Miscellaneous coins.

English tokens and coins.

English one half tokens.

Australia tokens.

Rebellion tokens.

Coins of Sweden, Norway, and Denmark.

Lot of war envelopes, different designs, Union and Rebel.

Collection of medals.

Collection of minerals.

Specimens of coins—Egyptain, Turkish, Hayti, Java, Dumps, Portugal, Uruguay, and Mexico.

Chinese and Japanese coins.

U. S. fractional notes. Two fine shields of fractional paper money.

Washington pieces.

Lot of gold coins. A full set of 3 dollar gold pieces ; very rare.

Gold from one quarter dollar to a $50 Unge.

Lot of Indian curiosities.

Dollars from 1795 to 1885, including the rare ones of 1858, 1839, 1836.

Half dollars from 1794 to 1885, excepting 1796 and 1797.

One fourth dollars from 1796 to 1885, excepting 1823 and 1827—very rare.

Twenty cent pieces—full set—from 1875 to 1878.

A set of U. S. proofs from 1858 to 1875—very rare.

The pattern pieces of the trade dollar—6 p.—a full set with many other pattern pieces, such as U. S. ring dollar, Feuchtwanger cent, 3 cent flying eagle, set of twelve cents, nickle Washington pieces.

Dimes, lacking a few of the rare ones to make a full set.

The one half dimes.

Silver three cent pieces—a full set from 1850 to 1873.

U. S. copper cents—a full set from 1793 to 1885.

One half cents—a fine set, lacking a few.

Early, D. S., Harrisburg:

Medical Botany, Strasburg. 1560.

German Bible, Zurich. 1565 Printed by Christoffel Froschoner.

German Hand Concordance. Owned by Benjamin Ohrle, now spelled Early. Printed at New Saltza, February 16, 1714.

German Testament. Printed in Frankfort and Leipzig. 1737.

The life, suffering and wounds of Jesus Christ. 1747.

Worthy Proverbs from Christian Gohlurg's Postilla Mystica of the Gospel, with short thoughts on each text. Christopher Saur, Germantown, 1748.

Nicolaus Luding, of Zinzendorf. Thoughts of Gospel Truth. Conrad Schilling, 1800.

Wandlenden Suele mit Adam. (Walks of the soul with Adam, Noah and Simon Cleophas,) by John Philip Shabalic. Print, Harrisburg, John S. Weistling.

German Westminster Church Hymn Book, with notes. Lancaster, John Baer. 1829.

Catechism and Confession of Faith of the Churches of Christ, reproachfully called Quakers. Printed in the year 1773 in Meric, Scotland, on the eleventh of the sixth month; reprinted by Joseph Cruikshank, in Market, between Second and Third streets, Philadelphia.

A conversation on the Plurality of Worlds. Bought by John Creigh Gray, at New York, August 10, 1776.

Wooden Cuckoo Clock, in perfect order, without case, that strikes and cuckoos. Very old.

French Silver Alarm Watch. Bought by John Shertzer, sr., of Annville, Lebanon county, Pa., in September 1796.

French pocket traveler's alarm; a family relic.

Steel flax-comb, owned by A. Runkle.

Set of old wooden cupping instruments and cups, made at different periods, of glass, brass, and silver.

Set of old wooden clock tools.

Hand made Pennsylvania Volunteer sword and leather scabbard, dated on plate 1799.

Musket and sword.

Silver scabbard, sword and belt.,

Large double lined pewter pitcher.

Tin tea-pot.

Pewter pitcher.

Tin tumbler.

Large tin soup-dish, seven pewter spoons, six pewter plates, stamped A. H. S. 1742.

Shell snuff-box.

Iron tallow-candle stick and snuffer.

Iron lard lamp.

Walnut bureau, 145 years old.

Silk self opening umbrella, patent spring; family relic.

Stove plate—six plate stove, weighs 115 pounds, with the following inscription in English letters joined together, but spelled in German, as follows: "Wohl den dar nicht wandled in road dar Gotlossen;" in English, 1 Psalm, 1 verse, "Blessed is the man that walketh not in the counsel of the ungodly." It measures twenty-seven by twenty-eight inches.

Four sets of brass standard coin scales, of different dates.

American politics before the Revolution. The works of Benjamin Franklin, printed and published by Wm. Duane, Philadelphia.

Leather hat-box lined and cushioned, with brass lock and key.

Pair of fire-tongs and shovel, and ash wood-stove scraper and rake combined. An old relic.

Old iron hand made locks with keys, and lock with screw key, and screw night key, chest lock, cupboard lock, cupboard catches, tongue latches, shutter holders and hinges, and catches inside and outside, folding door slides, and chest lock, all hand made, from the old log house on Walnut street, next to the Exchange building, where the U. S. Post Office now stands.

A corner stone found in the cellar wall, with date 1782.

Old Revolutionary musket, rifle, and shot gun, bullet-molds.

Continental silver plated buttons and brass handle buttons.

A scientific, vocal, and musical curiosity. A relic. Dr. Calcott's grammar of music, comprising a full explanation of all the notes and marks and treatises on the science of melody, harmony and rhyme. Printed at London by T. Hurst, St. Paul's Church-Yard.

Also a collection of old spelling books and readers.

Old cattle or cow bells.

Iron wood stove hoe. One pair steelyards.

One Buck-eye log cabin cane, presented to William Early in the Harrison hard cider campaign of 1840.

The law of evidence, by the late learned judge, Gilbert. Printed by Catherine Lintot, law printer to the King's Most Excellent Majesty, for W. Owen, at Homer's Head, near Temple Bar. 1760.

The Spectator. Bought by David Briggs, Apr. 17, 1798. Printed for Messrs. Bell & Bradford.

EGLE, CATHARINE IRWIN, Harrisburg:

Photo of old Hanover church.

Photo of old Derry church.

View of Camp Curtin hospital. 1863.

Daguerreotype of Henry Beader.

Pencil sketch of bridge over Paxtang creek at Market street in 1840, showing view at Eleventh and Market streets.

Pencil sketch of the warehouse erected by John Harris in 1790; afterwards called the "Hise House," Front and Barbara alley, now occupied by Washington avenue.

The Kelso Ferry House on the Cumberland side of the river—the oldest house in the Cumberland Valley.

The Masonic hall erected in 1825—located on the site of the new post office.

Surgeon Egle's headquarters in front of Richmond, Va., winter of 1864–65.

Photo of catafalque in the House of Representatives at Harrisburg on which remains of President Lincoln were placed, 1865.

The stump of mulberry tree as it appeared in 1839, sketched by David Lingle.

Portrait of George Beatty; born 1781; died 1862.

Pennsylvania currency. Ten shillings, 1771.

Continental currency of the denomination of
> One dollar.
> Two dollars.

Three dollars, (2.)
Four dollars, (2.)
Five dollars, (2.)
Seven dollars.
Eight dollars.
20, 30, 35, 45, 50, 55, 60, 65 and 70 dollars.

Spinning wheel of 1778, belonging to the great-great-grandmother of the owner. The distaff cut from a tree in Hanover, about 1790—the flax grown in Hanover in 1800.

Flax brake of 1810.
Wool carders of 1800.
Pin cushion of 1770.
Apron worn at the celebration of the Tercentenary of the Discovery of America in 1792.
Coverlet woven in 1778.
Straw-covered fancy box of 1820.

EGLE, SARAH BEATTY, Harrisburg:

Tea set of silvered ware made in 1810; five pieces.
Blue willow ware tureen. 1796.
Large china bowl. 1780.
Coffee pot of 1810.
Wedgewood Masonic pitcher. 1792.
Eight silver teaspoons. 1805.
One knee buckle.
Brass andirons of 1790.
Silver-plated candlesticks with snuffers and tray. 1812.
Tin snuffer trays of 1795.
Fire bucket of 1810—repainted in 1830.
Bellows and brush of 1810.
Bread tray 1810.
Silver shoe buckles purchased in 1778.
Parasol of 1810.
Parasol of 1825.
Bead purse of 1820.
Mexican needle work—old.

EGLE, DR. WILLIAM HENRY, Harrisburg:

The Humble Sinner Resolved what hee should do to be saved. By Obadiah Sedgwick, B. D., London, 1660.

The English-man's Treasure, with the True Anatomie of Man's Body. By Thomas Vicary, Black-letter, London, 1632.

Tagliches Hand Buch in guten and bosen Tagen; von Johann Friedrick Stark. Stuttgard, 1705. Brought from Switzerland by Ursula (Mœller) Thomas.

Des hocherlenchteten Lehrers Herrn Johann Arndts. Nuremberg, 1762. Beautifully illustrated.

Memoires de L'Amerique Septentrionale ou la suite des voyages de Mr. Le Baron de Lahontan. 2 volumes. A La Haye, 1709.

An historical review of the Constitution and Government of Pennsylvania, by Benjamin Franklin. London, 1759.

A True and Impartial State of the Province of Pennsylvania. Philadelphia, 1759.

Considerations on the Propriety of Imposing Taxes in the British Colonies. New York, 1765.

A New Essay (by the Pennsylvania Farmer) on the Constitutional Power of Great Britain over the Colonies in America. Philadelphia, 1774.

The Journal of a two month's tour in America, by Charles Beatty, A. M. London, 1768.

An examination of the Connecticut claim to lands in Pennsylvania. Philadelphia, 1774.

A Topographical Description of Virginia, Pennsylvania, Maryland, and North Carolina, by Thomas Hutchins. London, 1778.

An address to the Inhabitants of Pennsylvania, by those Freemen of the city of Philadelphia, &c. Philadelphia, 1777.

History of the Mission of the United Brethren among the Indians in North America, by George Henry Loskiel. London, 1794.

An Address to the People of the United States, from George Washington, President. New Castle, 1796. First copy of Washington's Farewell Address.

Der Blutige Schau-Platz, (the martyr book.) Printed by the Ephrata Brethren in 1748. [A fine copy of this remarkable and rare work.]

Biblia, Das ist Die Heilige Schrift. [The second edition of the celebrated Saur Bible, of 1763. This was the first Bible printed in America in a European language.]

History of the Holy Bible, adorned with cuts. Philadelphia, 1786. [Very curious; of the diminutive books of that period.]

Dickson's Balloon Almanac for the year of our Lord, 1805.

22

The Gentleman and Citizen's Pocket Almanack, for the year 1769. [Owned by Rev. John Elder, of Paxtang, and contains memoranda of marriages.]

Travels through the United States of North America in 1795-7, by the Duke de la Rochefoucauld Liancourt. London, 4to., 1799. [Contains an interesting account of Harrisburg, Fort Hunter, &c.]

Histoire Naturelle et Politique de la Pensylvanie et de L'Establissement des Quakers dans cette contrel. A Paris, 1768.

Vocabularius Rerum. Strasburgh, 1491.

A sermon preached at Christiana Bridge and New Castle, the 20th of July, 1775, being the day appointed by the Continental Congress as a day of fasting, humiliation, and prayer, by Joseph Montgomery, A. M. [The Rev. Joseph Montgomery was the first Register and Recorder of the county of Dauphin.]

Ausbund; Das ist Etlicke schone Christliche Lieder. Germantown. Christopher Saur, 1754.

Christliche Morgen-und Abend Bebaser auf alle Tage in der Mochen. Germantown. Christopher Saur. 1776.

Der Psalter des Konigs und Propheten Davids. Ephrata. 1793.

Specimen of Confederate Printing, 1865. Henry the 8th and his court.

The Oracle of Dauphin and Harrisburg Advertiser, 1792 to 1806. One volume of odd numbers.

Unparthenische Harrisburg Zeitung, (Morgenrothe,) from 1799 to 1808. First German newspaper printed at Harrisburg. 2 vols.

The Dauphin Guardian, from 1808 to 1811. 2 vols.

The Chronicle or Harrisburg Visitor from 1815 to 1818.

The Statesman for 1831 and 1832 subsequently merged into the Telegraph.

Pennsylvania Telegraph for 1832 and 1833.

Harrisburg Chronicle from 1822 to 1824.

Pennsylvania Intelligencer from 1820 to 1822. 2 vols.

Four Broadsides of the anti-Masonic Campaign of 1832.

Five military orders of the war with Mexico, 1846 and 1847.

St. Clairs' Defeat. A poem by Eli Lewis, Harrisburg, 1792. [This is probably the first book printed in Harrisburg.]

A correct account of the trials of Charles McManus and others, for murder. Harrisburg, 1798.

Memoirs of a Life Chiefly Passed in Pennsylvania, within the last sixty years. By Alexander Graydon. Harrisburg, 1811.

Another copy of the same with the MSS notes and additions by the author.

An accurate and interesting account of the hardships and suffering of the band of heroes who traveled the wilderness in the campaign against Quebec in 1775. By John Joseph Henry, Esq. Lancaster, 1812. [Although not printed in Harrisburg, it was there written, and gives an account of the Paxtang company who were on that expedition.]

Specimens of Toy Books, 1833, 1834 and 1835, printed in oil colors by Gustavus S. Peters, the inventor. The illustrations were designed and engraved by him.

Hinterlassene Predigten von Johann George Lochman, D. D. Harrisburg, 1828.

Letter of William Penn to Secretary Logan, 28th 4mo., 1702.

Petition of Marcus Hulings with rough draught of islands at mouth of Juniata—now Duncan's island, &c., dated May 17, 1762.

Two letters of Gen. Arthur St. Clair, of dates 1773 and 1774.

Certificate of Ordination of the Rev. John Winebrenner, V. D. M., founder of the Church of God. Sept. 28, 1820.

Call to Rev. John Winebrenner, by the churches at Harrisburg, Shoop's, &c. September 16, 1820.

Journal of George Croghan and Andrew Montour, to the Ohio Indians, in 1751.

Four pages of an old Missal of the 13th century, A. D. 1232. [Choice penmanship.]

Hessian sword captured at the battle of Trenton.

Sword of Sergeant George Beatty, of Harrisburg, in the war of 1812–14.

Wooden bowl carried through the war of the Revolution by an officer of the Patriot army.

Knife, fork, and spoon of an officer in the war for the Union, 1861–5.

Sixteen State buttons—Union and Confederate. 1861–65.

Mexican spurs presented to the owner by Gen. Miramon at Matamoras, in June, 1865. [Was an officer of the Imperial army, and shot at the time of Maximilian's doom.]

Blanket presented the owner by Gen. Canales, of the Liberal army at Mier, Mexico, in August, 1865. [The finest of Mexican blankets or ponchos, woven by hand—requiring 12 months in making.]

Mexican bridle. Presented the owner by Senor Don Careno, of city of Mier, Mexico, July, 1865.

One dozen Indian axes, (stone.)
Indian pestle fifteen inches long.
Indian arrow-heads.
Indian pipes found on the site of Chesapeake Nail Works.
Indian beads from a grave on site of Harrisburg.
Ornament worn by married women.
Bay of Biscay ax.
Quoits, (stone.)
Indian celts.
Gun cover made by Blackfeet Indians.
Moccasins from same tribe.
Indian whip, (Blackfeet.)
Indian whip, (Comanche.)
Needle case made by the Apache Indians.
Derry church collection box. 1740.

EMAUS ORPHAN HOME, Middletown :

George Frey's Family Bible.
George Frey's arm chair, which he brought with him from Germany, about 150 years ago.
George Frey's account books, dated 1783. Seven in number.
Mrs. Frey's brass cake turner and fork, over 100 years old.

GORGAS, WILLIAM R., Harrisburg:

Chronican Ephratenses. Ephrata, 1786.
MSS. Three books of Melodies. Ephrata, 1783.
History of the Apostles. Ephrata, 1764.
Christliche Bibiloth. Ephrata, 1792.
New Testament. Ephrata, 1787.
Life of Franklin. Ephrata, 1796.
German Grammar. Ephrata, 1772.
Almanacs from 1745 to 1751. Germantown.
Hymn book. Christopher Saur, 1787.
New Testament. Germantown, 1775.
Real Christian's Hope. Germantown, 1756.
Blumen Gærtlein. Germantown, 1800.
German Hymn Books. 1728, 1763.
German Bible. 1712.
Torborgene Leben. 1787.
Concordance Buchlein. 1710.

German Song Book. 1763.

Zionitscher. Germantown, 1739.

Temple Cottes in Christo. 1721.

Hamilton, Adam Boyd, Harrisburg:

MSS. Vol. Record of tickets drawn in the Presbyterian church lottery. 1809. John Wright, Esq., clerk.

MSS. catalogue of books in the Harrisburg Circulating Library. 1804.

Original parchment agreement of the founders of the Harrisburg Library. 1795. With autographs of the members. A very curious and valuable relic.

Two maps of Harrisburg, 1785, 1860; that of 1785 showing original boundary of the village.

Book of autographs of the early residents of Harrisburg, with notes.

Silver spoon of John Hamilton. 1772.

Silver spoon of Adam Boyd, manufactured by Geo. Beatty. 1805.

Satin vest of James Boyd, in girth six feet. 1800.

Cloth breeches of Adam Boyd. 1805.

Wedding dress, 1783, of wife of Adam Boyd, Jeanette Macfarlane.

Shawl, 1783, of same set.

Fan of 1790, with mottoes depicting the French revolution; belonged to Rosanna Boyd Hamilton.

Spectacles, 1712, of John Boyd, grandfather of Adam Boyd.

Silver thimble. 1793.

Steelyards, Adam Boyd. 1785. Also steelyards, with set of weights. 1783.

Steelyards, 1772, of John Hamilton.

Cut glass decanter, 1807, and wine glasses.

Papier mache snuffers and tray. 1827.

Blue bead satchel. 1830.

Green bead satchel. 1831.

Satin satchel. 1825.

Satin pin cushion. 1798.

Cloth pin cushion. 1790.

Linen pin cushion, flat. 1805.

Long pin cushion. 1770.

Sampler of Rosanna Boyd, of satin. 1798. Worked at Bethlehem.

Sampler of Brin. 1824.

Sampler of Margaret Hamilton. 1828. Worked at Miss Ross' school.

Handkerchief of 1790, showing ride and funeral of John Gilpin.

Handkerchief, "Sluggard," of 1805.

Two baby caps. 1786.

Two II. baby caps. 1808.

Sandwich Island cloth. 1831. Very rare and curious.

Bamboo chairs of 1783.

Fringes of 1829.

Hickory work basket. 1807.

Bronze jars. 1850.

Sconces of brass. 1741.

Sconces of bronze. 1841.

Flint lock from musket of 1812.

Portraits in oil by Eicholtz, of

 Catharine A. Hamilton. 1809.

 Hugh Hamilton. 1809.

 Arnold Naudain. 1850.

Cattle scene by Catharine L. Naudain. 1840.

High alabaster vases.

Large china vases.

Small china vases.

Looking glass handsomely ornamented, ' presented to Jane Allen upon her marriage with John Hamilton, in 1748, by Com. Thomas Allen, Royal Navy."

Looking glass, beveled edge, presented to Rosanna Boyd, upon her marriage with Hugh Hamilton, by her father. 1807.

Looking glass of Adam Boyd, 1780.

Block of the Harris Mulberry tree, presented exhibitor by George W. Harris, Esq. 1850.

Alabaster figures, vases, and pitcher.

A china inkstand formerly used by President Van Buren.

Smoking set—pale lead colored ware—3 pieces.

Silk shawl. 1805.

Pair of gaiters—1885—cloth.

Pair of gaiters—1805—Nankin.

Caps, slips, and other parts of infant clothing of 1808, and several articles as early as 1785.

Dinner plates. 1718.

Two china plates, time of Queen Anne, highly ornamented, of 1718.

Pair of tea dishes. 1800.

Tea pot, white china. 1861.

Tea pot of 1840.

Two tea sets. About 1800.

Blue china plates, a portion of the wedding outfit of my great grandmother Edmeston Alexander. 1732.

Blue bowl. 1799.

Tea pot, Japanese. 1785.

Tea pot, cups, saucers—1748—of Jane Allen Hamilton.

Tea pot, John Hamilton. 1772.

Tea pot, "Bee Hive." About 1790.

Tea pot, Elizabeth Boyd. 1767.

Tea pot, Rosanna Howard Macfarlane. 1754.

[These four articles wedding presents of my great grand parents.]

Two Japanese vases, large and small, brought in by the first Japanese expedition under Com. Perry, presented to exhibitor by Lieut. Whiting, U. S. N.

Bohemian glass, three pieces.

China toy. 1785.

Pewter dish. 1793.

One coffee pot. 1783.

Pitcher, china. 1809.

Three vases, bronzed, china.

Washington pitcher of 1790—a rare and valuable Wedgewood.

Furniture of Adam Boyd, described as follows:

12 Plates, willow pattern. 1800.

Great circular dish. 1793.

Sugar bowl, blue. 1805.

Toilet cup and dish. 1820.

Great dining dish. 1807.

One circular boarshead dining blue carving dish. 1789.

Blue soup bowl.

Blue sauce dish.

Punch bowl. 1787.

Three cups, old; fine china, dating from 1718 to 1748.

Tea plate. A slave with uplifted hands exclaiming: "Am I not a man and brother?" 1832.

Hess, Jacob, Susquehanna township:

Deed. 24th Sept., 1770. John Harris and wife to Philip Shreyner.

Deed. 8th Sept., 1794. Ex. of Philip Shreyner to Philip Adam Shreyner.

Deed. 14th Nov., 1763. Michel Wiedler and wife to George Hess.

Deed. 1st Aug. 1738. Patent to John Harris for 820 acres in Lancaster county, Province of Pennsylvania.

Deed. 10th Sept., 1761. William Harris, and Margaret, his wife to John Harris.

Deed. 19th Sept., 1761. Samuel Harris, and Elizabeth, his wife to John Harris.

Deed. 31st Dec., 1743. Patent to John Harris for 391 acres land, including island in Susquehanna river, in Lancaster county, Province of Pennsylvania.

Book of solved problems. 1731.

KEAN, Miss JANE D., Harrisburg:

Mahogany knife case. 1793.

Pot and pot hooks. 1785.

Frying pan with handle. 1785.

KELKER, RUDOLPH F., Harrisburg:

Fragments of the translations of the Old and New Testament, by ULFILAS in the *Moeso Gothic*, which is the earliest specimen extant of the Teutonic language, edited by H. F. MASSMAN, with the corresponding texts in Greek and Latin. Stuttgart, 1857. [ULFILAS was born among the Goths A. D. 311, died in Constantinople A. D. 381; belonged to a family of Christian Greeks whom the Goths had carried into captivity about A. D. 267. He became Arian Bishop of those Goths who dwelt between the Danube and Mt. Haemus.]

The Gospels of our Lord and Saviour in Gothic, A. D. 360. Anglo-Saxon, 995. Wycliffe, 1389, and Tyndale A. D. 1526. [Edited by Rev. Joseph Bosworth, D. D., F. R. S., F. S. A., London, 1865.]

Latin Bible; part second, beginning with Proverbs. Printed by Eggesteyn in Strasburg, A. D., 1469: Large Folio. [One of the rarest Bibles in existence. In the Catalogue of the Library of the Duke of Sussex, it is stated that this Bible, of which the first volume only is in the Duke's Library, is described in Bibliotheca Spenceriana and is supposed by Dr. Dibdin to be the second edition of the Latin Bible, printed by Eggesteyn at Strasburg. The work consists of two volumes. There are no signatures, catchwords or numerals, and the initial letters are written in. There is a copy of the first volume only in the Library of the British Museum. Eggesteyn was one of the earliest printers of Strasburg. This copy of the second volume has 245 leaves. The names of the Books, the chapters and the title on each page, are all inserted in red, by the hand, as in a missal. As a specimen of very early printing this rare and venerable volume is of the greatest value.]

Latin Bible, A. D. 1477. The second printed by Coburger, the celebrated printer of Nuremburg. The arrangement and readings correspond precisely with the first edition, but the Epistle of the Monk Mesnard, and the Canons of Eusebius have been added. Large Folio. [The type of this book is of a more elegant character than in the first edition. There was a copy in the collection of the Duc de Lavaliere. It is also fully described in the Catalogue of the Duke of Sussex. The work was finished as stated by Antonius Coburger, at the close of the New Testament August 3d, 1477.]

Latin Bible, A. D. 1480. Printed by Antonius Coburger in Nuremberg. Finished May 18, 1480. Large folio. [The learned compiler of the *Sussex Catalogue* says of this Bible: "This is the fifth edition of the Latin Bible printed by Coburger. It is the most elegant of all his Bibles. It is a beautiful volume and in the finest possible condition."]

Latin Bible, printed A. D. 1486. This is a very rare edition of the "Fontibus" series. There were two editions this year. This is the earliest and rarest. This was the first Bible which had a title page, and most likely printed at Venice by George D. Ravabenis, who is said to have been the first to have printed the Bible with a title page. Thick folio.

Latin Bible, 1556. Printed at Lugduni, (Lyons,) by Joan Tornæsium. Large folio. [Remarkable for the clearness of the type and of its illustrations.]

Latin Bible. Printed at Tiguri, (Zurich,) 1673. Old Testament from translation of Imman. Tremelio and Francisco Junio, and the New Testament from Theodoro Beza.

Gritsch de Basilia, Quadigesimal Tripartitum. Reutlingae Jo. Zeiner. 1476. Large folio volume.

Latin manuscript on vellum of the XIVth Century. Flores et Homilies Saint Bernard. (Born A. D. 1091; d. 1153.) [Written most beautifully on 322 pages. 8¼ by 12½ inches—two columns on each page.

Although five hundred years old, the ink and illuminated initials in various colors retain their original brilliancy.]

Latin manuscript XIVth Century. Written on parchment. Commentary on the Books of Esther and the Chronicles. [130 pages about 8 inches wide, 11¼ inches long. Bound volume.]

Latin Manuscript. Libellus Beati Misericordes. Small volume bound in Russia with gilt edges. Size 4 inches by 6 inches. 176 pages. [A very ancient and legendary manuscript on Vellum, thought to be about the period of Edward Third, (born 1312, died 1377.]

Wycliffite versions of the Holy Bible; 4 vols., quarto; with the Apocryphal Books in the English versions, made from the Latin Vulgate, by John Wycliffe and his followers. [Edited by Rev. Josiah Forshall, F. R. S., etc., late Fellow of Exeter College, and Sir Frederick Madden, K. H., F. R. S., etc., keeper of the manuscripts in the British Museum. Oxford, 1850.]

The New Testament, in English. Translated by John Wycliffe Circa, 1380. Now first printed from a contemporary manuscript formerly in the monastery of Sion, Middlesex, late in the collection of Lea Wilson, F. S. A. Printed in Cheswick by Charles Whittingham, for William Pickering. Piccadilly, London, 1848.

Biblia Pauperum. Conteynynge thirty and eight wode-cuttes illustrating the Liif, Parables, and Miraclis offe Oure Blessid Lord and Saviour Jhesus Crist, with the Proper Descrypciouns thereof, extracted from the Originalle Texte offe John Wiclif, Somtyme Rector of Lutterworth. (No. 111 of an edition of 375 copies printed for America by Unwin Brothers, London, England.) [This is not a *fac simile* of the famous Blook Book "Biblia Pauperum," printed in 1491, but a repro duction of a series of pictures printed from ancient blocks, with printed descriptions from Wycliffe's version of the Bible. It has received its title merely because its purpose resembles that of the Block Book, after which it is named. It represents the era of *early* printing; whereas the original Biblia Pauperum represents the era *before* early printing.]

Tyndales' Pentateuch. Verbatim reprint of the edition of 1530 (No. 217 of the first edition, limited to 500 large paper copies.) By Rev. J. I. Mombert, D. D. 1884.

The Coverdale Bible, A. D. 1535. The Holy Scriptures of the Olde and Newe Testaments, with the Apocripha. Faithfully translated from the Hebrue and Greke, by Myles Coverdale, sometime Lord Bishop of Exeter. Thick quarto. Reprint. S. Bagster & Sons, London.

The Book of Common Prayer. With the Holy Bible, (*King James Version.*) Printed by Thomas and John Buck, printers to the University of Cambridge, 1629. Small folio.

The Book of Common Prayer, with the Holy Bible. Printed at Oxford, by John Baskett; at the University, 1724. Quarto, bound in Russia, gilt edges, and profusely illustrated.

Holy Bible, containing the Old and New Testaments, together with the Apocrypha. Printed at Philadelphia, in two large folio volumes, for John Thompson and Abraham Small, (from the hot press of John Thompson.) 1798.

Complete Body of Divinity. By Thomas Stackhouse, A. M. London, 1755. Large folio.

The Holy Bible. The second of the six oldest German *Pre-Reformation Bibles.* Printed by John Mentel, of Strasburg, in 1466. One of the rarest German Bibles in existence.

The Holy Bible. Vol. 2d, beginning with the Book of Proverbs. The third of the six oldest German *Pre-Reformation* Bibles. Printed at Nuremberg, by Sensenschmidt & Frisner. 1470–1473. Large folio. [An inscription on a fly-leaf of this volume by *Barnheim*, designates it as " The so-called *Fourth* German Bible." This writer is, however, in error, as *M. Johannes Nast*, in his Critical History of the first six editions of the German Bible, all printed from 1462 to 1477, describes this copy, and clearly proves that it is the *third* and not the *fourth* of the six earliest editions. (See Nast's History, Stuttgart, 1767.) Nast states that it is the first Bible in which wood cuts are found.]

The Swiss German Bible. Translation made by the Swiss reform ers Zwingli and his contemporaries, and printed at Zurich in 1536 by the celebrated Bible printer, Christoffel Froschouer.

The Swiss German Bible. Translation made by the Swiss reformers, Zwingli and his contemporaries, and printed in Zurich in 1536, by Christoffel Froschouer, the celebrated Bible printer. [This copy bound with heavy brass corner pieces and shields.]

Holy Bible. German Wittemberg Bible. Translated by Martin Luther, and printed by Hans Luft, Wittemberg, 1583.

German commentary on the New Testament, by Erasmus, of Rotter dam, born 1467, died in Basle, 1536. [The title page of this volume is lost. The type and illustrations render it almost certain that it was printed by Froschouer, at Zurich, during the lifetime of Erasmus.]

Corpus Doctrinæ Christianæ, (Body of Christian doctrine.) In the German language, by Philip Melancthon. Printed at Leipzick, 1560, the last year of the celebrated reformer's life.

Jerusalem, *the Old Metropolis of the Jews*, situated in an Earthly Paradise, the Emblem of the future Eternal City of God. Printed at Franckfurt am Mayn, 1563.

Commentary on the Acts of the Apostles, (in German,) by Lindhammern. Halle, 1725.

Weltbuch. Spiegel und bildness des ganzen Erdbodens, von Sabastiani Franco Wordensi. Printed in 1534. [A large and comprehensive Geography of the World, published only 42 years after the discovery of America. Its statements in reference to the New World, then recently discovered, are very interesting.]

LaSainte Bible, with marginal notes, per David Martin. Amsterdam and Utrecht, 1712.

'T Groot Waerelds Tafereel, Verbeeldende in Konst-Prenton de Heilige en Waereldsche Geschiedenissen, zedert den Aanvang des Waerelds Tot het uiteinde van de Openbaring van Joannes. Amsterdam, 1721. [Events of Old and New Testament History, illustrated by most beautiful Etchings.]

Biblia Pentapla, A. D. 1711. The books of the Holy Scriptures, the Old and New Testaments in German, in five versions, viz:

1. The Roman Catholic, by Caspar Ulenberg, Theo. Sic.

2. The Evangelical Lutheran, by Martin Luther, Theol. D.

3. The Evangelical Reformed, by Johann Piscator, Theo. Prof.

4. The Jewish, the Old Testament, by Joseph Athie; the New Testament, by John Henry Reitzen.

5. The Hollandischen, by the authority of the Herren General Staaten.

Life size oil portrait of Frederick Kelker, born 1780; settled in Harrisburg, 1805, died, 1857. Painted by Eicholtz in 1814.

Columbus, with his brother and Roman Catholic priest, taking possession of the New World, and planting the cross, in 1492. A beautiful specimen of needle-work on silk, made by Catharine Fager, (afterwards Mrs. Frederick Kelker,) when sixteen years of age, at school in Harrisburg, in 1814.

Picture of Reformed and Lutheran church built in 1787, at the corner of Third street and Cherry avenue. The first house of worship erected in Harrisburg.

KELKER, WILLIAM A., Harrisburg:

Full set of chair-maker's tools used in Harrisburg in 1810, by Gilbert Burnett.

Baby coach of same style as stage coaches of olden times. Woodwork made by John Tomlinson, coach-maker; and iron work by John Geiger, blacksmith in Harrisburg, about the year 1825.

McCORMICK, JAMES, Harrisburg:

Reports of Sir Henry Yelverton, Kt. and Bart., 3d ed. corrected; Savoy. 1735.

Report of cases of King's Bench and Com. Pleas, time of King William, Queen Anne, Kings Geo. 1 and 2d; London, 1765. 2 vols.

Cases in Equity, in High Court of Chancery; Savoy, 1756. Vol. 2.

Gen. abridg. cases in equity, in the Savoy. 1756.

Reports of cases of King's Bench and Com. Pleas, from 1670 to 1683; Savoy. 1742.

He Sweit; C. M. S.; Eyppel; cloth antique.

Picture book scraps.

Murder trial; Harrisburg; John Wyeth. 1798.

Essays on law; Dublin. 1789. 2 vols.

Young clerk's magazine. 1799.

Clerk's English tutor; Savoy. 1733.

Cases in Court of King's Bench, time of late Lord Hardwicke; Dublin. 1769.

Doctor and student; Dublin. 1792.

Conductor Generalis for justices of peace; Woodbridge, N. J. 1764.

The law of uses and trusts; Savoy. 1741.

Crown circuit companion; Savoy. 1749. 2 vols.

Wright's English Bible. 1781.

A French-German dictionary; Leipsic. 1746.

A French-English dictionary; London. 1777.

David's psalms; Carlisle. 1804.

Biblesche historien, (Hubner;) Harrisburg. 1826.

Isabella Oliver's poems; Carlisle. 1805.

McDANIEL, JOSIAH, New Cumberland:

Indian tomahawk and knife.

Buckle and spoon.

Wedgewood pitcher. 1790.

Holy Bible. 1793.

Fac simile of ancient Indian tomahawk and pipe, in brass.

NEAD, BENJAMIN M., Harrisburg:

Letter from Wm. Penn. Dec. 9, 1700.

Letter from General E. Braddock. June 8, 1755.

Letter from Conrad Weiser, the Indian interpreter. July 6, 1758.

Brief of title to Penn'a ; opinion by Dudley. 24 Dec., 1739.

Ryder, attorney general of England ; Grant. March, 1680.

Fac simile of first Penn'a State paper. Aug., 1681.

Soldier's discharge, signed by Gen. Anthony Wayne. Jan. 29, 1781.

Late signature of Charles Wilson Peale, patriot artist of the revolution. Jan. 14, 1811.

Letter from Gen. Washington concerning Gen. Chambers, of Chambersburg. April 10, 1777.

First Penn'a State paper; oath and signatures of Lieut Gov. Markham's council. Aug. 3, 1681.

Receipt for soldiers' ferriage across the Susquehanna, at Harris' ferry. Dec. 17th and 18th, 1776.

Letter signed by the Viscount Noailles, brother by marriage to the Marquise DeLafayette. Feb. 20, 1794.

PARTHEMORE, E. W. S., Harrisburg:

Election certificate of John Parthemore, director of the poor for Dauphin county. 1815.

Summons—John Parthemore, and his wife Catharine, late wife of Martin Shell, to appear before John Gloninger, Lebanon. 1784.

Note given by Jacob Reeme to Rev. John Casper Stœver, minister at Lebanon, for his support. 1748.

Inventory of personal estate of John Philip Parthemore, deceased, Paxtang township. 1797.

Soldier's discharge—Henry Myer, from Capt. Stœver's co. Deed 1782. On a large parchment by Geo. Frey and wife Catharine to John Backenstow, carpenter, and Philip Parthemore, blacksmith, for a lot of ground, corner High and Pine streets, Middletown, for the use of the German Calvist (Reformed) for a burial ground, May 22, 1770. Written by James Burd, J. P.

Bible—Mormon, from W. D. Alleman, second cousin to the exhibitor, Springville, Utah.

Martin Luther's sermon book—printed in 1558, at Frankfort-on-the-

Main, by Weyant Han, "in derr Schurr, Gassen-Zum krug," and is 327 years old; belonging to Mr. Parthemore's great-great-grandfather, Matthias Winagle, and came into his possession the year he was born. 1716.

The True Christian—by Johann Arndt. 1730.

Surgeon's certificate exempting John Parthemore from military duty. 1801.

Parthemore Genealogy—by E. W. S. Parthemore. 1885. Printed by Lane S. Hart.

Voice of Warning—Mormon history.

Receipt for surveying land by land office prince of Pennsylvania. 1752.

Account book—John Parthemore, overseer of roads Paxton township. 1782.

Paradise Garden, by Johann Arndt. 1761.

Non Associators tax receipt of John Parthemore. 1777.

Bond given by John Parthemore and Christopher Shoop to Jacob Bomberger. 1772.

Constable appointment—Henry Meyer by court of Dauphin county for Paxtang township. 1796.

Non-associators certificate—Henry Meyer. 1777.

Bill of goods to Jacob Reeme by Johannes Musser, of Philadelphia 1755.

Envelope containing obligations, form of initiation, and list of 66 names of members of a Know-Nothing lodge in Dauphin county, Pa. 1854.

Leaf of a Bible—which is all that remains of John Frederick Parthemore's Bible containing his date of marriage, and to whom. 1721.

Receipt and letter to John Parthemore by Julius Zatzinger, of Lancaster. 1772.

Dismissal—John Frederick Parthemore from the Margravate of Baden Baden, Sprenglingen, Province of Rhein Hessen, Hesse Darmstadt, Germany. January 9, 1744.

Church certificate—John Frederick Parthemore from Rev. John Wilhelm Nisberger, pastor Reformed church, Sprenglingen. May 22, 1744,

Appraiser's certificate for gun made by Martin Shell for a member of Captain Green's company, Revolutionary war. Sept. 13, 1776.

Sword, epaulettes, and plume worn by Daniel Parthemore, of Highspire, as first lieutenant, National Blues. 1843.

Indian relics—pestle, hammer, and ceremonial ax, (very rare.)

POFFENBERGER, DR. A. T., Dauphin:

The family clerk and students' assistant—Bookkeeping by James Meginness; Harrisburg. 1817.
Das Neue Testament; Carlisle. 1824. Printed by Moser & Peters.
Der Geschwinde Rechner; Harrisburg. 1833. Printed by G. S. Peters.

SHANAHAN, RT. REV. J. F., Harrisburg:

St. Jerome's commentary on the Scriptures, Latin, Greek and Hebrew text; Paris. 1533.
The works of St. Gregory; Antwerp. 1572.
Bellarmin's controversial works; Lyons. 1599.
Baronius' ecclesiastical annals; Venice. 1611.
Joannis Maldonati Societatis—commentaries on the Gospels; Mayence. 1602.
Annalum Ecclesiasticum, Baronius; Cologne. 1627.
Complete works of St. Clement, of Alexandria; Greek and Latin text; Paris. 1629.
Geozalez commentaries on Decretals; Frankfort-on-the-Mayn. 1690.
St. Basil's works; French and Latin text; Paris. 1638.
Calmet's commentaries on the Bible; French and Latin text; Paris, 1724.
Liberius' controversial works; Milan. 1744.
Life and writings of St. Cyprian; Antwerp. 1568.
Rollins' ancient history in French. 1733.
Antonius Pius' works; Amsterdam. 1667.
New Testament; Greek text; first American edition; Worcester. 1800.
Paradise Lost; Boston. 1826.
Letters of Junius. 1814.
The Christian Companion; Harrisburg. 1831.
Biblia Sacra, Vulg. ed., Sixti V; Vienna. 1705.
The Lord's Prayer written in seventy languages by students of the Propaganda, Rome.
United States silver dollars, 1795 to 1799.

SCHMIDT, JOSEPH, Harrisburg:

Complete set of the new German Empire coin; one pfennig; 2 pfennig; 5 pfennig; 10 pfennig; 20 pfennig; 50 pfennig; 100 pfennig, (one mark;) 2 marks; 3 marks; 5 marks; old coins, German kreutzer, 1743; new kreutzer, 1870; 1 3-kreutzer, 1646; frauen thaler, patrona of Bavaria, with Holy Virgin and Jesus, 1763; Wurtemberg thaler, 1860; Austrian kulden, 1859; Austrian kronen thaler, 1788; Jolf shilling danake, 1711; Mexican dollar, 1827; Spanish quarter, 1807; Bremen 12-crotten, 1858; American dollar, 1799; American half dollars, 1795, 1801, 1806, 1808, 1810, 1811, 1812, 1813, 1814, 1817, 1818, 1820, 1824, 1825, 1827, 1828. Fractional paper currency of the United States: One yellow, 5 cents; one yellow, 10 cents; one yellow, 15 cents; one yellow, 25 cents; other kind, 25 cents; small dark color 50 cents; large last issue, 50 cents.

Stevens, Thomas H., Harrisburg:

Eleven lace bobbins in basket; of last century.
Armlet of eighteen agates. 1700.
Chinese tea pot. 1810.
Three china cups, of last century.
Collection of silver and copper coins, of various values and dates—some quite rare.

Strouse, Mrs. Joseph, Harrisburg:

Infant's cap, two hundred years old.
Pair of spectacles. 1730.
Lady's collar. 1800.
Lady's bonnet. 1800.
Gentleman's cane. 1810.
Lady's muff of 1825.
Lady's skirt of 1840.

Weir, Misses Annie C. and Sybil M., Harrisburg:

Letters to a young lady, calculated to improve the heart, to form the manners, and enlighten the understanding, "That our daughters may be as polished corners of the temple;" Rev. John Bennett; New York. 1716.

God's appearances for His church, under the New Testament; Mr. Robert Fleming, who died 1694. 1732.

New Testament in German; Beudingen. 1738.

Abrege L.'Histoire Universelle, depuis Charlemagne jusque a Charlequint; par Mr. deVoltaire, 2 vols. 1753.

23

Essais sur divers sujets de Literature et de Moral; par Mr. L'Abbe Trublet, 3 vols. ; Amsterdam. 1755.

Sermons on Christ's Famous Titles, and a Believer's Golden Chain, together with his Cabinet of Jewels, or a glimpse of Sion's Glory; Wm. Dyer, preacher of the Gospel; Belfast. 1761.

Sermons to Young Women, James Fordyce, 2 vols.; London. 1770.

Works of Jonathan Swift, D. D., D. S. P. D., with notes His. and Crit., by J. Hawkesworth, LL. D., and others; Dublin. 1774.

Works of Josephus, trans. by Sir Robt. L'Estrang, Kt.; 7th ed. English, vols. 1 and 3; vol. 1, pub. London. 1773. Vol. 3, New York. 1775.

Greek grammar, purchased in 1779.

The Gentleman's and Farmer's Almanack, 1782, being second after leap year and 22nd year of the reign of the King George III, 'till the 25th of Oct.; Dublin.

Human Nature in its Fourfold State, by Mr. Thomas Boston, late minister of the Gospel at Etterick. 1787.

The American Accountant, or Schoolmaster's New Assistant, Benj. Workman, A. M., Philadelphia. 1789.

Poems by Wm. Cowper, Esquire, Boston. 1791.

Schrevelliis Lexicon, London. 1791.

Holy Bible, Edinburgh. 1791.

Shorter Catechism, Air, Scotland. 1792.

The Pleasures of the Immagination by Dr. Akenside, to which is added, The Art of preserving Health, a poem by Dr. Armstrong, Exeter, Eng. 1794.

A Short History of the British Empire during the last twenty months from May 1792, to the close of the year 1793, by Francis Plowden; Dublin. 1794.

Friendship in Death, in twenty Letters from the Dead to the Living, to which are added Letters moral and entertaining by Mrs. Elizabeth Rowe, New York. 1795.

Selectæ e Veteri Testamento Historiæ, purchased 1792.

Selectæ e Profanis Scriptoribus Historiæ, Philadelphia. 1787.

Voyage dans les Etats-Unis d'Amerique, fait en 1795, 1796, et 1797, par LaRochefoucauld-Liancount; 8 vols. Pub. "L'an VII de la Republique, (with maps.)

Practical Philosophy of Social Life, or the Art of conversing with men; after the German of Baron Knigge, by P. Will, minister of the Reformed German Congregation in the Savoy, Lansingburg. 1805.

Ovid Delphini, cura Ioannis Andrews, D. D., in Academic Pennsylvaniensi, Phil. Mor. Prof. et V. Præfectus; Philadelphia. 1805.

History of the Civil War in Ireland, containing an impartial account of the proceedings of the Irish revolutionists from the year 1782, until the suppression of the intended Revolution. Rev. Jas. Gordon; Baltimore. 1805.

Travels and Adventures in Canada, and the Indian Territories, between the years 1760, and 1776, in two parts, Alexander Henry; New York. 1809.

German Testament; Germantown. 1819.

The Federalist on the New Constitution, written in the year 1788, by Mr. Hamilton, Mr. Madison, and Mr. Jay; Hollowell, Maine. 1826.

A Universal Geography, by M. Maltebrun. 3 vols.; Boston. 1834.

The Love of Jesus, a Dissertation on Baptism, Confirmation, and the Lord's Supper, by Frederika Misca, dedicated to His Excellency, Joseph Ritner, Governor of Pennsylvania, the Citizens of Harrisburg, and all subscribers, with a recommendation from Samuel Sprecher, pastor of Zion's church, Harrisburg. 4th edition; Harrisburg. 1838.

Testament in the Hawaiian language, presented by Mrs. Mary Alexander. Oahu. 1835.

CONTRIBUTIONS BY CLASSES.

Imperfect as the following records are, they will convey some idea of the varied character of the Antiquarian display. Although earnestly requested, some of the Committees failed entirely, to make a list of articles in their respective classes. Others gave but a small portion. This was owing to the fact that it was not ascertained until almost the closing hours of the exhibition that the proper parties had failed in the work confided to them. No records were preserved of the articles of silver, jewelry, household and farm implements, furniture, musical instruments, coins, etc., save those given in individual lists, which comprised but a small portion of the articles exhibited.

INDIAN RELICS.

ALTMAIER, HARRY :

Three stone axes, eight pieces Indian pottery, twenty-six arrow-heads one stone knife.

BAKER, ELLIS S., Middletown :

Bow and two arrows.

BALSBAUGH, HENRY :

Arrow heads.

BOYD, PETER K.:

Indian reticule, pair of moccasins.

CALDER, Mrs. WILLIAM J. :

Three water jars, used by Pueblo (New Mexican) Indians.

COMFORT, JOHN C.:

Ceremonial pick-ax, between two and two-and-a-half inches long— very fine.

DAVIS, A. J.:

Alaskan Indian exhibits, as follows :

Basket made of the fibrous roots of an Alaskan tree, an Alaskan lady's silver ear-ring, nineteen photographs of Alaskan scenery, horn spoon of fine workmanship, four Alaskan bracelets, abalena shells, money purse made of a swan's foot, with claws intact ; ten masks, carved box taken from a grave with the masks, gold quartz, sea otter skin, fur of a baby seal, kamalaka or water-proof coat, made of the intestines of a bear, land otter skin, yellow cedar board, covered bottle, cover made of same material as the basket, above described, floor mat made by an Alaskan Indian, of the inner bark of the yellow cedar, from Fort Wrangel, Alaska.

[The ten masks were worn years ago, by a Klinget Shamaan, at his incantations and were taken from a shamaan's grave, near Harrisburg, Alaska. These masks were hideous, and were intended to represent the faces of animals and human beings, in caricature.]

DEITRICH, FRANK :

Bow and four arrows, stone pipe, clay pipe, five arrow-heads, pair of moccasins, Indian vest, pair Indian pants, tobacco pouch.

EGLE, Dr. WILLIAM HENRY :

Stone axes, stone pestle, two stone hammers, one hammer-stone, one stone quoit, iron tomahawk, pair moccasins, pipe found in an Indian grave exhumed when excavating for a ditch at Chesapeake nail works. Ornament stone. It was made to resemble an animal with very prominent eyes, and, no doubt, was highly prized by its original owner. Celt neolithic, forty arrow-heads, consisting of fine jasper, obsidium, &c., stone pipe, Indian beads, Indian beaded case, beaded flint case, Indian whip, gun cover.

ENDERS, DR. L., Enders:

Ceremonial stone, seven spear-heads, three stone knives, two cutting stones, two stone borers, fifteen arrowheads.

FERTIG, ELIAS, Dauphin:

One iron tomahawk.

ENSMINGER, GEORGE, Strinestown, York county:

Stone tube, supposed to have been used by the "medicine man" in the curing of diseases. The medicine man placed the tube on or close to the diseased part, made a few draws and blows through it, accompanied with hideous contortions of face and body; this he repeated frequently, and if, by a natural course, a cure was effected, his fame, and the fame of his tube, became notorious. Ceremonial stone, sixty-five very fine arrowheads, six stone borers. These borers were used by Indians in making holes in hides. Various stone implements, &c., five scrapers, one cutting stone, stone pipe, eight stone axes, six stone hammers, one stone hoe, three celts, two scrapers, three cutting stones, one ornament stone, twenty-five pieces of pottery, seven spearheads.

FAGER, DR. CHARLES B.:

Three stone axes, one stone hammer, one stone pipe, Indian game bag of alligator skin, ceremonial pick-ax, one celt, three spearheads, stone pot, Indian bead, two arrowheads, Indian bone ornament, one iron spearhead, ceremonial stone, scalplock of a white woman killed and scalped by the Indians. [The stone pot, perfect, and a very rare relic, was found on Peter's mountain, and presented to Dr. John H. Fager.]

FISHER, F. D.:

Collection of arrowheads.

FISHER FAMILY, Swatara:

Indian hatchet, of iron.

GEETY, W. WALLACE, Dauphin:

Collection of arrow-heads, two stone axes, one pestle.

HARTAN, C., Dauphin:
Stone knife, Indian shot.
HAYES, MARGARET, Grantville:
Stone hammer.
HELLERMAN, Mrs.:
Pair of moccasins, beaded belt, (one of the finest we have ever seen,) beaded bird bag, Indian suit, consisting of a coat of deer skin, and a pair of pants, of same material, both nicely fringed.

[The above suit and accoutrements were purchased of an Indian, in the year 1855, and have been in the Hellerman family ever since. This suit, with the war bonnet, mentioned in Mrs. F. Wyeth's list constituted, in connection with an Indian false-face, the makeup of the "Cherokee Chief" placed on a pole at one end of the Indian relic department, and was an attractive feature of the Antiquarian, especially for the little ones.]

HILGART, P. W.:
Stone ax, of the neolithic age.
KERR, LYDIA, Highspire:
Arrow and spear-heads.
KIRK, W. E.:
Pair of moccasins, beaded neck-band, fifteen barbed arrow-heads one hundred triangular arrow-heads, two hundred and ten arrow-heads, spear-heads, and stone knives on cards, Indian war-paint stone, stone of unknown use, stone hatchet, two stone hammers, stone pestle, six stone axes, war-club, stone, stone of unknown use—supposed to have been used in making stone implements; stone ball, seven hammer-stones, four celts, pendant for fishing, three stone hoes, three stone scrapers, polishing stone.

LANDIS, GEO. C., Middletown:
Pair Indian breeches, worn by the "White River Utes."
McALLISTER, JAMES H., Rockville:
Stone ax.
McCORMICK, JAMES:
Piece of an Indian pipe of excellent workmanship. The whole pipe (which, judging from the part exhibited,] must have been very fine, was at one time in the possession of Mr. McCormick in perfect form. Stone hammer, stone ax.
McDANIEL, JAMES SAWYERS:
Brass tomahawk and pipe combined.

McDaniel, Josiah, New Cumberland:

Indian tomahawk, Indian scalping knife, both used in Indian wars.

Martin, Harry:

Comanche pipe bowl made of the knot of a tree. It was found in Yellowstone Canon, Texas and is a fine specimen of Indian skill.

Mason, William:

Stone mortar, found on an island near Harrisburg, many years ago; was formerly in the possession of Mr. Daniel Sheesley, sr., and by him presented to Mr. Mason. The mortar is seven inches in diameter and five inches high. The cup of the mortar is three and one half inches deep, the largest diameter being four and one half inches, and shaped like a cup.

Napier, Mrs. Eliza:

Indian bow, lot of arrows, eagle feathers, scalping-knife, case and whistle of antelope shinbone, Indian whip, beaded tobacco pouch, pair small moccasins, paint pouch and flint pouch, with steel, petrified wood and flint, belt with three pouches complete; piece of Indian skull, with beads attached, found in a grave at Chesapeake nail works.

[The former articles, with one exception, are relics of the "Custer massacre," and were obtained by a son of Mrs. Napier after the battle. The bow had thirty-one indentations on one side, which some of the Indians informed Mr. Napier indicated the number of buffaloes the owner had slain during his lifetime. The paint-pouch was filled with paint, some of which, no doubt, had been used to prepare the "braves" for the massacre. The body of a young man from Harrisburg was found by Mr. Napier on the battle-field, with three arrows deeply imbedded in the flesh. Several of these are included among the second articles.]

Norman, Philip A., Carlisle:

Sioux blanket, beaded and waterproof, pair of leggings, medicine bag, beaded wrist-guard, victory feather and string of beads, bow and six arrows, beaded tobacco bag, pipe made by "High Wolf," Indian scalp lock, breast-plate made of porcupine quills, knife scabbard, very finely beaded, pair of child's moccasins, boy's beaded vest, Indian chief's shirt, Navajoe blanket, child's vest adorned with brass beads, neck-lace of porcupine quills, perfume bags, perfume bottle, young buffalo hide.

[Mr. Norman was among the Indians as a soldier for years, and his collection was obtained under many circumstances unfavorable to

longevity; some of them representing not only historical, but blood
value. An arrow which he has in his possession struck him on the
head, between the eyebrows, and, although penetrating the skull, did
not touch a vital spot, but left a lifelong memento of the intentions of
the savage foe. The Sioux blanket was hand-knit, and was impervi-
ous to water for many hours. Many months were required for its completion. Custer's bloody massacre was represented in his loan as well
as other Indian battles.]

O'CONNER, HALDEMAN:

Pestle of stone two feet long, three axes, one of them a fine ax of
neolithic age.

O'CONNER, DR. MORTIMER:

Seventeen arrows, spears and fish-spears, four long bows; cassava
strainer used by South American Indians in preparing the juice of the
manioc plant for food. [What passes through the strainer goes into a
vessel prepared for its reception; on the surface of this strained juice is
found a deadly poison, which is carefully skimmed off and the substance
remaining, by preparation, becomes a very palatable food. Tapioca is
purified cassava.] Five war clubs, or insignias of office among South
American tribes. Case of poisoned arrows, used in hunting game.
Blow-pipe for blowing the poisoned arrows. Three specimens of S.
A. pottery; compares favorably with pottery made by white men. Pipe
and tobacco pouch; two bottles made by S. American Indians; three
calabashes adorned by Indians.

[The bows exhibited were over five feet long, as long, in fact, as the
Indian hunters who use them. Few men who visited the Antiquarian
could have used them effectively, but, in the hands of the Indian, who
from childhood is accustomed to their use in seeking his food and fight-
ing his enemies, they answer all requirements. The poisoned arrows,
(No. 5,) attracted much attention. They were placed in one of the
glass cases, and, in consequence of the danger attending their being
carelessly handled, no one but authorized members of the committee
were allowed to handle them. They were about one foot long, of the
thickness of a match, and made out of a reed found in S. A. These
arrows can be blown by an expert one inch into an oak board without
being broken, and poisonous as they are, constitute the only ammunition a South American Indian hunter desires. The poison with which
the points of the arrows are impregnated, paralyzes the game before it
kills it, but, strange to say, the flesh of the animal can be eaten with

impunity. The blow-gun is seven feet long, and requires months to complete it, in consequence of lack of tools.]

OTT, FREDERICK M. :

Three celts, five stone axes, four stone hammers, iron hatchet, piece of canister, supposed to have been used by the Paxtang Rangers.

PARTHEMORE, E. W. S.:

Indian pestle, very fine ceremonial ax, stone hammer.

PETERS, F. D. :

Silver breast-plate, made and worn by " Black Bear; " very unique, two arrow-heads.

POFFENBERGER, DR. A. T., Dauphin :

Stone ax, stone hammer.

POFFENBERGER, Miss MAGGIE, Dauphin :

Seven arrow-heads, stone hammer, stone hoe. (neolithic.)

PRATT, Mrs. Captain, Indian School, Carlisle :

Seminole head-band, Modoc bow, Kiowa bow and four arrows, one pair Caddo moccasins, one pair Sioux moccasins, one pair Navajoe moccasins, one pair Comanche moccasins, one pair Cheyenne moccasins, one pair Kiowa moccasins, one pair Arapaho moccasins, one pair Sioux moccasins, worked with porcupine quills, Pueblo sash, Sioux beaded cover, papoose cradle, Sioux necklace and ear-pendant of shells, necklace of brass beads, photograph of "Powderface," an Arapaho chief, photograph of an Indian camp, Navajoe blanket, birch toy canoe, photograph of an Indian girl, Omaha dolls, Comanche comb and awl case, pipe of peace, smoked in making a treaty between the Arapaho and Pawnee Indians, Modoc bow made by "Scarfaced Charley," watchguard made by the San Carlos Indians, two bowls made by Apache Indians, barkholder made by Menominee Indians, saddle-bags made by Shoshone Indians.

[Mrs. Pratt's collection was very fine, and much admired by all interested in such collections. The most of the articles were of great historical value, and were such an accumulation the value of which money cannot represent.]

SHENK & EIKER, Marsh Run :

Six stone scrapers, two stone knives, one stone hammer.

SNYDER, Rev. W. H. H. :

War-club, made with an elliptical stone, covered with tanned hide, attached to a stick, ready for use ; Indian papoose doll, owned, originally, by one of the children of the Crow Indians, of Montana. The doll was placed in a papoose cradle, and attracted much attention.

STROCK, WM. B.:

Indian violin, purchased by him of an Indian. It was eighteen inches long, and two inches in diameter, made of the limb of a maple tree, and painted with hieroglyphics. The harmonies it produced with its one string of sinew were no doubt very monotonous.

THOMAS, FINDLAY I.:

Pair moccasins, stone hammer, ornament stone, found in Susquehanna river.

TOMKINSON, Miss M. M.:

Ceremonial pick-ax, from Ohio. It was about three inches long, perfectly and symmetrically formed; stone ax.

MECK, H. R.:

Stone hatchet.

WYETH, Mrs. F.:

Pair Sioux garters, papoose cradle, brass tomahawk and pipe combined, beaded powder-case, bow and arrows, Indian bridle, Indian war bonnet made of eagles' feathers, pair moccasins, pair squaw's leggings, beaded pouch, Indian doll and paraphernalia, beaded bag, beaded money purse, musk bag, pair small moccasins; Indian war shield, circular in form, and made of buffalo hide, ornamented with feathers.

[Mrs. Wyeth's war bonnet was one of the finest made, being over six feet long and contained thirty-three eagle feathers on the back and twenty-seven on the head. These feathers were of eagles shot by the Indian from whom it was obtained, and as it represented his skill as a hunter, was highly prized by the original owner.]

OLD CHURCH RELICS.

DERRY CHURCH:

View of the log church erected about 1740, and a plan of the memorial church now being erected.

Pulpit of 1740.

Communion table and two chairs. 1740.

Communion service of 1785.

Two contribution boxes, about 1740.

Tokens, 1780. Mrs. Jacob F. Seiler.

Linen, 1785. Mrs. C. L. Bailey.

Original call of Paxtang and Derry churches to Rev. John Elder. Sept. 26, 1754.

Easel made of wood from the old church with ancient pew door on it.

PAXTANG CHURCH:

Old communion table and benches. Silas Rutherford.

Communion linen, home spun, over one hundred years old, consisting of two long table cloths, one square table cloth, and four napkins.

The old pewter communion service. John B. Rutherford.

Easel made of wood from the church, with ancient pew door resting on it. Mrs. Barber.

Neck band worn by Rev. John Elder.

HANOVER CHURCH:

Communion tray of 1780.

MARKET SQUARE PRESBYTERIAN CHURCH, Harrisburg:

Old arm-chair. 1790. Mrs. Isabella S. Kerr.

Portrait of Rev. William R. DeWitt, pastor of the church almost 50 years.

Church Bible. 1790.

Portrait of James W. Weir, superintendent of the Presbyterian Sunday-school, from 1834 to 1878.

Sunday-school superintendent's chair used from its first organization.

Sabbath-school bell, made from the old bell belonging to the church burned in 1858.

ZION LUTHERAN CHURCH, Harrisburg:

View of church built in 1814.

Baptismal bowl, in use a century ago.

Desk and table, two contribution bags, and two sconces.

Life-size portrait of Martin Luther, the reformer. Lutheran S. S. Association.

Engraving of " The Last Supper." William Sayford.

REFORMED CHURCH, Harrisburg:

Engraving of " Christ Blessing Little Children." Mrs. George Z. Kunkel.

The linen communion table cloth, purchased Oct. 2, 1795, and used on sacramental occasions afterwards for more than seventy years.

Communion service : tankard, cup and plates used by the Reformed and Lutheran congregations, from 1787 to 1816; and from 1816 to 1839, by the Reformed Salem church.

Walnut altar table of the Reformed and Lutheran (union) church, built in 1787, now used as the platform desk, in the lecture-room of the Reformed Salem church, of Harrisburg.

Two contribution boxes of 1787.

Tin sconce. 1787.

Charity box. 1820. R. F. Kelker.

Walnut chair. 1822.

View of Reformed and Lutheran church, Harrisburg. Built in 1787.

GRACE METHODIST EPISCOPAL CHURCH :

Two chairs used in the Methodist Church, Harrisburg, in 1810.

ST. STEPHEN'S P. EPISCOPAL CHURCH, Harrisburg :

The old arm chair in which the venerable Bishop White sat. 1828.

Two funeral biers, used in early days of burial.

Prayer book, published in 1696. Mrs. Catharine Boude.

The Book of Common Prayer. 1794. Mrs. Seneca G. Simmons.

ROMAN CATHOLIC :

* German Catholic prayer book, printed at Aschaffenberg, Bavaria, about 1756. This book used as "Bridal Prayer Book" by the great grandmother, grandmother, and mother of A. R. Kiefer, at their respective weddings.

Rosary 150 years old. Mrs. Nancy Magee.

Crucifix 475 years old. Mrs. John C. Delaney.

MISCELLANEOUS :

German communion tankard. Mrs. James McCormick.

Cherub from old Spanish church. Mrs. James McCormick.

WAR RELICS, 1776—1861.

BOUDE, Mrs. CATHARINE :

Sword of Capt. Thomas Boude, of the Revolution, presented to him by Gen. Washington.

CONRAD, JOHN B. :

Minnie ball taken from the skull of a Confederate captain, killed at the battle of Fredericksburg, December 13, 1862.

Portfolio found in Washington, D. C., in 1862.

Stone picked up at Gettysburg, on the spot where Gen'l Hancock was wounded when Picket made his charge.

COX, JOHN B. :

Blunderbuss. No history.

CRESWELL, FRANK :

Bullet, relic of the late war.

DAUGHERTY, Capt. ELI :

[A Bible and a gold watch that saved his life. A Confederate bullet struck the watch and chipped out a section, including the stem, like a crescent and then penetrated the Bible, stopping about half way; its course being then deflected, it passed out close to the lid tearing it somewhat. He found the bullet; cut it into three sections and placed them in his pocket-book, which he lost in Boston, Mass. Although offering a reward of twenty dollars for the recovery of the bullet, and no questions asked, he was unsuccessful.]

DETWEILER, Mrs. E. P.:

Two canes, owned originally by Benjamin Parke.

One sword, owned originally by Thomas Parke.

One pair of pistols carried through the Revolutionary war by Benjamin Parke.

EARLY, D. S.:

U. S. sword of iron and leather scabbard made in 1799—handmade.

Sword with silver and leather scabbard found on Gettysburg battlefield.

EGLE, Dr. WILLIAM H.:

Hessian sword captured at the battle of Trenton.

Sword owned by Sergeant Geo. Beatty, and used in 1812.

Wooden bowl used by a Revolutionary soldier.

Mexican spurs.

FAGER, Dr. CHARLES B.:

Gun-barrel.

Piece of a Revolutionary flag.

GEETY, W. WALLACE, Dauphin:

Confederate note, Winchester bank. Picture captured at the residence of Col. Stewart, of "Black Horse Cavalry" fame.

Rebel orders.

Fac-simile of the first paper printed in America.

Ulster County Gazette.

"Southern Rights," a paper printed by northern soldiers after they had possession of the office and printing press.

Grape shot which entered Mr. Geety's head at the base of the nose, breaking off a piece of his skull and lodging in his neck.

Spear of brass made from the sheathing of a locomotive destroyed by the Confederates at Martinsburg, Va.

Shell nipple.

Bottom of a shell fired at the Union forces, in the late war.

GEORGE, WILLIAM J. :
Gun of English manufacture, captured from the Confederates at Gettysburg.

GREENAWALT, THEODORE D. :
Grandfather's gun. The gun has an extraordinarily long barrel, and is eighty years old.

GUTSCHALL, RICHARD, Dauphin :
Sword and belt used in Revolutionary war.

HAYES, Mrs. MARGARET, Grantville :
Powder-horn used at the battle of Lexington, and brought to America from Ireland.

HAMILTON, A. BOYD :
Lock of a musket used in the war of 1812.
Sword bayonet used by Ellsworth's Zouaves.

HAMILTON, Dr. HUGH. :
Sabre from Camp Brookwood, Hannah's woods, war of 1861.

HICKOK, W. O. :
Flintlock pistol.

HINCKLE, GEORGE :
Gun 120 years old.

McALLISTER, JAMES H. :
Gun owned originally by John Harris.
Pistols presented by Gen. George Washington to Archibald McAllister, after the battle of Monmouth.
Grape canister, found above Harrisburg, and supposed to have been used by the " Paxtang Rangers," in a swivel gun.

MERSEREAU, JAMES :
Powder-horn used in Revolutionary war.

MIDDAUGH, J. K. :
John White's powder-horn, used in 1812.
Sword of 1812.
Sword of 1776.

NAGLE, Mrs. G. F., Philadelphia :
Very fine sword and scabbard presented to Colonel Geo. A. C. Seiler, when commander-in chief at Camp Curtin.

RINGLAND, Dr. JOHN, Middletown :
Pike made for the use of John Brown, at Harper's Ferry, and with which he intended to arm the slaves.

SAUL, J. M.:
Flintlock horse-pistol.
Sword, no history.

SCHAFFNER, DANIEL, Hummelstown :
Army blanket, used in the late rebellion.

STAUFFER, J. H.:
Old flintlock gun.

STONER, W. S., and MARY A., Highspire :
Gun used in 1776.
Cannon ball used in Revolutionary war.
Game-bag used in 1776.
Bayonet used in 1776.
Cartridge-box used in 1776.
Sword and holster used by Captain John Stoner, in the war of 1812.
Pewter fife.

THOMAS, FINDLAY, I.:
Sword captured in front of Petersburg, Va., and presented to Mr.
Thomas. The crape around it was placed there when President Lincoln was assassinated, and has never been removed. The belt was
presented by Amos Leschey, orderly to Gen. Grant.

TOMLINSON, Mrs. JOHN B.:
Yardstick 100 years old. Originally owned by Mrs. Elizabeth App,
who took tea with General Washington.

TOWSEN, HARRY H.:
Old gun. No history.

WEILLS, Dr. W. M. L.:
Indian tomahawk picked up at the battle of Tippecanoe.

WIKEL, JOHN:
Very old sword found in the Susquehanna river, near the C. V. R.
R. bridge, Harrisburg, Pa.

YOUNG, JOHN:
Gun in his possession 63 years.

OLD CHINA, POTTERY, &c.

Case table china from Foo Chow. Mrs. James Calder.
Collection of butterfly china. Mrs. John Keffer.
Collection of German china. Mrs. E. D. Klein.
Te 'te set Dresden ; present to her mother on her marriage, 1801.
Mrs. E. D. Klein.

China cup and saucer, 1775.   Mrs. E. D. Klein.

China cup and saucer, 1774.   Memento of a tomb of a dead friend. Mrs. E. D. Klein.

Flower bottles from Brazil.   Mrs. E. D. Klein.

Two majolica pitchers from Scotland, 150 years old.   Mrs. M. E. Brooke.

Pitcher 175 years old.   Kate McKee.

Large collection of vases.   Mrs. James McCormick.

Ancient tea pot.   Mrs. Jane Chester.

Part of a set of china presented to Jane Hamilton, on her marriage to Gen'l John Kean, December 10, 1789.

Two pieces Canton china.   Misses Weir.

English plate, 100 years old.   Mrs. Collins, Steelton.

Two vases imported from China, 1799.   T. D. Greenawalt.

Dark blue coffee-pot, 100 years old.   Mrs. James Mahon.

Dark blue coffee-pot, 74 years old.   Mrs. T. F. Mullen.

Two blue china plates, 125 years old.   Mrs. W. L. Trewick.

Purple china plate, over 100 years old.   Mrs. J. L. Stoey.

Purple china tea set 100 years old.   Mrs. Miller.

Plate from Wales.   Miss Fenn.

Very old flower vase.   Mrs. R. Hummel.

Turkey plate, 60 years old.   Mrs. J. R. Miller.

Very old platter.   Mrs. George Hoyer.

Blue china platter, 150 years otd.   Mrs. D. L. Jauss.

Black and blue china platter, 100 years old.   Mrs. Bidleman.

Two china cake plates, 80 years old.   Mrs. R. Hogan.

Purple amier plate, 50 years old.   Mary McCarroll.

Tea set, dark blue china.   G. B. Wiestling.

Large flowered soup plate, 80 years old.   Mrs. Kate Hammill.

Old china cream pitcher.   Miss Maggie Uhler.

Little Liverpool cream pitcher, 100 years old.   Mrs. Milleisen.

China cream pitcher, 70 years old.   Mrs. Robt. Vaughn.

Pepper-box, 150 years old.   John Wilver.

China cream pitcher, 106 years old.   Mrs. Clara Segelbaum.

One dark blue platter, 100 years old.   Mrs. S. H. Kennedy.

Turkey plate 75 years old.   Miss Maria L. Scheffer.

Light blue platter, 90 years old.   Charles Reel.

Coffee and tea set silvered pottery, made 1810.   Miss Sarah B. Egle.

Liverpool bowl, very old.   Mrs. Beard.

Common brown bowl, made 1807. Mrs. Witherow.

Sugar bowl, 100 years old. Mrs. J. L. Stoey.

Butter dish, 100 years old. Mrs. Corbett.

Pepper-bottle, made 1685. A. McKee.

Plaque of china, made 1685. Mrs. E. Haldeman Longenecker.

Image found in the streets of Ninevah, made of the ashes of a human being, 300 years old. H. A. Kelker.

Fish knives, 1774. Mrs. E. D. Klein.

Flower vase, silvered pottery, 100 years old. Mrs. D. Mumma.

Cream pitcher of Bombey ware of 1785. Mrs. Hage.

Antique plate, very rare. 1775.

A specimen of inlaid work of precious stone as seen on the interior of the Tap, the tomb of the Queen Argamund Banoo, wife of King Shahjehan, which was built in Agra, during Shehjehan's reign, and is the most beautiful tomb known. Mrs. Brown, missionary from India.

Set of lava plates, bronzed. Gen. Simon Cameron.

China ornament, 150 years old. Mrs. W. McGonigal.

Small cup and saucer. Mary Hogan.

Salt dish, 80 years old.

Chinese tea-pot. Thos. Stevens.

Chinese bowl, 100 years old.

Dark blue bowl with white figures, 100 years old.

Zuni pottery.

Very old cups. Mrs. H. M. Graydon.

Small cream pitcher, 80 years old.

Cup and saucer; after dinner cup, oil bottle, blue willow china. Miss Huston.

Cup, saucer and plate used by chief Beau. Mrs. Mather.

China cup, saucer, plate and tray. Mrs. B. L. Forster.

Small blue china plate, 252 years old.

Two custard cups and saucers 125 years old. Mrs. H. J. Armstrong.

Small blue tea-pot, willow pattern, 100 years old. Mrs. M. E. Brooke.

Three cups and two saucers 75 years old, cup and saucer 107 years old, cup and saucer 100 years old, cup and saucer 100 years old, cup and saucer 115 years old, cup and saucer 135 years old, cup and saucer 200 years old. Charles H. Small.

Cup and saucer owned by Lord Baltimore, and out of which Gener-

24

als Hancock and Gibbons, of the Union army, were treated to tea by the late owners, the Misses Scott, near Fredericksburg, Va.

Two china plates from Scotland. Mrs. M. E. Brooke.

China tea cosy. Miss R. Pollock.

Stone bottle, 100 years old.

Salad bowl, 50 years old. Mrs. John Kepple.

Egg shell china, brought from Japan at the treaty, in Commodore Perry's flag ship, Susquehanna. Mrs. B. L. Forster.

Tea cup, 100 years old. Mrs. D. L. Jauss.

Tea pot, 80 years old. Mrs. John Kepple.

Cream pitcher, cup and saucer. Mrs. LeRue Lemer.

Two china cups from Scotland. Mrs. M. E. Brooke.

Plate owned by Wm. Penn. Mrs. Chas. A. Boas.

Tea caddy, 100 years old, was in Chicago fire.

China bowl. Mrs. H. M. Graydon.

Pickle dish, 150 years old, Mrs. Thomas S. Weirman.

Sugar bowl, 105 years old.

House idol brought from India 40 years ago. Miss G. F. Huston.

Stone bowl, 140 years old. John Wilson.

Four pieces of china used 60 years ago by Catharine Shelly. Mrs. J. R. Miller.

Three china cups of last century. Thos. Stevens.

China ring, 100 years old. Mrs. Chas. H. Small.

Plate, cup, and saucer, brought from Wales, 1710. Mrs. Fenn.

China tea cup and metal receiver, also rice cup. Fred. Kelker.

Cameo cream pitcher, 1820. Mrs. S. M. Forster.

Sugar bowl, 100 years old. Mrs. Chas. H. Small.

Majolica pitcher very old. Mrs. M. E. Brooke.

Cream pitcher owned by James Alricks. Mrs. B. L. Forster.

Plate, cup, and saucer from Wales. Mrs. Fenn.

China vase. Mrs. B. L. Forster.

Blue china gravy bowl and plate. Mrs. Geo. Hoyer.

Blue water pitcher. John K. Small.

Blue plate, 100 years old. Mrs. Milleisen.

Cream pitcher, 75 years old. Mrs. W. A. Zollinger.

Plate, 75 years old. Mrs. R. Ricker.

Cream pitcher, 75 years old. Mrs. D. L. Jauss.

Old tea pot. Mrs. E. Demmy, Middletown.

Sugar bowl, 100 years old. Mrs. Gipe.

Light blue tea pot, 105 years old. Mrs. Donecker.

Light blue gravy bowl, 100 years old. Mrs. J. W. Stofer.

Two mugs from the family of Lord Wellington. Mrs. M. E. Brooke.

Blue plate. Mrs. Jane Chester.

Flowered plate. Mrs. Herbert Morrow.

China flower vase, very old. Mrs. Phœbe Brown.

Masonic pitcher, (wedgewood,) 1792. Miss Sarah B. Egle.

Dark blue platter, 100 years old. Mrs. Mary Corbet.

Platter bought on Market street near the Square, 98 years ago. Mrs. Rachel Stocy.

Small cream pitcher. Miss Mary Small.

Mexican water bottle. Mrs. J. C. Kunkel.

Cream pitcher, 130 years old. Helen Johnson.

Blue platter, 150 years old. Mrs. D. L. Jauss.

Mexican water bottle. Miss Pollock.

China tea pot, 100 years old. Miss Annie Kendig.

Dark blue platter, 100 years old. Mrs. B. G. Peters.

Dark blue soup plate, landing of LaFayette. Mrs. J. S. Weaver.

Dark blue dinner plate, 100 years old. Mrs. D. D. Boas.

Dark blue dinner plate. Mrs. Adam Reel.

China bust of Plato, bought by Christian Kunkel, 100 years ago. Exhibited by his grandson, J. P. Keller.

Cups and saucers, 70 years old. Dr. J. H. Coover.

Plate, 100 years old. Dr. J. H. Coover.

Pitcher, bought by Christian Kunkel over 100 years ago. J. P. Keller.

Lot of Egyptian pottery. Mrs. A. S. McCreath.

Duck, taken from an Indian tomb of Peru. Dr. Hugh Hamilton.

Large china bowl, 1782. Miss Sarah B. Egle.

Pitcher, 125 years old.

Pitcher, 1842. Mrs. O. F. Johnson.

Blue and white china butter dish, 1810, blue and white cup and saucer, 1810, soup turreen. Mrs. B. L. Forster.

Two old china tea pots, 100 years old. Miss Annie Kendig.

Cup and plate, 1790. Mrs. B. L. Forster.

Tobacco jar of 17th century. Thomas Stevens.

Very old bowls. Mrs. Oyster.

China tea pot and cream jug. Mrs. John Kepple.

Plate, 100 years old. Mrs. J. R. Stoey.

Egyptian pottery. Mrs. J. C. Kunkel.

Cream pitcher, 125 years old. Mrs. Anna M. Mohler.

Bowl, 100 years old. Mrs. S. R. Parker.

Water and cream pitcher, 80 years old. Mrs. R. Hogan.

Dark blue dinner plate, 100 years old. Mrs. S. Stormfeltz.

Light blue plate, 100 years old. Mrs. Milleisen.

Light blue soup turreen, 150 years old. Mrs. Beidleman.

Dark blue plate, 60 years old. Mrs. Martin Shaffner.

White and yellow tea set, tea pot, cream jug, cups, and saucers. Mrs. Olewine.

Cake dish, 50 years old. Mrs. Emily D. Brooks.

Child's china cradle. Mrs. Emily D. Brooks.

Baby tea set.

Blue coffee pot, 100 years old. Mrs. Dr. Fager.

Small blue plate. Mrs. Martin Shaffner.

Dark blue breakfast plate, 100 years old. Mrs. C. A. Boas.

Blue sauce dish, 100 years old. Mrs. I. M. Kelker.

Soup turreen. Mrs. I. M. Kelker.

Two red and white stone saucers and plates. Mrs. B. G. Peters.

Mexican water bottle. Mrs. J. C. Kunkel.

China pitcher and vase. Mrs. Wm. Calder.

Red and white coffee pot, 55 years old. Mrs. J. R. Miller.

Syrup pitcher, 110 years old. Katie Hand.

One china vase, 50 years old. Mrs. John Killinger.

Blue platters, 115 years old. Charles Reel.

Blue platter, 100 years old. Mrs. B. G. Peters.

Blue platter. Mrs. Christie Boak.

Blue platter, 100 years old. Mrs. C. A. Boas.

Dark blue coffee pot, dark blue bowl, sugar bowl. Mrs. I. M. Kelker.

Pair Dresden vases.

Very old tea pot. Mrs. LeRue Lemer.

Two china plates, 100 years old. Mrs. Eliza Napier.

Pottery cup and saucer, 50 years old. Mrs. A. Fox.

Pickle dish, 60 years old. Mrs. E. D. Klein.

China plate and two cups and saucers. Chas. E. Fox.

Majolica plate, 1701. Mrs. Wm. Buehler.

Little china plate, 100 years old. Mrs. Chas. Wollerton.

Two china plates, 1806.   Mrs. Martin Schaffner.

Old Dresden flower basket, 200 years old.   Mrs. E. D. Klein.

Old Dresden card plate, 200 years old.   Mrs. E. D. Klein.

Modern doulton cream pitcher.   Mrs. J. C. Delaney.

Modern plaque, lower lakes of Killarney.   Mrs. J. C. Delaney.

Old majolica coffee pot, 60 years old.   Mrs. Le Rue Lemer.

Old china flower vase.

Dark blue plate brought from Germany by exhibitor's grandmother. Mrs. H. B. Weand.

Large mug, 100 years old.   Mrs. Le Rue Lemer.

Water and cream pitcher.   Mrs. B. G. Peters.

Small cream pitcher.   Helen Johnson.

Dresden flower basket.

Plate and cup and saucer, 75 years old.   Miss Boas.

Old Dresden tete-a-tete set brought to America by Count Zinzendorf in 1741, and sold by him for the benefit of the Moravians.   Mrs. J. B. Cox.

Very old pitcher, white, with blue band.   Mrs. H. M. Graydon.

Molasses jug.   Miss Boas.

Blue china cup and saucer, 75 years old.   Mrs. J. Fox.

Green band gravy bowl.   Mrs. I. M. Kelker.

Small china mug, 115 years old.   Mrs. A. Fox.

Decorated cup and saucer.   —— Fisher.

Very old saucer.   Mrs. John Kepple.

Two cups and saucers, and pitcher, (blue stone.)   Mrs. B. G. Peters.

Liverpool ware coffee pot, 1810.   Miss Sarah B. Egle.

Cup and saucers, 100 years old.   Mrs. Sue Wise.

Dining plate for serving mutton; the base to be filled with hot water. Manufactured about 1815, at the Herculaneum pottery, near Liverpool, when it was in charge of Rev. John Tomkinson.   Miss Tomkinson.

Liverpool ware water pitcher.   Mrs. I. M. Kelker.

Red Liverpool ware, covered vegetable dish.   —— Fisher.

Blue china coffee pot.   110 years old.   Mrs. W. H. Zollinger.

Large china vase, 50 years old.   Mrs. John Killinger.

China plate, 100 years old.   Mrs. Dunkle.

Large brown china platter.   Mrs. John Napier.

Blue gravy turreen, willow pattern, 105 years old.   Mrs. Donnecker.

Old blue water pitcher, 120 years old.   Josiah S. McDaniel.

Dark blue tea pot, very old.

Gravy bowl. Mrs. I. M. Kelker.

Blue ware soup turreen, 1780. Mrs. Donecker.

Purple Liverpool ware soup plate, 100 years old. Helen Johnson.

Two water jars used by the Pueblo Indians. Miss Lucy Hoerner.

Part of a set dark blue willow pattern. Mrs. Fred. Biery.

White stone plate from which George Chester sold oysters over fifty years ago, at Third and Walnut streets, at twelve and a half cents per plate.

Reproduction of the Elder Brewster tea pot; the original was brought over in the Mayflower, 1620. Mrs. Francis Wyeth.

Cup owned by Mrs. Judge Carson, 95 years old. Mrs. Francis Wyeth.

Blue plate, 100 years old. Mrs. A. Fox.

Turkey platter, view of West Point. Henry Ebersole.

Gray pitcher brought from Scotland. Henry Ebersole.

Small plate, 100 years old. Miss Carrie Schaffner.

Purple tea pot, 100 years old. Mrs. A. Fox.

Wedgewood Masonic punch-bowl. Henry Ebersole.

Mexican water jar. Mrs. Wm. Calder.

Two large Dresden china vases, 1830. Mrs. Wm. Calder.

Case of very fine modern china; some painted by young ladies of the city, and some loaned by Mrs. Thos. Hammersley, Mrs. J. C. Kunkel, Mrs. T. Rockhill Smith.

Alabaster plate, with black medalion heads of prominent Italians. Dr. J. H. Coover.

Large doll, 60 years old. Mrs. Thos. Elder.

GRANDMOTHER'S ROOM.

" Grandfather's clock."

A flint-lock musket.

Powder horn, old coat, pipe and snuff-box, 1756.

Linen towel, thread spun on the small spinning-wheel, by Mrs. George Lentz. 1780.

Large spinning-wheel made by Mr. George Lentz, 1775.

Small spinning-wheel and reel, over 100 years.

Ancient lamp and candle-stick. 1780.

Rug of 1800, sewing-box and silver finger-shield, 1785; lady's saddle, looking glass, 1770; three chairs over 100 years; one a solid mahogany, (inlaid,) from Holland.

Inlaid solid mahogany breakfast table and small inlaid mahogany stand; two pewter plates, 1770; five books printed in the years 1719, 1750, 1727, 1729, 1763, and book of common prayer, 1794. '

Brass andirons, fender, shovel and tongs, brush and bellows, ages unknown; copper tea kettle, over 100 years, brass snuffers and tray, very old; wooden mantle, china vases and silver candle sticks, patterns for worsted work, over 100 years; bronze candle stick, map of Lebanon and Dauphin, 1816.

Harris Memorial Room.

Picture of the attempt to burn John Harris, the Indian trader, about the year 1720. Miss Carrie Pearson.

Picture of the log house and stockade erected by the first John Harris.

Plan of the Harris mansion erected by the Founder of Harrisburg in 1766. Miss Nellie Pearson.

Mahogany table owned by Mrs. Hanna, daughter of John Harris, the Founder. Mrs. John J. Pearson.

An ancient sideboard, about two feet high and four long; made of solid mahogany, of English manufacture, inlaid with satin wood. Is supposed to have been brought to Philadelphia, by the trader, John Harris, in 1685, and descended through him to the second John Harris, and thence to Robert Harris, and used in the Harris family ever since. Mrs. Elizabeth Kerr.

A solid mahogany bureau, four feet high, with four drawers, plain in construction, descended from the Founder to his son Robert, and now in the family of the late George W. Harris. Belonging to the bureau is what is called the eagle mirror, a glass in a frame of unique make.

One of two dozen chairs, which were a wedding gift to John Harris, the Founder, in 1768.

John Harris, the Founder's, knee buckles, in the style of the period, and of solid silver.

Two cut glass decanters and six wine glasses which were in one of the drawers of the sideboard descending from John Harris.

The Harris china, fifteen pieces. In the collection is a custard cup which belonged to a set owned by John Harris, the trader. In the collection of china are heirlooms of the Harris family, owned by descendants, among whom are Mrs. John J. Clyde, Mrs. John J. Pearson and Mrs. Kerr.

An oval dish-shaped silver castor of John Harris, the founder.

Dress of brocade silk worn by Mrs. Hanna, one hundred years ago. Silver chatelaine worn by Mrs. Hanna.

A beveled edge mirror, when first bought by John Harris the Founder of great beauty and value.

Brass fender, tongs, and shovel, used in the Harris stone mansion from the time it was built until it passed out of the Harris family.

Pin cushion, scissors and knitting needles belonging to Mrs. General Hanna, daughter of John Harris.

Four silver plated candlesticks.

Four India vases, writing and work-box brought from England during the reign of George IV.

Willow-ware plate from a dinner set belonging to Rev. John Ewing, D. D.　Miss Nellie Pearson.

Wedding veil of Miss Caroline E. Briggs, daughter of Gen. John Andre Hanna and his wife, Mary Harris.　Mrs. John J. Pearson.

China bowl and cream pitcher, part of tea set belonging to Mrs. Caroline E. Briggs.　Miss Nellie Pearson.

Child's quilt made by Mrs. Caroline E. Briggs.　Miss Carrie Pearson.

Two Swiss caps embroidered by Miss Henrietta Hanna.　Miss Carrie Pearson.

Celery glass over one hundred years old.　Mrs. John J. Pearson.

Old china sauce boat.　Mrs. John J. Pearson.

China coffee pot and slop bowl, a wedding present from Governor McKean, to Elizabeth Ewing, daughter of Rev. Dr. Ewing, of Philadelphia, at her marriage to Robert Harris, son of the Founder.

A mirror from the family of William Maclay, who married a daughter of John Harris the founder, and who erected the stone house at the corner of Front and South streets.　Mr. Maclay was one of the first two Senators who represented the State of Pennsylvania in Congress.

The John Harris silver, consisting of a collection of forks and spoons.

A hand traveling-box, belonging to Jane Maclay, marked 1806, who married John Lyon, and was the mother of William Maclay Lyon, of Pittsburgh.

Copy of Blackstone printed in 1772, once the property of Senator William Maclay.　Wallace DeWitt.

Wooden cup made from the tree to which John Harris was tied by the Indians in 1720.　Miss Carrie Pearson.

Portrait of Gen. Washington, presented by himself to a lady of Philadelphia, during the Revolutionary war, and given by her in 1840, to Judge Pearson.

Coke's Institute, printed in London in 1642. Hon. John J. Pearson.

Hobart's Reports, printed in London in 1658. Judge Pearson.

Reports by Jean Latch, of cases tried during the reign of Charles I. Printed in London, in Law French, in 1661. Hon. John J. Pearson.

Postlethwayt's Dictionary, printed in 1766. Mrs. John J. Pearson.

Part of a tea set, painted by Miss Nellie Pearson.

PORTRAITS.

Kirkpatrick, William, painted by Eicholtz. Mrs. Espy.

Elder, Thomas, painted by Eicholtz ; Elder Mrs. Thomas, painted by Eicholtz. Mrs. Boude.

Findlay, Governor, painted by Eicholtz; Findlay, Mrs. Governor, painted by Eicholtz. William Findlay Shunk.

Snyder, Mrs. Governor. Mrs. C. C. Rawn.

Cameron, Gen. Simon ; Cameron, Mrs. Simon.

Hummel, Judge Valentine ; Hummel, Mrs. Mrs. Richard Hummel.

Crain, Richard M., painted by Eicholtz ; Crain, Eleanor Whitehill, painted by Eicholtz. Mrs. W. W Rutherford.

Wallace, Rev. Benjamin J., painted by Lambdin. Dr. Hugh Hamilton.

Graydon Alexander, first prothonotary of Dauphin county. H. Murray Graydon.

Hamilton, A. Boyd. Dr. Hamilton.

Forster, Gen. John. Mrs. John Forster.

Forster, Gen. John, (when a young man.) Benjamin L. Forster.

Grube, Bernhard Adam, Moravian missionary to the Indians. Augustus Beck.

Roberts, Col. John. Mrs. Henry A. Kelker.

Kelker, Frederick, painted by Eicholtz. Rudolph F. Kelker.

Coleman, G. Dawson, photograph.

Beatty, George, photograph in oil. Dr. William H. Egle.

Rutherford, Dr. William Wilson.

Rehrer, Major Thomas J. Mrs. Clara Rehrer Dock.

Bucher, Hon. John C. Mrs. Susan Bucher Ray.

McAllister, Capt. John C. Mrs. Fanny McAllister Morley.

Herr, Col. Daniel. Mrs. Dr. Weistling.

Ninninger, John. Mrs. Agnes Kemp.

Roumfort, Gen. Charles E. Roumfort.

Nelson, John, painted by Eicholtz; Nelson, Mrs. John, painted by Eicholtz. Mrs. Valentine Hummel.

Pearson, Judge John J., photograph.

Full length portrait, in water color, of Alexander Ramsey, when four years of age, taken at his birth-place, Hummelstown, Pa. Mrs. Irwin J. Boas.

Books and Newspapers.

Arndt's Warhes Christhenthum.

German Bible, 118 years. John Cline.

German Bible. 1683.

The Psalter. 1758. Samuel Selser.

Psalter. 1771. Harrison Dean.

Doddridge's Rise & Prog. 1788.

Doc. & Dist· M. E. C., 1808.

Hist. of O. & N. Test. 1784, by C. J. Reese.

New & Uni. Gazetteer, by Jos. Scott. 1800.

Ger. Bible. 1530. Mary J. Stoner.

Ger. Bible. 1765. Henry Walters.

Eng. Bible with Paraphrase, by Rev. John Brown. 1813.

Philadelphia Paper. 1789.

Huntingdon Gazette. 1829.

Ger. Alma. from Europe. 1847. A. F. Boone.

Penn. Intel. 1828–29–30–32.

Penn. Repub. 1830 to 32.

Penn. Reporter. 1828 to 1851.

The Harmony of the Divine Attributes in the Contrivance of Man's Redemption. Rev. W. R. H. Deatrich.

Montgomery's Poems. Vol. 4. Boston. 1825.

Book of Prayers, (German.) Gmuend. 1814.

Lieder Cammlung, (German.) Germantown. 1803.

German Testament, about 150 years old. Mrs. C. J. Moore.

New System of Modern Geography, by Elijah Parish, D. D. Newburyport, Mass. 1812. Y. M. C. A.

Letters by a Turkish Spy in Paris. 1637 to 1682; 8 Vols. London. 1741. Y. M. C. A.

Treatise of Practical Surveying by R. Gibson, Philadelphia. 1803.

The Churchman. April 16, 1876; Nov. 6, 1880; Oct. 22, 1881; 32d year, 36th and 37th years.

The Christian Union, Dec. 10th, 1873.

Fac simile copy of Gen. Washington's account of expenses during the Revolutionary war.

The New York Herald for Saturday, April 29, 1854.

The following of Christ, by Thomas A. Kempis. Printed in Cologne, 1767. A. R. Keifer.

Rules & Regulations for the Government of Public Schools—Lancasterian System.

Two book marks made in 1812 by Minnie Yingst, when three years old.

Lane S. Hart, autograph album.

The Grave, Royal English Grammar, Schema Sacrum. Miss Whiteside.

Prompvarium Satinitatis Probatae et Exercitae. Leipsic. 1753.

Fac simile of the Egyptian Court in 1302. James McCormick.

Deed for a farm in Lower Paxtang township, property now owned by the widow of G. G. Miller. [This deed was buried during an Indian raid, in the sack in which it is enclosed.]

Patent to Jacob Stricker for the White Hunter Cabin, 200 acres, situated in Upper Paxtang township, Lancaster county, 1767.

A draft notice of 1814.

Ye Olden Times, containing New England Weekly Journal, 1728, The Boston Gazette, 1770; New York Morning Post, 1783, &c., &c. J. C. McCreery.

Mementoes of the war of 1861.

Pieces of native cloth brought from the Sandwich Islands by the first missionaries to that place. Mrs. Alexander, *nee* Graydon.

German Bibles printed at Nuremberg in 1760 and 1712.

Bible printed in London in 1708, containing also the Psalter & Prayers & Thanksgiving for deliverance from the Gunpowder Plot— For Martyrdom of Charles 1st—For Restoration of Charles 2d—For the Accession of Queen Anne to the Throne, & Prayers for the Ceremony of healing by the Royal touch. Miss G. F. Huston.

The Holy Bible abridged—being a valuable present for a little Son or Daughter. Philadelphia. 1794.

Facultas P. Provincials. 1679. Rhine Bros.

Bible & Prayer Book. Mrs. Lowe.

New Testament. 1601. Rhine Bros.

History of 3 Judges of King Charles I. 1794.

German Bible. 1752. Agnes Snyder.

Paradise Lost. 1753. Eliza H. Clyde.

The Narrow way to Life ; (Ger.) Thos. Scheppard. 1762.

German Hymn Book & Bible together; 142 years. Mrs. S. A. Poulton.

German Bible. 1798.

Scriptural Book. 1779.

L. His & D. of Martin Luther. 1770. Cath. Von Boren.

German Psalter; 1749. Nuremburg. Joseph Miller, Fisherville.

Martin Luther's Edition Old Testament. 1720.

Life, History & Death of Martin Luther. 1755.

Book of Martyrs; T. J. V. Braght. 1748. Ephrata.

German Bible. 1716. Jacob Smith.

Eng. & Ger. Dict. 1843. Harrisburg. Amelia Fox.

Ger. Bible. 1761.

George Frey's Bible. 1530.

N. Test. 1802. New York.

Military Order of Release in 1781, from Gen. Geo. Washington.

Pass of Mr. Brown and negro, from Gen. Geo. Washington. 1778.

The Gentleman's Magazine. London. 1737.

Journal of the first session of the Senate of the U. S. 1789. New York.

Elementa Philosophica. Phila., 1752.

The Gentleman's Magazine. London. 1758.

One of the first books written by Martin Luther, when twenty-two years of age, in the year 1572.

Der Andr-Teil.

Bible belonging to Michael B. Fry.

German Bible. 1788.

Medical Botany. Strasburg. 1560.

German Bible. 1798.

Book of Common Prayer. Oxford. 1791

Book rest brought to America in 1828.

German Bible. Zurich. 1565.

Fac simile of Mass. Spy. 1775.

Fac simile of N. Y. Morning Post. 1783.

Fac simile of Continental currency.

Fac simile of New England Weekly Journal. 1728.
Fac simile of Boston Gazette & County Journal, 1770.
Prayer Book. Reuttejrger. 1768.
The Book of Martyrs. Ephrata. 1748.

[In the antiquarian collection of the Dauphin County Centennial exhibition were no less than six copies of this, the rarest of American
ante-revolutionary publications. These bear the imprint of the Ephrata
press, the volume being Der Blutige Schau-Platz. Of these, two
copies were in unusual condition. The volumes are huge folios, weighing
about fourteen pounds each, and containing 1,550 pages, printed on
thick, strong paper. Originally they were heavily bound in boards
covered with calf, brass corner plates fastened on with brass rivets, a
pair of heavy brass and leather clasps keeping the book closed, while at
the top and bottom of the back were two studded brass straps for the
purpose of giving additional strength. One of the copies alluded to is
in as good condition as it was when it left the press of the Mennonite
Brotherhood, at Ephrata, Lancaster county, one hundred and thirty and
six years ago, saving the yellowing of the leaves by age. In two is the
well known copper-plate engraving, while one copy contained a pen
and ink picture of the crucifixion.]

Soci Communes Theologici. 1541.
Regens Collecti et Recognitia.
Philippo Melanthona; pub. Wisdenberg. John Abel.
Autograph Album, Constitutional Conv. of Penn. 1872–73.
German Bible. 1776. Germantown.
N. Y. Trans. from Greek into old Ger. Rev. Abele.
Old German Psalter. 1820.
Whole duty of Man. 1791.
German Book. 1782.
German Prayer Book. 1814.
Communion Book. 1809.
Testament found at Petersburg, 1864.
German Hymn Book. 1755.
Presbyterian Hymn Book. 1822.
Astronomical and Geographical Essays. 1795. Geo. Adams.
Dictionary of Quotations. 1828.
German Bible. 1784. John C. Tittle.
Immortal Mentor. 1815. Carlisle.
German Paper Published in Harrisburg, 1803. C. Heater.

Penny Magazine. 1834.

Old Curiosity Shop. Dickens, 1841. Philadelphia.

Fables, John Gay. 1784.

Ready Reckoner. York. 1798.

Old Arithmetic.

Book of Job—First pub. 1609 ; reprint, 1796.

Songs of Solomon. 1803.

Grammar. 1826.

Penn. Intel. 1841. Mr. Weand.

Tel. & Intel. 1839.

Phil. Ind. Balance. 1820.

Saturday Eve. Post. 1825.

The Oracle of Dauphin. 1802.

Loskiel's History of Indian Missions. 1794.

Testament found on Sailor's creek, 1865. J. W. Collins.

Diary of War. T. A. Dent. 1865.

Explication of 50th Psalm. 1655.

Bavarian Pass Book for Hired Help. 1830.

Homer's Iliad. 1807.

Military Surgery. 1814. Baltimore. Dr. Witman.

Defense of Christ. 1728.

Antiquities of Rome. 1785. Hamilton Aldricks.

Religious Visitor Harrisburg. 1824. Joshua M. Wiestling.

Bible in German. 1776. Mrs. S. Johnson, Middletown.

German Bible. 1534. Zurich. Daniel Hake, Middletown.

German Bible. 1761.

German Hymn Book. 1800.

Letters to a Young Lady. 1786. Robt. S. Jones.

Young Man's Best Companion. 1773.

English Grammar. 1750.

Amer. Pol. by Benj. Franklin. 1800.

Short His. of Paper Money & Banking. 1833.

Ger. Bible. 1776. Germantown; E. Fox.

Ger. Bible. 1789.

Uni. Letter Writer. 1798. London.

Bible Ger. 1792.

Book of Job. Ger. 1711.

Life of Christ. Ger. 1720.

Two Ger. Test. 1775. M. J. Stoner.

Taufscheins of years, as follows: 1745, 1783, 1790, 1783, 1796, 1780, 1801. 1784, 1807.

Receipt for 1811. John Stauffer.

A writ of 1816.

German Almanack for 1823.

Engraving of Gov. Simon Snyder. 1809.

Old note of 1847.

Bible. Edinburg. 1787.

Quaker Catechism and Confession of Faith. Philadelphia. 1773.

German Hymn Book. Germantown. 1829.

German Hymn Book. Germantown. 1785.

Bible. Berwick. 1793.

By-Laws of the Union Fire Company. Harrisburg. 1819.

German Book. Harrisburg. 1776.

Spelling Book. Ephrata. 1795.

German Bible. Philadelphia. 1836. Thomas Beidleman.

Political Works of Thomas Paine. Springfield. 1826.

Lutheran Hymn Book. German. Philadelphia. 1814.

A Survey of Spiritual Anti Christ. 1648.

A Paraphase of the New Testament in 6 vols., by P. Doddridge. Edinburg. 1772.

Pamphlets. Harrisburg. 1829 to 1834.

Musical Monitor. Ithica. 1825.

Laws of the Borough of Harrisburg. 1813.

Music Book. London. 1699.

Latin & German Bible. 1574.

German Sermons, Postilla Mystica. Germantown. 1748.

German Life of Christ, by Grasin of Zendorf. 1747.

Buchner's Hand Concordanz. (German.) Jena. 1776.

Manuscript Arithmetic. 1789.

Book of Songs. 1793.

German Manuscript. 1789.

German Book. 1757.

Clarke's Hand Book, German. Philadelphia. 1834. Hymn Book, German. 1815.

German Interest table. Harrisburg. 1833.

Luther's New Testament. Carlisle. 1824. German.

The Family Clerk. Harrisburg. 1811.

A Hand Book for Riflemen. Philadelphia. 1813.

German, Christian Commentary. Ephrata. 1792.

The Universal Letter-writer, by the Rev. Thomas Cook, A. B. London. 1798.

German Bible. Mengeringhausen, 1789. Mrs. Cunkle.

Medical Recipes. Germantown. 1771.

Lives of early Christians. 1720.

The laws of the U. S. of America. Philadelphia. 1796.

Melish's Travels, 2 vols. 1812. D. M. Davidson.

Monatliche Unterredungen Eineger Buten Freunde, Januarias, 1690. Henry F. Lutz.

The Instructor, or Young Man's Best Companion. Edinburgh. Printed by Alexander Donaldson. 1773. William Lutz.

Phil. Saturday Courier. 1838.

First Directory of Harrisburg. 1839. L. G. Poulton.

New Testament, original print. Frankfort & Leipsic. 1737.

Commentary of the Book of Genesis, (Latin.) 1633. A. P. W. Johnson.

Deeds—Patent. Hugh Swan, "The Two Springs," Lancaster county, and Hugh Swan and wife to Robert Elder.

German Bible. 1758.

German Book of Sermons. Manheim. 1736. Mrs. J. R. Miller.

Italian Play. 1606. A. P. W. Johnson.

Blackstone's Commentaries. Dublin. 1796. John F. Lee.

Medical Work of 1686. Dr. C. B. Fager.

- Geography. 1711. A. B. Rupp.

Framed colored picture of the Reading of the Declaration of Independence, on July 4th, 1776, at Philadelphia.

Letters of Junius. Baltimore. 1814.

The Christian Companion.

An increased edition of Morning, Evening, Lenten & Spiritual Hymns in German. Zurich. 1739.

High German American Calendar for 1742. Germantown.

Mystical & Prophetic Bible. German. Marburg. 1712.

A collection of all the laws of the Province of Pennsylvania, now in force, published by order of the Assembly. Philadelphia. Printed and sold by B. Franklin. 1792.

Lives of the Dukes of Wurtemburg. 1739.

Book of Melodies; manuscript, by the Sisters of Ephrata. 1783.

Ahiman Rezon. Philadelphia. 1783.

A compendious, pleasant, and methodical tract of modern Geography. 1749.

German Testament. 1545.

Latin Testament History. 1807.

The Humbled Sinner's Resolve. London. 1560.

The Lord's Prayer in 70 Languages, manuscript, by students of the Propaganda, Rome. Bishop Shanahan.

A conversation on the plurality of the Worlds, bought in 1776.

Martin Luther's translation of the New Testament, in German. Nuremburg. 1782.

The Hidden Life of Christ, in German. Gotingen. 1747.

A German Hymn Book. 1728.

A Grammar of Music. London.

German Concordance. New Saltza. 1714.

Book of Daniel in the Chinese language.

R. R. contract for building Lykens Valley R. R. Dec. 1st, 1832. James Miller, Elizabethville.

Chinese Books.

The Centennial Song of The Old Hill Clock, by Mrs. Nellie Eyster of San Jose, Cal. MSS.

Newspapers from Algeria, North Africa. Arabic language.

Almanack of 1783. Mrs. Annie Miller.

The City of Harris. Miss Gabrielle Jacobs.

Legend of the Mound. Mrs. F. K. Witman.

Watt's Psalms. 1740.

A Celebrated Psalm Tune, sung by universal applause in the Presbyterian Church, by Miss Allen. Written in 1817 by Francis R. Shunk, afterwards Gov. of Penna.

Baltimore American, Aug. 20th, 1773.

Dauphin Guardian, Nov. 14, 1809.

Bible, in 4 small vols., printed in Oxford. 1739.

Constitutional Convention of Pennsylvania for 1872 and 1873.

Ulster County Gazette, (fac-simile,) containing Gen. Washington's funeral obsequies. Mrs. J. R. Miller.

Almanacks from the year 1834 to 1885. Mrs. Joseph Ball.

The Works of the Ancient Fathers, Barnabas, Clement, Hermas, Ignatius and Polycarp, with the history of their doings and martyrdom. (Latin.) Edited by J. C. Cotolivius. Second edition annotated by Joannes Clerigus. Amsterdam. 1724.

25

Geographical Dictionary. 1680. W. P. Deuchey.

Old papers containing messages of Thomas Jefferson, President of the U. S., and Thomas McKean, Governor of Pennsylvania. 1805. Miss M. Hays.

The Aboriginal Port Folio, or a collection of Portraits of the most celebrated Chiefs of the North American Indians. Philadelphia. 1836–38.

The History of England, Ecclesiastical & Civil. London. 1726. Miss A. Fisher, Middletown.

Latin Dictionary; Folio Edition. London. 1758. Miss A. Fisher.

English–German & German–English Dictionary. Lancaster. 1812. Two volumes.

Medical Museum. Philadelphia. 1805. Dr. H. O. Witman.

Virginia Gazette, from January 5th, 1776, to May 11th, 1776. Miss Meily, Middletown.

German Bible of 1763.

Picture of the Home of John Harris, the first settler of Harrisburg, and the Indian assault.

Music Book, copied by Jacob Baab when eight years of age, at Reading, Pa. 1809.

German Evangelical Truth. 1800.

German Hymn Book. 1814.

Geography of the World. Hartford. 1807.

The Family Clerk and Students' Assistant. Harrisburg. 1817.

The Art of Reading. Boston. 1806. Mrs. F. K. Witman.

German Bible. Christopher Sauer. Germantown. 1763.

Book of Sermons, written by forty-nine different ministers.

Book of Psalms, German. Miller.

Photograph Album. Hamilton Alricks.

An Atlas of Ancient & Modern History, by J. W. Tyson, A. B. Philadelphia. 1845.

Pedacii Dioscoridis Anazarbari. 1598. Jacob Smith.

Address published in "Harrisburg Chronicle," July 6th, 1831. Remarks of Benjamin Parke, previous to the reading of the Declaration of Independence, at the celebration of the 55th anniversary of American Independence, near the Great Spring, on Peter's Mountain, Halifax township.

Memoirs of Jefferson, 2 vols. 1809.

Pitcairn's Island, an eventful History of the Mutiny of the Bounty. New York. 1832.

The New American Spelling Book. A. F. Boone. Philadelphia. 1808.

New Testament. (German.) Leipsic. 1818.

German Hymn & Prayer Book. 1811.

A Greek New Testament. Amsterdam. 1762. Valentine Feeman.

French New Testament, with the Psalms of David set to music. 1761. Valentine Feeman.

New Testament. New York. 1827. Valentine Feeman.

Pike's Expeditions. Philadelphia. 1810. Mrs. F. K. Witman.

Journals of Congress. 1780–85. John E. Carmony, Middletown.

Comments on the Suffering and Crucifixion of Christ. German. 1770.

German Newspaper of 1823.

German Prayer Book. 1829.

A Sacred Scheme of Natural & Revealed Religion. Lancaster. 1776.

A Preservative against unsettled notions in Religion, by John Wesley, M. A. Bristol. 1770. Mrs. F. K. Witman.

The Life of Wicliffe. New York. 1832. Mrs. F. K. Witman.

The Letters of Pliny the Consul. London. 1763.

German Bible. Christopher Saur. Germantown. 1743.

Prayer Book brought from Scotland in 1772. John Hamilton Alricks.

Original Poems by John Dryden, in two vols. Aberdeen. 1776.

Anecdotes of some distinguished persons chiefly of the Present and two preceding Centuries, in 2 volumes. 3d edition. Dublin, 1796.

Poetical Works of James Montgomery. Boston. 1825.

The Psalms of David. Boston. 1819.

The Grave. A Poem by Robert Blair. Philadelphia. 1791.

The History of Physick from the time of Galen to the beginning of the 16th Century. 2 vols. London. 1726.

Old Plays. London. 1695.

Commission of Abdiel McAllister, (son of Col. Richard McAllister, of Hanovertown, York county, Pa., who was with Arnold's Expedition against Canada, and was taken prisoner.)

German Day Book, No. 5; Sept. 20th, 1775, to 30th Sept., 1778.

German Journal, March 1st, 1774, to Oct. 28th, 1774.

Bound volume of Extra Globe, 1840. D. S. Early.

German Ledger. Copier Buch.

Music Book, printed by John Wyeth. 1826. Harrisburg. John S. Vandling.

George Frey's account Book from 1767 to 1790.

American Bravery displayed in the Capture of 1400 Vessels of War and Commerce since the Declaration of War by the President. Carlisle. 1816.

Enquiry concerning Political Justice. Philadelphia. 1796.

German Book on Religious Subjects.

Hymn and Prayer Book. German. 1760. Mrs. D. F. Jauss.

German Bible. Halle. 1781. Mrs. Martin Schaffner.

Latin Grammar.

The Original 2nd Message to the 1st Congress by George Washington. June 8th, 1790. Mrs. Hogan.

Certificate of good character given to Rose Chestnut and James Walker, her son, when coming to America from "County Antrim, Kingdom of Ireland," in 1760; also the pocket book in which it was carried.

The original wood cuts, cut by Gustave Sigismund Peters, the first printer of oil color toy books in America. Estate of Theo. F. Scheffer, successor to Gustave Sigismund Peters.

Boston Recorder. 1820.

Deed from Robert Harris and wife to Henry Ruthrauff for a piece of ground in Harrisburg, corner 2d and Walnut. 1792.

The Democratic Press. Philadelphia. 1827.

Two Albums. 1830. Mrs. Seneca G. Simmons.

The History of Queen Esther and King Ahasuerus, on vellum, brought from Germany, by Mr. Joseph Lowengard, and supposed to be 300 years old. Hebrew.

Old Testament in Hebrew and German. Joseph Lowengard.

Bill of sale of a negro slave at Huntingdon, Pa. 1803. A. P. W. Johnson.

Letters from Lafayette. Gen. Cameron.

Two German Bibles and Hymn Book. 1759.

German Book. 1629.

German Psalm Book. 1797.

Fac simile of the accounts of G. Washington with the United States, commencing June, 1775, and ending June, 1783. Mrs. Richard Hogan.

COMFORT, JOHN C.:

Pindari. 1620.

Cavite Criminalis. 1682.

Bloody Martyr Book. Ephrata, 1748. Contains a full page pen and ink drawing of the Crucifixion.

New Testament. Carlisle. 1823. Moser & Peters.

Indian Narratives. Carlisle. 1812. Three copies of volume two.

Letters of an Italian Nun and an English Gentleman. Harrisburg. John Wyeth. 1809.

Book of Fate. 1542. Once the property of Napoleon Bonaparte.

Six German publications, by Saur, of Germantown.

MAURER, CHARLES W.:

Deed of William Penn of Norminghunt, in the county of Sussex, England, to George Keith of the city of Edinburgh, kingdom of Scotland, for five acres of land "within the province of Pensilvania," dated 19th day of October, A. D. 1681.

Deed from the Commissioners of property, Richard Hill, Isaac Norris and James Logan, to Edward Farmer of the county of Philadelphia, for 1713 acres, part of the Manor of Springfield, bearing date "the twenty fourth day of the fourth month" A. D. 1714. (The wax seal is in excellent preservation.)

MISCELLANEOUS:

A saddle of 1830. Mrs. Joseph Whisler.

Bible of 1820. Mrs Dicker.

Reel. 1770; 125 years old. Mrs. McCarroll.

Flax heckel. J. L. Swartz.

Two pewter plates. Mr. Swartz.

Nutmeg grater. Miss Hogan.

Flax and yarn. Mrs. Catharine Wertz.

Cane of 1800. Mrs. Strouse.

Shuttle. 1800. Mr. Wilber.

Small trunk. Miss H. Johnson.

Paper knife, inlaid with gold.

Razor of 1750. Mrs. Fisher.

Spectacles of 1730. Mrs. Fisher.

Old waiter. 1600. Mrs. Ulrich.

Necklace and pin. 1700. Miss Whiteside.

Tea and tray. 1750. Miss Whiteside.

Candelabra. 1770. Mrs. Segelbaum.

Spectacles. Isaac Barr.

Cigar stand. 1830. Snuff-box found at Waterloo. Dr. Fager.
Shoe of 1800. Dr. Fager.
Cane made of a jaw-bone of a whale. D. F. Jauss.
Hank of flax. 1775. D. M. Davidson.
Fireman's belt. 1784. J. W. Grove.
Sugar cane from battlefield of New Orleans.
Cane cut on Antietam. Name of principal battles cut on with pen knife.
Sword-cane from Perry's Flag Ship, Lawrence. Wm. Lathe.
Cedar cane. 1780. Henry Ebersole.
Self opening umbrella. D. S. Early.
Model of old time whipping post.
Old hat box, with lock and key.
Settee belonging to Winfield Scott Sellers. Mrs. C. Rhodes.
Clothing of Lilliputian, Winfield Scott Sellers. Mrs. C. Rhodes.
Two pewter plates. Mrs. Wertz.
Pewter teapot.
Long kid gloves. 1840. Julia Fenn.
Stone from Susquehanna river, in shape of a foot. Jos. Greenawalt.
Old trunk. 1770.
Tin box. 1810. Mrs. Mary Barringer.
Decorated table. 1800. Mrs. P. K. Boyd.
Flask. T. A. Dent.
Small Japanese slippers.
French brass waiter.
Knives and forks. 1785.
First keys of Harrisburg Bank.
Piece of turf from Ireland. Eliza Napier.
Tin box for inkstand.
Work box. 1810. Mrs. Jane Keenan.
Flax brake. Mrs. J. McCormick.
Flax brake.
Stone fruit. Mrs. J. Baab.
Brass candle sticks. A. Boyd Hamilton.
Small basket. A. Boyd Hamilton.
Indian club.
Part of the mulberry tree under which the first John Harris was buried. 1840. A. Boyd Hamilton.
Photograph of Winfield Scott Sellers. Mrs. Rhodes.

Saddle bags. 1700. Miss Mary Stoner.

Work basket containing calico needle case, pincushion, and patches. 1600. Miss Mary Stoner.

Scales and weights used in the year 1700. Miss Mary Stoner, Highspire.

Razor. 1810.

Tooth extractor. 1730.

Hammer from Ireland. 1785. A. P. W. Johnson.

Collection of Japanese idols and ornaments. Fred. Kelker.

Snuff-box from Waterloo.

Chinese shoes. Fred. Kelker.

Two old newspapers. Mrs. C. A. Lee.

Old neck-lace.

Piece of the Washington Monument.

Relics of Gettysburg. Dr. J. H. Coover.

Piece of wood that Col. Ellsworth was shot on.

Shoe last of 1785. Mrs. J. W. Stofer.

Old coach and pair. Miss M. Boas.

Rolling pin. Miss Tomkinson.

Indian Saucer. Mrs. Lenhart.

Fine enameled water jar. Mrs. Wm. Calder.

Chess from China. Mrs. Wm. Sergeant.

Old slippers. C. F. Showers.

Old belt. Mrs. C. Boude.

Gen. Washington's shaving case. Mrs.' C. Boude.

Tinder box.

Cocoa nut.

Tortoise shell combs. M. J. Leonard.

Tortoise shell comb. Mrs. M. Espy.

Two Chinese jewel boxes. Mrs. Charles Wollerton.

Reel in bottle. Solomon Gorgas.

Reel. Lydia Kerr.

Lacquer bowl from Japan.

Old razor. 1800.

Tortoise shell knife.

Spectacles.

Little trunk.

Spectacles.

Piece of marble from Catacombs of Rome.

Waiter, or tray. Mrs. Forster.

Old lamp. 1780.

Fan. 1805.

White swan bone. 1825.

Chinese Goddess of Mercy. Mrs. I. M. Kelker.

Case containing ivory tablet, with alphabet. Ivory patch box. Mrs. M. R. Meck.

Fan. Old English relic. 1830. Mrs. C. Boude.

Kitty Kapp's doll; 80 years old. Amos Kapp.

Kitty Kapp's toy dishes. Amos Kapp.

Two pieces gold mosaic.

Piece of column from First Presbyterian church, destroyed by fire March 30, 1858.

Silk bag. 1840.

Tea box. 1750.

Silk bag. 1840, Mrs. J. Ball.

Pocket book. 1780.

Needle book. 1810.

Two silhouettes. 1740.

Vase from Vienna. Mrs. Smith.

Beads from Chicago fire.

Bell from Chicago fire.

Spectacles worn 100 years ago.

Doll. 1805.

Porridge cup used in the year 1700.

Fan. Mrs. Johnson.

Specimens of lava from Mt. Vesuvius.

Tortoise shell spoon. 1810.

Vertebra of a snake.

Specimen of marine algae tree growing out of a stone.

Work box and spool case. 1840.

Small trunk. 1810.

Copper tea kettle.

Hog's tooth, twelve and a half inches long. 1830.

Brass spoon and cake turner. Mrs. B. G. Peters.

Silver snuff box of the Revolution. John H. Alricks.

Tea caddy. Mrs. D. D. Boas.

Marble from Pompeii. Dr. J. H. Coover.

Cocoa pod. Dr. O'Connor.

Porridge cup.   Mrs. Ward.

Two pipes.   Mrs. Brown.

Home made buttons.   1799.   Miss Mary Stoner.

John Roger's lamp.   J. W. Simpson.

Indian tea saucers.   J. W. Simpson.

Jaw bone of a whale taken off Charleston harbor.   Lewis Abel.

Britannia tea set.   1800.

Pewter meat plate.   Mrs. Deller.

Egyptian waiter.   1500.   Mrs. A. S. McCreath.

Pewter pitcher and bowl.   1790.   Mrs. Hogan.

Egyptian teapot.   1650.   Mrs. Andrew S. McCreath.

Brass candlesticks.   Mrs. D. D. Boas.

Brass snuffers and tray.

Brass tray.   Mrs. R. J. Haldeman.

Two pewter breakfast plates.   Miss Bella Hays.

Two small brass candlesticks.   Miss Clara Johnson.

Bronze idol.   Mrs. James McCormick.

Russian samavar.   1300.   Mrs. R. J. Haldeman.

Brass warming pan.   Miss Anna Weir.

Two Roman lamps.   Mrs. James McCormick.

Steel snuffers and tray.   Miss M. Robeck.

Pewter plates.   Mrs. J. Goldsmith.

Pewter plate.   1785.   Mrs. Hogan.

Leather fire bucket.   Dr. Egle.

Old lantern.   James McCormick.

Silver snuffers and tray.

Two scarfs.   Mrs. Mary Espy.

Ancient fork.

Mexican basket.   Mrs. Seneca G. Simmons.

Mexican bridle.   Dr. Egle.

Chinese lantern.

Wreath of ivy leaves made in Andersonville prison.   Joseph Kahn-weiler.

Ancient sign of "Glover, Taylor."

Umbrella.   Mrs. E. Zollinger.

Silk reel.   Mrs. McCarroll.

Dragon head.   James McCormick.

Chinese god of war.   Mrs. I. M. Kelker.

Soapstone ornament.   Mary E. Williams.

Straw covered box. Dr. Egle.

Five stem candalabra. Mrs. C. Segelbaum.

Case Indian curiosities. Mrs. Brown.

Three bronze lamps. James McCormick.

Bread basket and gourd. James McCormick.

Steel snuffers and brass tray. Miss Clara Johnson.

Pewter plate. Mr. Breslan.

Red tray. Mrs. Ulrick.

Chinese tablet. Frederick Kelker.

Products of gold and silver from Colorado. Wm. B. Whinnery.

Marble inlaid vase. John Hendrickson, Middletown.

Coffee pitcher. Mrs. Jacob Boyd.

Chinese pillow.

Spiral candlestick. James McCormick.

Gen. George Washington and Martha, his wife, in a bottle. Chas. Bingaman.

Reel in a bottle. Miss Boas.

Rattlesnake skin. William G. Ball.

John Rogers, a silhouette.

Clock that was in the first Senate of Pennsylvania. Mrs. Wm. F. Shunk.

Clock that was in the first House of Representatives of Pennsylvania. Mrs. George Dock.

Chinese junk in ivory. Frederick Kelker.

Doll in case, 1830. Mrs. John W. Gray.

Chinese picture. Frederick Kelker.

Silver candelabras. Mrs. T. J. Dunott.

Photographs of Barbara Fritchie, house and flag, pincushion made from B. Fritchie's wedding dress in the year 1806. Mrs. T. J. Dunott.

Red bellows. Mrs. George Dock.

Baby in cradle, 1740. Mrs. Peter August.

Certificate of the Society of the Cincinnati. Mrs. C. Boude.

Whip, 1800

Fac simile of Declaration of Independence.

Old bracket. Mrs. Hendrickson.

Pewter pitcher. D. S. Early.

Wedding fan used in 1816. Mrs. C. Boude.

Cider mug. Mary Stoner.

Iron inkstand made at Gov. D. R. Porter's furnace. Miss Boas.

Pewter cream jug.
Pincushions. M. J. Stoner.
Brass candlestick, 1810. David Cassel.
Chinese razor.
Small wooden house, a family relic. Mrs. J. R. Miller.
Iron goose used in 1812. D. Martin.
Knife and spoon box. Mrs. Power and Miss Kean.
German jewel case. Mrs. Hendrickson.
Chest. Mrs. Gipe.
Mahogany work box. Mrs. Zimmerman.
Dough scraper. Mrs. Gipe.
Small bureau. Mrs. P. K. Boyd.
Shoe last. M. J. Stoner.
Old copper hammer. Mrs. Ricker.
Two Chinese umbrellas. Fred. Kelker.
Flint and steel. M. J. Stoner.
Moonstone idol. James McCormick.
Two pewter plates. Lucy Hoerner.
Epaulette of the war of 1812–14.
Old tea chest. Mrs. V. Hummel.
Wooden last.
Toy drum.
Ancient fork.
Knitting needles.
Stone lava.
Opium pipe.
Indian canoe.
Candlestick.
Breast plate and buttons of the year 1600 and 1700.
Gilt buttons before the Revolution.
Card containing necklace, wax, &c. Miss Mary Stoner.
Wheel of fortune.
Fan. 1830.
Pewter teapot. Mrs. Scott.
Home-made fife. 1799.
Hickory cane. 1825. John Alter.
Hone. 1820.
Pistol. 1822. W. O. Hickok.
Trunk made in Glasgow. 1750. L. C. Bryan.

Fan. Miss Alricks.

Campaign cane.

Candlesticks brought from Ireland in 1826. Mrs. Sarah Murray.

Work box. 1810. Mrs. Sarah Murray.

NEEDLE WORK, EMBROIDERY, &c.

Boas, Mrs. Daniel D. :
  Home-made towel, dress, two bags.

Boas, Miss Margaret :
  Bureau cover, toilet cover, infant cap.

Bowman, Miss Maggie, Millersburg :
  Toilet table cover.

Boyd, Mrs. Jacob M. :
  Sampler, piece of embroidery, pitcher, six large tablespoons.

Boyd, Mrs. James :
  Sampler.

Brooks, Mrs. Emily D. :
  Bed spread, two infant caps.

Buehler, Mrs. Jacob :
  Pair of shoes and stockings, bead bag, sampler.

Buffington, Mrs. Thomas W. :
  Two bags, knit quilt.

Cameron, Mrs. James :
  Sampler.

Cartwright, Mrs. Jacob :
  Sampler.

Cowden, Mrs. William K. :
  Two night caps, bead bag, sampler.

Cramer, Mrs. Nat., Millersburg :
  Two towels.

Dare, Mrs. Nora P. :
  Veil, sampler, patch-work quilt, woolen quilt.

Deller, Mrs. :
  Bead purse, pair of slippers, two pair cotton mittens.

Egle, Mrs. Hiram :
  Home-made linen towels, table-cloth, and sheeting, 1790; infant cap, 1810; black embroidered veil, 1820; ladies' capes, 1830; lace tie, 1800.

Ehling, Katharine :
  Towels.

Elder, Mrs. Rebecca O. :
  Sampler, pin cushion.
Elder, Mrs. Thomas :
  Pin cushion.
Etter, Mrs. B. Frank :
  White quilt.
Fahnestock, Miss :
  Table cloth, baby dress, old needle-work, two towels, silk shawl.
Fisher, Mrs. Adolphus, Middletown :
  Two towels, three tea pots, cream pitcher, gravy tureen, shoe last,
  gilt bracelet, infant cap and dress.
Fox Mrs. Adelaide :
  Bag and needle-case, bead bag.
Forster, Mrs. J. Montgomery :
  Two needle-cases, two baby dresses, necktie, gentleman's card
  case, towel, two collars, patches for quilt.
Fry, Mrs. William H. :
  Two towels.
Gilbert, Miss Jennie, Millersburg :
  Two samplers made by Rebecca Dechat.
Haldeman, Mrs. Richard J. :
  Night cap, quilt patches, red and white quilt, bead purse, silk scarf,
  bag, two gentleman's collars, four mustard spoons, tea spoon, salt
  set, embroideries on cloth, Russian samavar.
Houston, Miss Georgianna :
  Two fans, sampler, painting on velvet, chain and hook, bead bag,
  three pieces of embroidery.
Hoyer, Mrs. George :
  Two vandyke collars, three baby caps.
Hummel, Miss Emma :
  Two samplers, framed, sewing cushion.
Groh, Miss Nancy, Millersburg :
  Ball pin cushion.
Hummel, Mrs. Albert :
  Two samplers.
Hummel, Mrs. Eliza B. :
  Two pairs of undersleeves, night cap.
Ingram, Mrs. Samuel D. :
  Three pieces of embroidery.

Jauss, Mrs. C. E. :
> Home made check linen, linen sheets, towels.

Johnson, Miss Hannah I. :
> Pin cushion, pin cushion and chain.

Johnson, Mrs. A. P. W. :
> Baby dress, silk handkerchief, towels.

Kapp, Amos, Northumberland :
> Two dresses belonging to Miss Kitty Kapp.

Keenan, Mrs. Jane :
> Silk quilt, thread lace veil, two samplers, fan, night cap, belt, infant shirt, two fine laces.

Kelker, Mrs. Rudolph F. :
> Sampler.

Keller, Mrs. John P. :
> Three stocks.

Kennedy, Mrs. S. H. :
> Pin cushion, two card cases, two bags, bead bag, pin cushion.

Killinger, Mrs. John W. :
> Woolen quilt.

Leibrich, Miss Hannah :
> Cape, collar, bonnet, quilt.

Linn, Mrs. Erasmus :
> Two vandyke collars, shell comb, two samplers, wedding veil, two baby caps, fan.

Longnecker, Mrs. Elizabeth :
> Infant dress.

McCarroll, Mrs. William :
> Table cloth, towel, pair of gloves, lace cape, lace veil.

Martz, Mrs. Daniel, Millersburg :
> Sampler, baby cap, hand embroidered dress.

Maurer, Mrs. Daniel C. :
> Lace sampler.

Maurer, Mrs. Fred. C. :
> Tobacco pouch.

Metzgar, Mrs. LaRue :
> Patch of darning, pewter dish.

Rawn, Mrs. Charles C. :
> Shell comb, two samplers, collar, baby cap, veil, fan.

Rutherford, Miss V. :
> Two caps.

Scheffer, Mrs. Theo. F. :
   Table cloth, napkins.
Schmidt, Mrs. :
   Three double capes.
Simon, Mrs. John B. :
   Sampler.
Snyder, Mrs.
   Baby dress.
Stofer, Mrs. J. W., Middletown :
   Shoe last.
Thompson, Miss, Middletown :
   Handkerchiefs.
Ulrich, Mrs. Abram :
   Embroidered home made linen towels and table cloth, hank of
   flax, wedding veil, silk sash, handkerchiefs and collars, two
   bureau covers.
Vaughan, Mrs. George :
   Sampler, pocket-book, knitter, white crape shawl, red crape
   shawl, embroidered apron, infant shirt.
Ward, Mrs. Silas :
   Silk embroidered apron, bead bag, porridge bowl, old laces.
West, Miss Linda, Millersburg :
   Baby cap worn by George M. Brubaker, made 1825.
Wilson, Mrs. Thomas :
   Dress, three baby caps, two baby dresses.
Wolfersberger, Mrs. Catharine :
   Quilt.
Zimmerman, Mrs. C. O. :
   Doll quilt.

THE ANTIQUARIAN FUND.

SAMUEL W. FLEMING *in account with the Dauphin County Centennial for Receipts and Expenditures at the Antiquarian Hall, from September* 10, 1885, *to February* 20, 1886 :

DEBTOR :

1885. September 10, for receipts,		$	23 50
" 11, " "			132 00
" 12, " "			225 00
" 13, " "			332 67
" 15, " "			395 03
" 16, " "			1,103 32
" 17, " "			917 71
" 18, " "			338 95
" 19, " "			222 75
1886, February 16, " A. B. Hamilton,			18 17

Total receipts, $3,709 10

CREDIT, SEPTEMBER 1885, ORDERS NUMBERED AS FOLLOWS:

1. S. W. Fleming, pay-roll of employees,	$132 65
2. A. M. Cleveland, on account of rent,	300 00
3. Carpenters' account,	177 03
5. D. Bacon, use of show cases,	284 90
6. A. M. Cleveland, on account of rent,	300 00
7. S. W. Fleming, pay-roll of employees,	260 58
8. S. W. Fleming, pay-roll of employees,	207 73
9. S. W. Fleming, pay-roll of door-keepers,	134 00
10. S. Boyd Martin, cleaning hall,	29 37
11. LeRue Lemer, sundries,	85
12. Geo. W. Buehler, freight, &c.,	2 25
13. H. J. Steel, posting bills,	2 25
14. Rutherford Ice Co., ice,	1 50
16. Barringer & Bannan, painting,	18 32
17. M. G. Einstein, muslin, &c.,	30 86
18. A. R. Sharp, material and labor,	17 00
19. L. Poulton, hanging pictures,	4 00
20. O. P. Grove, calico,	3 11
21. E. A. Fisher, lettering signs,	19 35
22. Joseph Montgomery, lettering signs,	16 80
24. S. W. Fleming, sundries,	10 77

25. F. W. Liesman, Harrisburg, advertising, ... $1 50
26. Reinhard & Sharp, Lebanon, advertising, ... 4 50
27. Samuel M. Fenn, Lykens, advertising, ... 3 00
28. Penn'a Staats-Zeitung, advertising, ... 4 85
29. J. B. Seal, Millersburg, advertising, ... 2 00
30. Wm. M. Breslin, Lebanon, advertising, ... 6 50
31. Patriot Pub. Co., printing, &c., ... 50 25
32. Harrisburg Pub. Co., printing, &c., ... 43 65
33. E. Z. Wallower, printing, &c., ... 39 65
34. Theo. F. Scheffer's estate, printing, ... 3 85
35. Lane S. Hart, printing, &c., ... 88 85
36. R. M. Sturgeon, printing, &c., ... 52 25
37. A. M. Cleveland, bal. of rent, ... 100 00
38. J. A. Work, Steelton, advertising, ... 2 50
40. J. M. Place, Telegram Co., advertising, ... 90
41. J. H. Light, Lebanon, advertising, ... 4 00
42. Estate of A. King, boxes, ... 45
43. J. O. Nissley, Middletown, advertising, ... 2 25
44. Dr. J. Ringland, services Antiquarian display, ... 10 00
45. W. H. H. Sieg, Steelton, advertising, ... 4 00
46. Harrisburg Pub. Co., printing, ... 4 00
47. Frank R. Leib, chairman, balance owing by committee, . 5 00
48. William H. Egle, expenses of office, and services, . . . 300 00
49. Samuel W. Fleming, services, ... 75 00
50. William Bellman, for watch lost, ... 15 00
51. Wilson Elder, services rendered, ... 5 00
52. General Secretary, for preparing centenary volume, . . 200 60
53. W. K. Cowden, coal for office, ... 2 50
55. Samuel W. Fleming, postage, expressage, ... 18 87

$3,003 70
March 6, 1886, balance due, ... 705 40
April 17, 1886, Order 56 drawn in favor of James M. Lamberton, treasurer Dauphin County Historical Society—
balance on Antiquarian Fund, ... 705 40
Balance medal account, ... 66 25

$771 65
NOTE—For orders Nos. 4, 15, 23, 39, and 54, see medal account, p. 74.

26

GENERAL CENTENNIAL ACCOUNT.

The general Centennial account of cash received and expended by the general committee of the Dauphin County Centennial, as audited and approved, is as follows:

T. D. Greenawalt, treasurer, cash received,* $4,160 00
Samuel W. Fleming, received from rink exhibition, . . . 3,709 10
Samuel W. Fleming, medals sold, ... 569 50

$8,438 60

Orders paid. Balance.

T. D. Greenawalt, treasurer, ... $4,154 60 $5 40
Samuel W. Fleming, rink, ... 3,003 70 705 40
S. W. Fleming, medals, ... 503 25 66 25

Balance, ... 777 05

$8,438 60

All the above accounts were audited, approved and certified to by the Historical Society of Dauphin county, as correct, March 11, A. D. 1886.

GEO. J. SHOEMAKER,
Centennial Auditor.

*This includes $260 30 paid for medals, and refunded by the treasurer of Antiquarian Exhibition. For the same reason the amount received from all sources was in reality $8,178 30, instead of the amount given.   W. H. E.

NEWSPAPERS OF THE CITY AND COUNTY.
1885.

The newspaper editors of Anno Domini, 1885, are herewith given. We desire to embalm them. Ninety-five years ago the first newspaper was published at Harrisburg. Not a copy is in existence. We only have the name, *Harrisburg Advertiser*, with its editor, Major Eli Lewis. So with the *Harrisburg Phœnix*, edited by James Philip Puglia. Perchance there were other newspapers not so fortunate even as to have the names preserved. Our county has been the mausoleum of a hundred newspaper ventures, and it is probable of those now in existence, none having the honored names familiar to us, will continue to herald the day's news a century hence.

Our newspapers gave themselves the credit for the success of the Centennial Celebration, and yet there were some of these which within two weeks of the time prophesied a failure throughout. To the newspaper press of Harrisburg, nevertheless, are we greatly indebted for the valiant service they accomplished, and especially for preserving the very complete record of the Centennial proceedings. We have used these reports pretty freely in making up our account of the different days displays. In A. D. 1985, there will be no writer who will give more graphic descriptions of Centennial days, than Thomas M. Jones, "ye City Editor of ye *Telegraph*"—nor a more faith-

ful chronicler than Robert M. Sturgeon, " ye Reporter for ye *Call*"—of that of A. D. 1885. Whatever is
lacking in color, or may be omitted, in the records we
have given, *they* are responsible. Our duties at the
time were elsewhere; the "greatest show on earth,"
as Artemus Ward said, was then open. The newspapers of 1885 deserve to flourish for a century at
least, and we hope they may, and in this wish we
but echo the voice of all the people of "ye City of
Harrisburg and ye county of Dauphin."

HARISBURG TELEGRAPH:

Editor and Publisher—Matthias Wilson McAlarney.
Editor—John Tomlinson.
News Editor—Samuel C. Miller.
City Editor—Thomas M. Jones.
Assistant City Editor—E. J. Stackpole.

HARRISBURG PATRIOT:

Editor and Publisher—Benjamin F. Meyers.
Editors—George D. Herbert, John Youngman.
News Editor— Chas. O. Bernheisel.
City Editor.—John P. Dahoney.

HARRISBURG INDEPENDENT:

Editor and Publisher—Elias Z. Wallower.
Editor—Wien Forney.
City Editor—John Robertson.
Assistant City Editor—Charles O'Donnell.

HARRISBURG MORNING CALL:

Editor and Publisher—Robert M. Sturgeon.
Editor—Edward C. Jones.
Reporter—Adam H. Baum.

HARRISBURG SUNDAY TELEGRAM:
Manager—James M. Place.
Editor—John Moore.
City Editor—Hiram Schoch.

CHURCH ADVOCATE :
Editor—Rev. C. H. Forney, D. D.

PENNSYLVANISCHE STAATS-ZEITUNG :
Editor and Publisher—Naudain Hamilton.

DAUPHIN COUNTY JOURNAL:
Editor and Publisher—Frederick W. Liesmann.

MIDDLETOWN JOURNAL:
Editor and Publisher—J. W. Stofer.

MIDDLETOWN PRESS:
Editor and Publisher—J. O. Nissley.

MILLERSBURG HERALD :
Editor and Publisher—John B. Seal.

MILLERSBURG SENTINEL :
Editor and Publisher—Frank S. Bowman.

LYKENS REGISTER :
Editor and Publisher—Samuel M. Fenn.

HUMMELSTOWN SUN :
Editor and Publisher—W. R. Hendricks.

STEELTON ITEM :   '
Editor and Publisher—J. A. Work.

STEELTON REPORTER :
Editor and Publisher—W. H. H. Seig.

PUBLICATION COMMITTEE.

Adam Boyd Hamilton.

George Wolf Buehler,

William Henry Egle, M. D.

GENERAL INDEX.

www.ingramcontent.com/pod-product-compliance
Lightning Source LLC
Chambersburg PA
CBHW030857270326
41929CB00008B/462